Thomas Henry Huxley

Thomas Henry Huxley

Thomas Henry Huxley
Communicating for Science

J. Vernon Jensen

DELAWARE
Newark: University of Delaware Press
London and Toronto: Associated University Presses

Associated University Presses
440 Forsgate Drive
Cranbury, NJ 08512

Associated University Presses
25 Sicilian Avenue
London WC1A 2QH, England

Associated University Presses
P.O. Box 39, Clarkson Pstl. Stn.
Mississauga, Ontario,
L5J 3X9 Canada

The paper used in this publication meets the requirements
of the American National Standard for Permanence of Paper
for Printed Library Materials Z39.48-1984.

Library of Congress Cataloging-in-Publication Data

Jensen, J. Vernon (John Vernon), 1922–
    Thomas Henry Huxley: communicating for science / J. Vernon Jensen.
      p.   cm.
    Includes bibliographical references and index.
    ISBN 0-87413-379-3 (alk. paper)
    1. Huxley, Thomas Henry, 1825–1895.   2. Naturalists—Great
Britain—Biography.   3. Orators—Great Britain—Biography.
4. Science—Philosophy.   I. Title.
QH31.H9J46   1991
574′.092—dc20   89-40762
[B]   CIP

PRINTED IN THE UNITED STATES OF AMERICA

*To our grandchildren, Danny and Mikey
and in memory of our first,
Sally Kathleen*

Contents

Preface

The purpose of this rhetorical biography is to explore in detail the life of Thomas Henry Huxley who was a communicator for science in the late nineteenth century. It seeks to get inside his public rhetoric, inside important rhetorical events in his life, and inside his interpersonal communication networks, leading up to a more insightful view of his rhetorical legacy. In addition to analyzing his published speeches and essays, it is important to have Huxley and his contemporaries speak for themselves as much as possible, in order to get at the personal and private dimension, as well as at the public persona. To achieve this goal, it was necessary to consult primary materials, such as letters, journals, diaries, lecture notes, minute books, newspaper articles, and miscellaneous documents, both in Britain and the United States.

I have thoroughly examined the Huxley Papers, housed in the archives of the Imperial College of Science, Technology and Medicine in London, and have used primary materials in other London archives and libraries, such as the Royal Institution of Great Britain, the Royal Society, the British Library, the University of London, and the Wellcome Institute for the History of Medicine. In addition, I have used primary materials in the Cambridge University Library, the Bodleian at Oxford, Trinity College in Dublin, the American Philosophical Society in Philadelphia, and the Huntington Library in San Marino, California. I am grateful to these institutions for permission to consult and quote from their holdings. Using these rich primary resources, many of which have not been consulted in other works on Huxley, I have tried to create a fresh and intimate view of Huxley and his rhetorical contributions.

I am deeply appreciative to the following librarians and archivists who greatly facilitated my research: particularly, Professor Stoddard, Mr. Weston, Mr. Stallybrass, Mr. Friday, and Mrs. McCabe of the Royal Institution. My very special thanks goes to Mrs. Jeanne Pingree, recently retired archivist of the Imperial College, whose expertise with the Huxley Papers and whose many kindnesses through two decades have in so very many ways made my research more successful and more enjoyable than would otherwise have been the case. The members of her staff have likewise been unusually helpful.

I also want to acknowledge those British and American colleagues whose interests bridge the study of communication and the history of science, particularly the life of T. H. Huxley. I especially wish to express my gratitude to Douglas J. Foskett, the retired head librarian of the University of London, with whom I have shared three decades of friendship and interest in Huxley and communication. I also want to thank Donald K. Smith, who was present at the beginning.

I wish to thank Carol Hargarten, who typed this manuscript, a task that she performed with expertise, speed and pleasantness.

I appreciate the helpful suggestions of the anonymous reviewer, the steady guidance of the managing editor, Michael Koy, and the careful work of the copyeditor, Marilyn Silverman.

Finally, I wish to express heartfelt gratitude to my wife, Irene Khin Khin, who has performed with excellence and grace her varied roles as wife, mother, supportive companion, and professor of history. To her I am deeply indebted and for her eternally grateful.

Acknowledgments

For permission to draw on my previously published articles, I am grateful to the editors of the following publications:

Notes and Records of the Royal Society of London
"Thomas Henry Huxley's Lecture Tour of the United States, 1876." 42 (1988): 181–95.
"Thomas Henry Huxley's 'Baptism into Oratory.'" 30 (1976): 181–207.

British Journal for the History of Science
"Return to the Wilberforce-Huxley Debate." 21 (1988): 161–79.
"The X Club: Fraternity of Victorian Scientists." 5 (1970): 63–72.

Royal Dublin Society. "Tyndall's Role in the 'X Club.'" *In John Tyndall: Essays on a Natural Philosopher* (Dublin: The Royal Dublin Society, 1981).

Historical Studies (Melbourne, Australia)
" 'The Most Intimate and Trusted Friend I Have': A Note on Ellen Busk, Young T. H. Huxley's Confidante." 17 (1977): 315–22.

Dalhousie Review (Halifax, Nova Scotia)
"Interrelationships Within the Victorian 'X Club.'" 51 (1971–72): 539–52.

Western Speech
"The Rhetorical Influence of T. H. Huxley on the United States." 31 (1967): 29–36.

Today's Speech
"Hewers of Only One Root." 13 (1965): 20–22.

Speech Monographs
"Thomas Henry Huxley and Robert G. Ingersoll: Agnostics and Roadblock Removers." 32 (1965): 59–68.

Thomas Henry Huxley

Introduction

Thomas Henry Huxley (1825–95), the English biologist-educator-rhetorician who became perhaps the leading expositor and advocate of science, and of Darwinism in particular, was one of the most eloquent of Victorian communicators, both in speaking and in writing. In public lectures, classroom teaching, convention presentations, commemorative addresses, after-dinner speeches, articles, essays, books, book reviews, and letters to newspapers editors, he clarified and defended the world of science as he saw it, usually dueling en route with orthodox theologians. Friend and foe attested to his rhetorical expertise. In 1888 the *Pall Mall Gazette* cited Huxley as the premier scientific orator of the era,[1] and that reputation remains intact to the present time. Recently, a leading American scientist, not entirely friendly to Huxley's views, wrote that Huxley was "the greatest public spokesman for science in his century . . . the most eloquent spokesman that evolution has ever known."[2]

Huxley was born on 4 May 1825 at Ealing, Middlesex, then a small village about six miles from London's Hyde Park, where his father, George Huxley, was an assistant school master. When Tom was about ten years old, his father moved the family back to Coventry and worked in a bank. Young Tom had an unhappy, lonely childhood. His father suffered from mental illness and was uncommunicative. His mother, Rachel, played a more important role in the young boy's life and he was very devoted to her, but she wasn't an affectionate person. The Huxleys had eight children, but only four sons and two daughters survived: Eliza, Ellen, George, William, James, and Thomas. Tom was the seventh child and youngest survivor. There was little harmony in the family, and except for Tom's deep fondness for his eldest sister, Eliza, his links with his family were not strong.

Discussing his parents in his brief autobiography written at the age of sixty-four, Huxley gives us an insight into his own nature:

Physically and mentally I am the son of my mother so completely—even down to peculiar movements of the hands. . . . I can hardly find any trace of my father in myself, except an inborn faculty for drawing, which unfortunately, in my case, has never been cultivated,[3] a hot temper, and that amount of tenacity of purpose which unfriendly observers sometimes call obstinancy. My mother was a slender brunette, of an emotional and energetic temperament, and possessed of the most piercing black eyes I ever saw in a woman's head. With no more education than other women of the middle classes in her day, she had an excellent mental capacity. Her most distinguishing characteristic, however, was rapidity of thought. If one ventured to suggest she had not taken much time to arrive at any conclusion, she would say, "I cannot help it; things flash across me." That peculiarity has been passed on to me in full strength; it has often stood me in good stead; it has sometimes played me sad tricks, and it has always been a danger. But, after all, if my time were to come over again, there is nothing I would less willingly part with than my inheritance of mother wit.[4]

In 1850, shortly after returning to England from his four-year voyage on HMS *Rattlesnake*, Huxley reported in a letter to his sister Eliza: "All the family are well. My father is the only one who is much altered, and that in mind and strength, not in bodily health, which is very good. My mother . . . is . . . the same amusing, nervous, distressingly active old lady she always was."[5]

Huxley himself was about five feet ten inches, with a slender build, straight black hair, sparkling black eyes, high forehead, rather prominent nose, a determined look, and a self-confident manner. Throughout his life he suffered from serious indigestion, a condition he traced in part to a violent illness brought on at about the age of thirteen when observing his first postmortem dissection: "For years I suffered from occasional paroxysms of internal pain, and from that time my constant friend, hypochondriacal dyspepsia, commenced his half century of cotenancy of my fleshly tabernacle."[6] He suffered from chronic headaches, depression, and in later years, liver and heart ailments.

He felt his early schooling was very unsatisfactory and instead he decided to become self-educated. He voraciously read books on English and ancient history, mathematics, geology, philosophy, physics, and physiology. He studied Greek, Latin, German, and French. Though he had an inquiring mind, his readings were sporadic and random with no real direction. He admitted in his autobiography that he had not been a disciplined student.

I should distinctly warn ingenuous youth to avoid imitating my example. I worked extremely hard when it pleased me, and when it did not—which was a very frequent case—I was extremely idle (unless making caricatures of one's pastors and masters is to be called a branch of industry), or else wasted my energies in wrong directions. . . . I read everything I could lay my hands upon, including novels, and took up all sorts of pursuits to drop them again quite as speedily.[7]

His experience on the *Rattlesnake* was very instrumental in giving him disciplined habits and a basic appreciation for, and direction in, life. He wrote in his autobiography:

The cruise was extremely valuable. It was good for me to live under sharp discipline; to be down on the realities of existence by living on bare necessities; to find out how extremely well worth living life seemed to be when one woke up from a night's rest on a soft plank, with the sky for canopy and cocoa and weevilly biscuit the sole prospect for breakfast; and, more especially, to learn to work for the sake of what I got for myself out of it, even if it all went to the bottom and I along with it. . . . I am inclined to think that my naval life was not the least valuable part of my education.[8]

As a youngster he was drawn into the study of medicine by the examples of his two brothers-in-law who were doctors, and he served as an apprentice with Eliza and her husband, Dr. John G. Scott, who had moved to the Regent's Park area in north London. He attended lectures at the Sydenham College in Chelsea, prepared for the matriculation examination of the University of London, received a scholarship from the Charing Cross School of Medicine, and in 1845 received his M.B. in London University. But he cared little for the practice of medicine. In his autobiography he later wrote:

My great desire was to be a mechanical engineer, but the fates were against this, and while very young, I commenced the study of medicine. . . . But . . . I am not sure that I have not all along been a sort of mechanical engineer *in partibus infidelium*. I am now occasionally horrified to think how very little I ever knew or cared about medicine as the art of healing. The only part of my professional course which really and deeply interested me was physiology, which is the mechanical engineering of living machines.[9]

In 1846 he was accepted into the Medical Service of the navy and was assigned to Haslar Hospital in Portsmouth.

An ideal opportunity soon emerged. His superior at Haslar, Sir John Richardson, had been asked by Capt. Owen Stanley, who was to command the HMS *Rattlesnake*, to recommend "an assistant surgeon who knew something of science,[10] and Richardson recommended Huxley, who "jumped at the offer."[11] The *Rattlesnake*, a 113-foot frigate with a crew of 180 officers and men, was soon to sail on a lengthy expedition to northeastern Australia, to study inshore waters and the natural history of the Great Barrier Reef, Torres Strait, the Louisiades Archepelago, and the New Guinea coast. Huxley rightly anticipated that his rather limited duties as assistant surgeon would give him time to engage in his own personal experiments on specimens of invertebrate sea life in that distant part of the world. As he wrote to his sister Eliza prior to departure:

> We shall form one grand collection of specimens and deposit it in the British Museum or some other public place, and this main object being always kept in view we are at liberty to collect and work for ourselves as we please. Depend upon it unless some sudden attack of laziness supervenes, such an opportunity shall not slip unused out of my hands. ... I must confess I do glory in the prospect of being able to give myself up to my own favourite pursuits without thereby neglecting the proper duties of life.[12]

Like Darwin's voyage on the *Beagle*, in 1831–36, this was to be a fundamental stepping stone into a life devoted to science, and Huxley was destined to become a leading player in the unfolding drama of Victorian science.

Much was happening in the last half of the nineteenth century, which opened the way for Huxley's contributions and that he in turn helped to shape. The accumulation of much new data and insights in the biological and physical sciences, in biblical studies, and in comparative religion, seriously challenged traditional views of orthodox Christianity, and a vigorous rhetorical battle ensued with Huxley in the forefront. Darwinism seemed to question the origin, nature, and status of humans, the nature of God, and the meaning and purpose of life. Geology challenged biblical accounts of creation and chronology; astronomy continued to shrink human beings as it opened the heavens; and physics proposed materialistic explanations for religious concepts. Higher criticism of the Bible questioned the sources, accuracy, and validity of much biblical material, the authorship and chronology of some of the books, and the unity of "God's Word." The study of comparative religion challenged the uniqueness and preeminence of Christianity.

Underlying these findings lay a basic conflict in procedure. Insisting on the right to investigate all of life, to be free to accumulate and classify materials, to be free to formulate and publicize hypotheses, insisting that truth was to be found not by accepting on faith past authorities, but by accepting through reason present investigations, and insisting that doubt was a sail not an anchor, adherents of the scientific method produced a revolution in thought that presented a basic challenge to organized Christianity. Scientific procedure was worshiped. It was not certain what would be discovered, what would be at the end of the journey, but the important thing was to keep the roads open, lead where they may. Implicit throughout was the optimistic, and perhaps naive, faith that the inevitable destination was progress, peace, human enrichment, and happiness.

It is this intellectual historical milieu in which Huxley lived and moved and had his adult being. This book will focus on in-depth descriptions and analyses of important specific rhetorical events in Huxley's life, and will apply rhetorical criticism to his numerous writings and speeches in his advocacy of science, especially Darwinism, defending the same against attacks from orthodox theology. His rhetorical stance and strategies will be analyzed, as will some of his significant interpersonal communication networks. All will build toward a better understanding of his legacy.

One chapter discusses in detail, the first public lecture he delivered in 1852 at the prestigious Royal Institution of Great Britain, which he considered to be his "baptism into oratory."[13] This lecture was a continual source of confidence for him throughout his life, and it helped him in his effort to secure a position in the world of science.

A second event to be analyzed is Huxley's "debate" with Bishop Samuel Wilberforce at Oxford in 1860, which continues to draw the attention of academia and the general public as a symbol of the conflict between science and orthodox theology. It projected Huxley into broad public view more quickly than would otherwise have been the case, and it reinforced for him the importance of public speaking. The remaining thirty-five years of his life were accordingly spent as an active "bulldog," defending Darwinism and science in general, and the public as well as scientific circles became acquainted with him. This historic confrontation is explored in greater detail than has heretofore been done.

His lecture tour of the United States in 1876 is the third important rhetorical event to be analyzed. He visited American scientists, attended a meeting of the American Association for the Advancement of Science, delivered a lecture on geology in Nashville, three widely publicized lectures on evolution in New York, and a lecture on science education at the opening of Johns Hopkins University in Baltimore. While in Nashville he enjoyed a reunion with his sister Eliza and her family. This seven-week tour strengthened his influence outside of Great Britain as a spokesman for evolution and science education, and furthered his reputation as a highly skilled public speaker.

Dwelling on the details of these three rhetorical events, each in a different decade, permits us to see Huxley more intimately, to get underneath his role as a public communicator for science.

I then devote a chapter to a broad survey of his numerous rhetorical contributions after his Oxford encounter. Through these years he delivered lectures at the Royal Institution, at various universities, to London workers and to various general audiences. He presented papers at the meetings of the British Association, the Metaphysical Society, and at learned societies. In various cities in England and Scotland he drew large audiences. Essays and articles appeared in various periodicals and magazines, and during his retirement years he energetically dueled with Gladstone and other defenders of orthodox Christianity in the *Nineteenth Century*. His books and his prefaces to books, spread his views, as did his letters to the *Times*. Thus, in writing and in speaking, he was in the front-lines in the rhetorical battle with those he perceived to be the enemies of Darwinism and science in general.

Having descibed his contributions, it is then necessary to get inside his rhetoric by analyzing his rhetorical stance and strategies. His rhetorical efforts were cast in a two-valued dramatic format of a struggle between the forces of good and evil, science and orthodox theology, respectively. He created a vivid drama in which the roles of hero and villain were sharply drawn. His was the rhetorical stance of an inspired messenger much like his theological foes, but his "revelations" were not from Scripture or some inner voice, but rather from nature, from observation and experimentation. An overarching metaphor that portrays his stance is that he saw his rhetorical efforts as those of a roadblock remover. That is, he was trying to get rid of the obnoxious and dangerous theological roadblocks standing in the pathway of science.

But focusing on one's public rhetoric does not fully get inside the person and into his role as a communicator. With whom was that individual communicating behind-the-scenes, sharing his thoughts, worries, hopes, and plans? The first chapter of this volume explores Huxley's interactions with his closest confidantes in his early years, three women who were central figures in keeping his focus on his commitment to a life of science. Another chapter provides a detailed analysis of Huxley's frequent and regular interactions with eight of his closest scientific friends, which crystallized in the formation of the "X Club" in 1864, a monthly dining club, which continued until his death. This network of leading scientists of the time became an abundant reservoir for good fellowship and intellectual stimulation, and a significant forum for exchanging ideas and information about each other's work. The group successfully marshaled their efforts in furthering the cause of science in general, and specifically in the affairs of the Royal Society, the Royal Institution, the British Association for the Advancement of Science, and various other scholarly societies.

The final chapter summarizes Huxley's rhetorical legacy. For well over a century he has had an abiding rhetorical impact on Great Britain and on the United States. As an articulate, intelligent and courageous spokesman for an initially unpopular cause in which he thoroughly believed, he has stood as a model and as an inspiration to those who were committed to freedom of expression. He stimulated the use of the extemporaneous method of delivery both on the public platform and in the university classroom. He has demonstrated that a speaker can be effective without having a strong commanding voice or a flamboyant manner. He has served as a stimulating model of clear exposition and effective argumentation, and is still heralded as one of the most outstanding examples of a scientist who has been capable of rendering complicated subject matter understandable and interesting to a lay audience, without sacrificing accuracy. He exemplifies the importance of thoroughly understanding one's subject matter, expressed in as few words as possible. His firm integration of ideas, data, words, and style gave an integrity and strength to his messages. He is a master of using colorful analogies and metaphors without distorting his scientific information. He integrated literature and science with ease, and his works abound with insightful literary references and allusions. He used concrete illustrations and examples effectively, defined terms and concepts carefully, constructed rhythmical phrasing, and displayed clear organization. He demonstrated that high ethos generated by mirroring important cultural values of one's society can contribute significantly to one's rhetorical success. The many tributes to Huxley during his lifetime and after his death eloquently testify to his rich rhetorical legacy.

1

Early Confidantes

In studying the lives of historical figures, we often tend to focus on their adult years, when their ideas are crystallized, their actions are structured, and their influence becomes pervasive. This is understandable, for, after all, posterity is interested in the mature, fleshed out ideas, the accomplishments, and the impact of those who went before. We skim lightly over their younger years when they were stumbling along, beset with all sorts of hesitancies and doubts while setting and resetting their goals. In so doing, the uncertainty, frustration, and agony connected with early decision making and employment seeking is lost from sight. It is important to examine the early years of Huxley's struggling.

Between the ages of fifteen and twenty he sporadically made brief entries in a journal he entitled "Thoughts and Doings." In his last entry he reminisced about his largely unhappy existence up to that point. "Remembrances of physical and mental pain ... absence of sympathy, and thence a choking up of such few ideas as I did form clearly within my own mind."[1] But then he chided and bolstered himself. "Oh, Tom, trouble not thyself about sympathy; thou hast two stout legs and young, wherefore need a staff?"[2] But he did have a staff in the form of his eldest sister Eliza, and in the next decade he added two more, his fiancée Henrietta Heathorn, and his close friend Ellen Busk. They formed a tripod that steadied his professional focus, calmed his personal anxieties, and kept his dreams alive. This chapter will explore the significant role played by these highly trusted confidantes. He owed much to their advice and encouragment. Those years of indecision and frustration and eventual success were fruitful because, to a large degree, of the counsel and presence of these three women.

Eliza Huxley Scott

During childhood a close bond developed between Eliza (Lizzie) and

Tom, separated by eleven years in age, and it held firm throughout their lives despite many years of being apart. As Huxley's biographer-son, Leonard, wrote, she was the "one member alone of his family [who] felt with him that complete and vivid sympathy which is so necessary to the full development of such a nature."[3] When he was sixteen he went to live in London with Lizzie and her husband, while pursuing medical studies. In the summer of 1842 Huxley decided to enter a public competition for a botany medal, and, as he later reminisced:

> The day of examination came and as I went along the passage to go out I remember dear Lizzie half in jest half in earnest throwing her shoe after me, as she said for luck. She was ... almost as anxious as I was. ... [Weeks later I was surprised] on returning home one afternoon to find myself suddenly seized and the whole female household vehemently insisting on kissing me. It appeared an official-looking letter had arrived for me, and Lizzie ... could not restrain herself from opening it. I was second, was to receive a medal accordingly and dine with the Guild on the 9th November to have it bestowed. I dined with the company and bore my share in both pudding and praise, but the charm of success lay in Lizzie's warm congratulation and sympathy. Since then she always took on herself to prophesy touching the future fortunes of "the boy."[4]

For almost four years Huxley enjoyed the security and happiness of Lizzie's home.

In 1846 Huxley began the practice, that was to continue to be the only link with Lizzie for many years, that is, to write lengthy letters in which he summarized what he was doing, successes he had reaped, problems he had encountered, and his hopes for the future. In letters in May and October 1846 he told her of his impending expedition on the *Rattlesnake*. This might well lead, he wrote, to significant results, so that "some of Sister Lizzie's fond imaginations [may] turn out not altogether untrue"[5] about his future success.

Within two weeks after the arrival of the *Rattlesnake* in Sydney in July 1847, he wrote to Lizzie, about what he had accomplished in the way of scientific papers he sent to London, and indicating his plans for more sophisticated papers as he gathered more data. He concluded, "Five years ago you threw a slipper after me for luck on my first examination, and I must have you to do it for everything else."[6] That memorable episode remained a symbol of Lizzie's ever-present concern and pride, and of his ever-present desire to vindicate her faith in him.

Huxley's annual, or semiannual, letters to Lizzie become almost like periodic reports to stockholders, whereby company officials report on the accomplishments and problems of the past year, and give projections for the coming year, hoping to convince the stockholders that their investment is being wisely used. Lizzie had invested much love and interest and faith in her young brother, and he was anxious to report that all was well with her investment. As he wrote in his *Rattlesnake* journal on Christmas Day 1847 off the coast of Australia: "You once said 'my highest hopes are centered in that boy' and may the Almighty forget me when I forget you or shrink from serving you or yours."[7] It was not an idle commitment, for the desire to measure up to Lizzie's expectations seemed to always be in the background of his endeavors. On the same day, the lonely young man wrote in his journal:

Where [on board ship] is the social ease, the comfort, the heartfelt kind words, the friendly influences of a home circle? It is now two years since I formed part of such an one and that one alas! was but the last ray of a happy sun, followed by a dark night of misfortunes. Oh Lizzie! dear Lizzie, dearer to me than any but one[8] in this world, what endless misery hast thou seen since then—would that I could have been ever by you—I would have tended you and cheered you with a care passing that of a brother—for of all of us, you and I were the only two I believe who really loved and therefore understood one another. Where shall I ever find another sister like you at once endowed with more than man's firmness and courage in adversity and you gifted with tenderest heart, and mind and taste capable of the highest cultivation? And yet we may never meet again, nay in all human probability never shall.[9]

That pessimistic prediction was based not only on his service in the navy, but also on the fact that the Scotts, due to unhappy but unexplained reasons, early in 1846 had emigrated to Germany, and would soon leave for the United States.[10]

In March 1848 he wrote not only about his scientific accomplishments and plans, but also about his engagement to a girl in Sydney, Henrietta Heathorn ("Nettie"), a step taken with Lizzie's advice in mind. "Of all [the] people in the world," he wrote, "I must tell you. ... Do you remember how you used to talk to me about choosing a wife? Well, I think that my choice would justify even your fastidiousness."[11] He was desirous not only of meeting Lizzie's standards, but also of assuring her that she was not now being pushed aside.

Do not suppose that my new ties have made me forgetful of old ones. On the other hand, these are if anything strengthened. Does not my dearest Nettie love as I do! and do I not often wish that you could see and love and esteem her as I know you would. We often talk about you, and I tell her stories of old times.[12]

Lizzie was not losing a brother; she was gaining a sister. In March 1849, in addition to summarizing what the *Rattlesnake* had done, he wrote of Nettie and his hopes of marriage.[13]

In November 1850, three weeks following his return to London, he wrote a long letter to Lizzie, who was now in the United States, bringing her up-to-date on his dismal employment possibilities. Nevertheless, he boldly asserted; "I will leave my mark somewhere, and it shall be clear and distinct."[14] He comforted her in light of a number of severe misfortunes she had had to bear, including the death of her little daughter and the rigors of emigrant life. He commended her for "the brave woman's heart you always had."[15] He expressed his great affection for her family as usual, which was an important factor in keeping their bond strong. As Lizzie's last letter had been sent to London, he had not heard from her for a long time. "I will honestly confess,' he wrote, "that I was half puzzled, half piqued, and altogether sulky at your not having answered my last letter containing my love story, of which I wrote you an account before anybody."[16] After summarizing Nettie's virtues, he described how lonely he was, being separated from her—and from Lizzie. "[Nettie] loves me well, as well as I love her, and you know I love but few—in the real meaning of the word, perhaps, but two— she and you."[17] Now they were both far away.

In May 1851, he again summarized his problems and his successes; the latter included this time the wonderful news of his election to be a Fellow of the Royal Society.[18] A year later he had to inform Lizzie of their mother's sudden death, and he also reported on his successful lecture at the Royal Institution of Great Britain. He vented his discouragement at having no scientific employment in view, and lamented his separation from Nettie and their uncertain future. He concluded by longing for Lizzie's "brave heart and clear head to support and advise me. . . . Pray write to me more often than you have done."[19]

In February 1853, he wrote: "Many thanks, my dearest sister, for your kind and thoughtful letter—it went to my heart no little that you amidst all your trials and troubles, should find time to think so wisely and so affectionately of mine."[20] He then proceeded to give his usual report, which contained his assurance that success had not inflated his ego nor changed their relationship.

I have acted in the spirit of your advice, and my reward, in the shape of honours at any rate, has not failed me, as the Royal Society gave me one of the Royal medal's last year. It's a bigger one than I got under your auspices so many years ago, being worth £50 [about $240], but I don't know that I cared so much about it. ... In the eyes of the world I, of course, am greatly the bigger—but I will confess to you privately that I am by no means dilated, and am the identical Boy Tom I was before.[21]

He said that in his next letter "I will tell you more at length about my plans and prospects,"[22] for at the moment he only wanted some quick advice on how to send money to her, since he wanted to help her now that he had a small income. Two months later he sent the money, and wrote about his unsuccessful attempts to obtain grants to publish his *Rattlesnake* materials, about his writing and lectures, and his applications for positions in Toronto, Aberdeen, and King's College (London). He concluded on a disgruntled and indecisive note.

Something I must make up my mind to do, and that speedily. I can get honour in Science, but it doesn't pay. ... In truth I am often very weary. The longer one lives the more the ideal and the purpose vanishes out of one's life, and I begin to doubt whether I have done wisely in giving vent to the cherished tendency towards Science which has haunted me ever since childhood. Had I given myself to Mammon I might have been a respectable member of society with large watch-seals by this time.[23]

Putting his head on her shoulder, figuratively, seemed to be therapeutic, clearing his mind, healing his wounds, and strengthening his will.

In November 1854, his letter began with an explanation for his long silence and an assurance of his unbroken tie with her.

When a man embarks as I have done, with nothing but his brains to back him, on the great sea of life in London, with determination to *make* the influence and position and the money which he hasn't got, you may depend upon it that the fierce wants and interests of his present and immediate circle leave him little time to think of anything else, whatever old loves and old memories may be smouldering as warmly as ever below the surface. So, sister mine, you must not imagine because I do not write that therefore I do not think of you or care to know about you, but only that I am eaten up with zeal of my own house, and doing with all my heart the thing that the moment calls for.[24]

This time there was much success to report, for in 1854 he had finally secured a government grant and his first permanent professorship (in natural history at the Government School of Mines), which, together with income from writing, enabled him to look forward to a definite career in science and to marriage. His one deep sorrow was the sudden death of his friend and benefactor, Prof. Edward Forbes. In a long list Huxley summarized the writing and lecturing in which he was engaged.

> Now, my dearest Lizzie, whenever you feel inclined to think it unkind I don't write, just look at that list, and remember that all these things require strenuous attention and concentration of the faculties, and leave one not very fit for anything else.[25]

All in all, 1854 was the great breakthrough, vindicating all his work and patience and suffering. As he put it in a letter to Lizzie, he finally had rounded the Cape (he had experienced Cape Horn on his return to England in 1850).

> There is always a Cape Horn in one's life that one either weathers or wrecks one's self on. Thank God I think I may say I have weathered mine—not without a good deal of damage to spars and rigging though, for it blew deuced hard on the other side.[26]

The presence of Lizzie in these letters, helped to no small degree in making it through that dangerous passage.

The following summer Nettie arrived from Australia and she and Huxley were married. Understandably Lizzie was not needed for counsel and comfort as much now, but periodic letters between them still kept the bond firm. He was anxious that it not be weakened. For instance, in 1858 he wrote within a month after receiving a letter from her, admonishing her:

> Do not be silent so long again; it is bad for both of us. I have loved but few people in my life, and am not likely to care for any more unless it be my children. I desire therefore rather to knot more firmly than to loosen the old ties, and of these which is older or stronger than ours? Don't let us drift asunder again.[27]

Their correspondence continued, with their only reunion being in 1876 when Huxley, on a lecture tour of the United States, arranged for a three-day stay in Nashville with Lizzie and her family, which will be discussed in a later chapter. In 1895, she died only a few weeks after him,[28] as if symbolically seeing her favorite young brother through to the very end.

In the period prior to 1855, then, young Huxley had an important confidante in his eldest sister, Lizzie, from whom he gained strength, which enabled him to struggle with his personal and professional uncertainties. During the years 1842–46, when he lived with her family in London, and during 1846–55, when they kept up a correspondence when she was in Germany or the United States and he on the high seas, in Australia, or in Britain, the bond was firm. As he rode the waves in the South Pacific, bent over his microscope, wrote at his desk, strode to the lecture-table, or walked the streets of London, she was there, her spirit ever urging him to do his very best, comforting him in sorrow, rejoicing with and praising him in success, advising him with the wisdom and courage of an older sister who had experienced much in life and in whom he had complete faith and trust. He was anxious to live up to her expectations, and that he did so, was in part a tribute to Lizzie and her role as his first important confidante.

Henrietta Ann Heathorn

At most ports into which the *Rattlesnake* called, Huxley's naval commission permitted him to mingle socially with many of the important local people. This was certainly true also in Sydney, where, at a party in a private home in August 1847, he met William Fanning, a leading merchant, and his young sister-in-law, Henrietta Heathorn. Late in life Henrietta wrote in her "Reminiscences":

> My first meeting [with] the young officer was at a private party at Mrs. Campbell's where, after our introduction by one of the midship (men) to one another, we later on only exchanged a few words, he asking me for a dance and my brother-in-law who stood by declaring it impossible as his wife (my sister) had already gone to put on her wraps & the horses cd not be kept waiting. "Never mind," said Mr. Huxley, "we shall meet again & then remember—you are engaged for the 1st dance."[29]

After meeting again at a ball, Huxley was soon riding horseback to the Fanning home, Holmwood, in New Town, just outside of Sydney, attracted by the friendship with the Fannings and with his rapidly growing attachment to Henrietta, a feeling that she likewise, shared.[30]

The Heathorn family had lived near Maidstone, in Kent, but in 1842 Henrietta's father had sailed to Australia where he eventually established a brewery and sawmill about ninety miles from Sydney. Henrietta studied in Germany for two years, and in December 1843, together with her mother and a stepsister, Oriana, arrived in Sydney to join him. The next year Oriana married William Fanning, and

Henrietta came to help her keep house. The friendship of the Fannings, and the immediate "at-one-ness" he felt with the sensible, sensitive, German-educated Henrietta, made Huxley feel very much at home at Holmwood. Invited to dine with the family on one occasion, he wrote later in his journal, "I never spent a happier evening. We sat around the fire and I told no end of auld wives tales—there was something that put me in mind of the happy old days at S's [Scott's in London]. . . . On my ride home that night I felt happier than I had for months."[31] Held back by ship duties, by social functions in Sydney, and by illness, Huxley was together with Henrietta only on a very few occasions before they became engaged in October, shortly before the *Rattlesnake* was to depart on its first surveying expedition.

On board ship, almost two months after their engagement, Huxley reflected on their relationship.

> We found corresponding events in our past life, we found that taste and habit of thought in each harmonised, and more than all each found that the other was loved . . . I felt awakened to a new life, pledged by all the confiding tender love of that dear girl, to a new course of action—nobler and purer. My personal character, my personal devotion is all I have to offer her in return. And shall not that be made worthy of her? The thought that it is my duty to discipline myself for her sake, that she may have less reason hereafter to repent her choice, nerves my better feelings—and often her image is my good genius, banishing evil from my thoughts and actions. Bless you, bless you, dearest, a thousand times. You have purified and sweetened the very springs of my being which were before but waters of Marah, dark and bitter were they. And strangely enough, too, not merely is your influence powerful over my heart, but my intellect is stronger, my thoughts more rapid, my energy less exhaustible, I never could acquire more rapidly or reason more clearly.[32]

When he chides himself later in his journal for writing so much about his love life instead of about the supposedly important subject of what the expedition was accomplishing, he answers himself, "Not events merely but those which influence a man, are of importance. These [socializing events with Henrietta] formed a new era in my life, a matter to me of much more importance than all H. M. navy put together."[33]

What was she like, this girl his same age who had such a strong hold on the twenty-two-year-old Huxley and who was to retain that hold for the rest of their lives? He wrote in his journal on board ship: "There was something inexplicably pleasing to me in the expression of her mild . . . countenance, in the tone of her voice, and still more in her sensible and yet thoroughly womanly conversation."[34] A year later, he described her in a letter to his mother.

> She is exceedingly fair, with the Saxon yellow hair and blue eyes. Then as to face, I really don't know whether she is pretty or not. I have never been able to decide the matter in my own mind. Sometimes I think she is, and sometimes I wonder how the idea ever came into my head. Whether or not, her personal appearance has nothing whatever to do with the hold she has upon my mind, for I have seen hundreds of prettier women. But I never met with so sweet a temper, so self-sacrificing and affectionate a disposition, or so pure and womanly a mind.[35]

Late in 1850, back in London, he summarized the characteristics of Henrietta ("Nettie") in a letter to Lizzie.

> Someone in whom I can place implicit confidence, whose judgment I can respect, and yet who will not laugh at my most foolish weaknesses, and in whose love I can forget all care. All these conditions I have fulfilled in Nettie. With a strong natural intelligence, and knowledge enough to understand and sympathise with my aims, with firmness of a man, when necessary, she combines the gentleness of a very woman and the honest simplicity of a child.[36]

Actually, they didn't spend much together in Australia. The *Rattlesnake* was in Sydney on only five occasions, and of course much of that time Huxley was not free to visit Nettie. Following their engagement, the *Rattlesnake* sailed on several surveying expeditions up the northeastern coast of Australia, north to the Torres Straits, and northeasterly to the Louisaides and New Guinea. But even though they were separated most of the time, they were together in spirit. During those years, Nettie replaced Lizzie as his premier confidante.

In his journal and in his letters to Lizzie and his mother during these years away from England, he makes manifest his great love for, commitment to, and reliance on, his fiancée. Together they struggled with what was the best thing to do regarding their marriage and regarding his life's vocation. In February 1848 he wrote in his journal that if his scientific papers he was sending to London did not meet with success, "I will give these things up and try some other channel towards happiness for dear Menen [his pet term of affection for her] and myself."[37] Three months later in his journal he expressed the inner agony with which he was grappling.

Have I the capabilities for a scientific life or only the desire and wish for it springing from a flattered vanity and self-deceiving blindness? Have my dreams been follies or prophecies? If in old times these questions have pressed themselves painfully upon my mind when my own fate was all that hung in the balance, how shall I cease to think over them now that the fate of one whom I love better than myself, depends upon their right or wrong solution.[38]

In March 1848 he wrote to Lizzie of his engagement, of the happiness Nettie had brought him, and of his new "home" in Sydney.[39] A year later he wrote to Lizzie of how he was looking forward to returning from his current expedition to his "home" in Sydney, and he reports that Nettie is "full of hope and confidence, and to me her love is the faith that moveth mountains."[40] At that same time, he wrote to his mother: "With my present income, of course, marriage is rather a bad look out, but I do not think it would be at all fair towards N. [Nettie] herself to leave this country without giving her a wife's claim upon me."[41] As he walked the decks of the *Rattlesnake* at night, no matter what he thought about, Nettie always came to the fore.[42] In his journal shortly before departure for England, Huxley spoke of "the influence of a pure and devoted love,"[43] which had become so central to his life, and he of course agonized over the lengthy separation to which they now would have to look forward. As the *Rattlesnake* approached England, Huxley closed his journal (which it was understood Nettie would read in lieu of letters) with the realization that he was *not* coming "home."

I feel most truly, that where you are there is my true home. There is where all my loves and all my anxieties are centered. Those whose care and affection reared me into manhood seem but as aliens, compared with you. The scenes of my childhood and youthhood seem but as strange compared with dear old Holmwood, and the bush paths where we twain have walked hand in hand.[44]

In the meantime, Nettie was also writing in her journal, which likewise it was understood he would read at some future time. In it she revealed her mutual love, commitment, reliance, and guidance. As he feared he was being unfair to her, so she worried that she was being unfair to him. "I would so gladly have the happy knowledge that nothing could separate us," she wrote in July 1849, "but I so fear it would not be right to burden him with myself under his present circumstances—God guide us."[45] The next month she wrote:

How happy am I in having one who loves me so much and who in every sorrow will truly sympathize with me. Dear dear one, he has my whole affection and it seems to me as if none other could have drawn forth so much love. Our tastes and thoughts and feelings agree and in all things he answers the ideal my heart told me I could love—before I knew him. My love, based upon esteem and reverence, clings to the dear object with a happy consciousness of his worth. He is my life, my all—God ever bless him.[46]

Shortly before he left Australia she wrote:

I told him that I reverenced as much as I loved him and believed that success or non-success was no criterion of merit, but he replied [that] he would not give anything for the ability that could not compel fortune— Oh Hal,[47] dear one, how wrong you are—many gifted ones who should have succeeded have failed and if you should, after doing your best, is it right to repine? You are so young too—if you have health and long life what may not your determined will accomplish? Dearest of all was your assurance that could you only have me with you you would yet be fully happy.[48]

Only one major obstacle existed: his critical approach to religion. Here his guidance was, in this early stage, looked upon as misguidance. She recorded in her journal in June 1849: "Dear Hal—God guide him to the perfect light for I am often very unhappy about his sentiments—I have so much need of leading unto holy things, am so dilatory luke-warm and dreamlike myself that I fondly hoped he would have been the guide and instructor unto more perfect ways—but here my hopes have borne bitter fruit."[49] However, she gradually grew to be at one with Huxley's views, and in fact her grandson, Julian Huxley, was startled to learn of her early religious anxieties. When he knew her in her old age, he wrote:

She had fully adopted the agnostic position, expected no personal survival after death, and was facing this anticipated extinction with complete equanimity. However, until she was fifty, she went regularly to Church and insisted on her children accompanying her. . . . She provided in her own person a lesson in how to grow old, serene in spite of her infirmity and her lack of what is usually called faith. Indeed, the mellow age of the grandmother is in strong contrast with the troubled soul of the young woman.[50]

Once Huxley was back in England, he and Nettie had to be satisfied with communicating via letters for four and a half years before she was able to come and join him in marriage. Their mutual love stood that test of time and separation, just as it had the long intervals when the *Rattlesnake* had been away from Sydney. Everything now was in an interlocking chain. He must work hard to acquire scientific qualifications; he must write and lecture as much as possible to gain attention and employment in the world of science; income was needed in order to become married. As he expressed it in a letter to Lizzie shortly after returning to England, "I have no ambition except as means to an end, and that end is the possession of a sufficient income to marry upon."[51] But he was also propelled by a craving for excellence. In November 1852 her wrote to Nettie:

> I do not think that I am in the proper sense of the word ambitious. I have an enormous longing after the highest and best in all shapes—a longing which haunts me and is the demon which ever impels me to work, and will let me have no rest unless I am doing his behests. . . . My demon says work! You shall not even love unless you work.[52]

Work he did, and that most diligently. But though he accumulated an increasing amount of praise, he was frustrated time and again in his hope to secure the needful income.

In his moments of triumph her praise was valued above all other plaudits, and honors were placed in the context of how they would hasten the wedding day. For instance, as soon as he finished his successful maiden public lecture at the prestigious Royal Institution on 30 April 1852, he hurried to his lodging to share his euphoria with Nettie: "My own pet, if you were here would you not . . . put your arms around my neck and give me a dear kiss, and call me your own Hal! You do not know Menen, how much more I would give for that reward than for all others."[53] When he received the highly revered Royal Society Medal in November 1852, he wrote to Nettie that it would be "a fine lever to help us on,"[54] and that no honor "would give me the pure and heartfelt joy and peace of mind that your love has given me, and, please God, shall give for many a long year to come."[55]

In frustration, disappointment, loneliness, and sorrow he relied on her steadying encouragement and comfort. He shared with her his frustrations at his lack of success in frequent efforts to secure a grant from the government or the Royal Society to enable him to publish his *Rattlesnake* materials, and he shared his disappointments over his unsuccessful candidatures for professorships. He constantly lamented to her about the general lack of financial opportunity in science and the abundance of politics in science. He poured out his sorrow to her at the sudden death of his mother. He occasionally wavered in his commitment to waiting for some position in science to open up, and thought seriously of returning to Australia to practice medicine or to undertake anything that would bring in enough money to permit their marriage. He wrote to Nettie in January 1852:

> I think of all my dreams and aspirations, and of the path which I know lies before me if I can only bide my time, and it seems a sin and a shameful thing to allow my resolve to be turned; and then comes the mocking suspicion, is this fine abstract duty of yours anything but a subtlety of your own selfishness? Have you not other more imperative duties? ... I must come to some resolution about it, and that shortly. I was talking seriously with Fanning the other night about the possibility of finding some employment of a profitable kind in Australia, storekeeping, squatting, or the like. ... I wish I understood Brewing, and I would make a proposition to come and help your father. You may smile, but I am as serious as ever I was in my life.[56]

But more often he stood firm, feeling that the pursuit of some scientific position

> more than any other enables me to lead the intellectually active life, which seems to be one of the very deepest wants of my nature. I feel that I am going on—that the Necessities of life do not come and say to me, "Turn your mind away from all the great problems of thought and action—put down the cup of knowledge just tasted and give up your thoughts and your strivings to us." Menen, I confess to you frankly that I am as yet too full of youth and hope and conscious power to do this without in a measure losing my own self-respect.[57]

In May 1852 he wrote to Lizzie: "I dare not face the stagnation—the sense of having failed in the whole purpose of my existence—which would, I know, sooner or later beset me, even with her [Nettie], if I foresake my present object [to secure a position in science]."[58] In a letter to Nettie in September 1852, he marveled at the growth in maturity and purpose he had experienced in the last six years thanks to Nettie, his naval experience, and his two years of labor in London. "It is quite strange to me now to look back upon my state of mind when I left England. ... I was honestly disgusted with life and careless of all it had to offer. In reality, I knew nothing about it. ... I believed in nothing and I cared for nothing."[59] Winning the Royal Society Medal in November 1852 helped to convince him "as clearly as anything can what is the true career that lies open before me. ...

It only strengthens and confirms the conclusion I had come to [to pursue patiently a position in science]."[60] By mid-1853 he could write to Nettie that he now was firm in his resolve to pursue a life in science.

> My course in life is taken. I will *not* leave London—I *will* make myself a name and a position as well as an income by some kind of pursuit connected with science, which is the thing for which nature has fitted me if she has ever fitted any one for anything. Bethink yourself whether you can cast aside all repining and all doubt, and devote yourself in patience and trust to helping me along my path as no one else could.[61]

Finally, in July 1854 he was able to write his "come home" letter. Two years earlier in July he had written his familiar lament to Nettie: "Menen, darling, I want you here to help me on my way—more than ever," followed by the familiar litany, "it is impossible so far as I can see, that you should come until I am in a position to give you a home."[62] Suddenly in the middle of 1854 employment opportunities began to open up. In May his friend and benefactor Prof. Edward Forbes was appointed to a chair in Edinburgh, and had to leave his London duties at once just as he was beginning a course of lectures at the Government School of Mines. Huxley wrote to Nettie in June:

> He [Forbes] had spoken to me of the possibility of his being called away long ago, and had asked if I would take his place, to which, of course, I assented, but the whole affair was so uncertain that I never in any way reckoned upon it. ... [O]n Friday the 25th May I took his lecture, and I have been going on ever since, twice a week on Mondays and Fridays. Called upon so very suddenly to give a course of some six and twenty lectures, I find it very hard work, but I like it and I never was in better health.[63]

This temporary employment was made permanent in July at a salary of £200 a year (about $960). On 30 July he reported to Nettie that the lectures had been successfully completed, and he rendered her a lengthy detailed account of his decidedly brightened financial picture.[64] With additional income from writing for periodicals, being released from the navy's rolls, and obtaining a grant from the Royal Society to enable him to publish his *Rattlesnake* materials, he now had the freedom and financial resources necessary for him to write to Nettie:

So my darling pet, come home as soon as you will—thank God I can at last say those words to you. . . . I feel now that I have all along hoped—that I have been right in doing as I have done—in spite of all the pain it has cost us. You will think that also will you not, Menen?[65]

Actually, Nettie's father had decided about this same time to come to England,[66] so she would have been coming anyway, but Huxley's sudden harvest of jobs enabled the marriage to be finalized.

Within two more months he had been appointed naturalist to the Geological Survey to study the Welsh and English coastal areas, and he had been asked to lecture on comparative anatomy at St. Thomas's Hospital and to lecture at the School of Science and Art at Marlborough House. Shortly before his marriage in July 1855 Huxley learned of his appointment as Fullerian Professor at the Royal Institution; his friend John Tyndall exulted: "May the gods continue to drop fatness upon you."[67]

During these months and years from late 1850 until their marriage, letters were extremely crucial in keeping their bond strong. He increasingly limited correspondence to only Nettie. "I find it getting more and more difficult," he wrote in February 1852, "to sit down and write a long letter to anybody but you—and I have pretty nearly stopped all my other correspondents."[68] As important as the correspondence with Nettie was during those years of working and waiting, "Correspondence," as Huxley once expressed it to a friend, "however active, is a poor substitute for personal communication."[69]

Huxley needed someone on the scene with whom he could counsel on matters of life and vocation. As he forlornly wrote to Lizzie upon returning to London from Australia, he really loved only two people in this world, her and Nettie. "And now she is away, and you are away."[70] To whom could he turn? There could be no substitute for Nettie without violating their special relationship, but Huxley did discover a surrogate Lizzie shortly after returning to England. Enter Mrs. Ellen Busk.

Mrs. Ellen Busk

Soon after Huxley's return to London late in 1850, he struck up a close friendship with Dr. George Busk, the surgeon of the HMS *Dreadnought*, at Greenwich. Huxley called Busk "a thoroughly honourable and good as well as able man who wouldn't do a dirty action if he tried."[71] But whereas Busk was "a man in a thousand," Mrs. Busk was "a woman in ten thousand,"[72] and it was mainly from Mrs. Busk that the lonely young Huxley received the intimate, sympathetic, and stimulating counseling that he so needed at this stage in his life.

The first time Huxley spent a long period of time with the Busks was in late summer 1851 when, following the meeting of the British Association in Ipswich, a small group of scientists and their families, including the Busks and the bachelor Huxley, decided to spend some time at the village of Felixstowe, on the seacoast near Ipswich. Telling of this outing in a letter to Nettie on 1 September 1851, Huxley mentioned the Busks for the first time, and from then until the end of 1854 Huxley's letters to his fiancée in Australia contained frequent comments about the Busks, especially Mrs. Busk. These letters become the major source of information about the Huxley-Busk friendship, and the only source of insight into the counseling role played by Ellen Busk in the life of Huxley during those crucial years, an important role hitherto overlooked.

Huxley had frequent contacts with the Busks during that period. He spent many weekends at their home in Greenwich,[73] was there for a Christmas gathering in 1852,[74] and had been invited to visit them at Sandown, Isle of Wight, in September 1852.[75] Late in 1852 and early in 1853 Busk and Huxley were engaged in the translation of Albert von Koelliker's *Manual of Human Histology* (a textbook on human anatomy) from German into English, for the Sydenham Society, which published the English version in the summer of 1853.[76] The income from this enterprise was important to the struggling young Huxley, but even more important perhaps was being linked with an older established scholar like Busk. Huxley did, however, bring to the translation the prestigious "FRS" after his name. Early in 1853 Busk was attempting to help Huxley secure a professorship of Physiology at King's College,[77] but without success. From August to November 1854, Huxley was at Tenby, South Wales, engaged in his geological survey work, preparing lectures, and relaxing; most of the time he was living with the Busk family.[78] In April 1855 Huxley was relying on some of Busk's findings for the Maritime Natural History of Great Britain, which Huxley was planning to formulate.

Huxley described Mrs. Busk to Nettie in various letters. Ellen Busk was seven or eight years older than Huxley.[80] In a letter in September 1851 shortly after their two weeks together at Felixstowe, Huxley described Ellen in some detail.

[She is] ... tall, very refined and ladylike ... with black hair—and anything but pretty, but with a most singular pair of ... grey eyes. The mouth somewhat large but highly expressive—a slight stoop in the figure ... kind and gentle manner. ... The words that flow from the mouth are sharpwitted, spirited and playful. They *can* be sarcastic enough—and on occasion show evidence of no little thought and no little suffering. ... She has four children—girls—the eldest ... has hair just like yours, and is altogether not unlike you. I make a pet of the child—can you tell why?[81]

In February 1852 Huxley again described her:

She ... has a very remarkable but by no means pretty face—In fact a mask of the face would be very plain, so you need not be jealous of my admiration (fancy the pout!!!) ... all her ways are exceedingly truthful—and yet graceful and fascinating. Though if she likes she can say as severe things as anybody I know. In fact I am not sure that your big boy is not a little bit afraid of her switch ... [She] possesses all the womanly feelings and even prejudices and yet is not afraid to face a logical consequence.[82]

Comparisons of Ellen and Nettie give interesting insights into both—and into the values of Huxley, especially his love for truthfulness.

She is as different from you, Menen darling as one human being can be from another—and yet I know you would be great friends, for there is the same foundation of truth and earnestness at the base of both your characters. ...[83] Though you are as different as any two people can be—there are numberless points in which you would be of essentially one mind—The basis of each of your characters is thorough truthfulness—and that harmony entails all others.[84]
... [As] different as you are you are both *true*—and that is the best common ground.[85]

The special and intimate rapport between Huxley and Mrs. Busk, which grew steadily, was very therapeutic for Huxley. The first time Huxley mentioned the Busks to Nettie, he said that Mrs. Busk "is a great ... ally of mine."[86] Three weeks later, on 23 September, discussing the Felixstowe vacation, Huxley spoke of "my friend Busk" but then commented much more on Mrs. Busk.

Busk and his charming wife are just two people after my heart,—their tastes harmonised so well with mine that I enjoyed everything the more.

I say *their* tastes which may surprise you, but Mrs. Busk is almost as enthusiastic a Naturalist as her husband. ... I have fallen into friendship with her in a manner quite unusual for me—and laid bare my heart to her in a way that astonishes me when I think of it. In truth, Menen, I know no one except yourself to whom I have talked as I have to her.[87]

In February 1852 Huxley wrote:

I think I have told you about her [Mrs. Busk] and her husband. They are the only intimate friends I have except the Fannings[88] and I often go down [to Greenwich] on a Saturday and stop till Monday. ... I do not make new friends in a hurry in general, and I have too much to do to wish to go into society of any other kind, except that in which it is politic to be seen [to further his chances of securing some position in science]—so that I know not how it is I have taken to the Busks so kindly. ... She does me a world of good and is the only person except Fanning with whom I can really take counsel. ... I should much like you to know her—as indeed I trust you will some of these days.[89]

With the Fannings returning Australia in the summer of 1852, Huxley turned even more to Mrs. Busk for counsel. In July, Huxley wrote to Nettie:

I wish you knew Mrs. Busk—I was down there yesterday, and had some long talks with her that did me good. Of all my friends over here she is I feel the only one who thoroughly understands the good and evil of me—and the only one who properly comprehends my aims—you will like her very much, and she would like you.[90]

In December 1852 he wrote:

She is I think next to yourself Menen, the most intimate and trusted friend I have. The friendship we commenced two years ago has become more and more intimate—until now she is a sort of elder sister to me—In this respect, my relation with her is so different from that with my dear little Polly [his brother George's wife]—who in spite of the very slight difference in age between us is and was and always will be a sort of child in my eyes—whom I love, but whom I don't counsel. Some of these days you shall know Mrs. Busk. You will love her and she will love you.[91]

In a letter to Nettie in July 1854 it becomes apparent that Huxley's friendship with Mrs. Busk had continued unabated, and had grown even warmer. At this joyous moment when Huxley could tell Nettie that he now had sufficient income to ask her to come to England to become his wife, he is quick to acknowledge his debt to Mrs. Busk for her counsel through his difficult years.

> And when you come to know her you shall love this sisterly friend who has more than any other helped me to be stedfast in my purpose. I have often spoken to you of Mrs. Busk—She has been my great friend and adviser in all my troubles—A wise, noble and trueminded woman, my pet, who has been your best friend as well as mine—I do not know anything I have so much at heart as that she and you should love one another.[92]

One of the most significant subjects on which Mrs. Busk served as a trusted counselor was Huxley's sadness at separation and his hopes for marriage. She is the only one with whom he confided his innermost thoughts on his relationship with Nettie. In four different letters from September 1851 to September 1852 Huxley wrote to Nettie:

> I have even told her all about you—a marvelous proof of my confidance. . . . You go by the name of "my wife" and form sometimes a very important element in our discussions. . . . I often talk to her about you— more unreservedly perhaps than to any one else, for she alone comprehends all my aims and struggles internal as well as external;— things I never can feel myself to talk about unless I am met halfways. . . . No one but Mrs. Busk knows anything about our engagement and she keeps my secret.[93]

Another crucial subject on which Mrs. Busk gave him an understanding ear was religion. Huxley's growing skepticism left him uneasy, because he knew that Nettie was greatly disturbed by his rationalist views. In September 1851 Huxley wrote to Nettie:

> We had much talk about theological matters. It did me good to open the ———— of my skepticism under her ————. She did not start back affrighted Menen as you did—for she has passed through it herself, and is familiar with its darkness. . . . I have rarely spoken of these things to you, darling, for I know that this is one of the anxieties I have brought you, but I have not the less thought—and sought for light.[94]

Earlier in 1851 he had been greatly heartened by evidence of growth in Nettie's religious questing: "You thrilled me, dearest, in one of your letters by telling me that the thought came upon you to think what you really believed."[94]

From early August to early October 1854 Huxley was living with the Busks at Tenby, and this prolonged closeness strengthened the bond between Huxley and Mrs. Busk. In September, Huxley wrote to Nettie:

> The Busks made up their mind to spend their holidays here —a few days before I left[96] and so I am much more comfortable than I should otherwise be—as we have set up a communistic establishment in a large house— ... Mrs. Busk feeding us and poking us up with the stick sometime too. ... You would have been amused the other day to hear Mrs. Busk and I ——— how we would have communistic establishments hereafter, when you were my dear little wife.[97]

On 14 October Huxley wrote:

> The Busks have been here with me up to last Wednesday when they returned to town with bag and baggage and left me solitary. Their being here has made my sojourn very pleasant in more ways than one and the raging cholera in London kept them here longer than they would otherwise have been.[98]

That is the last we hear of Mrs. Busk's counseling. Knowing of Nettie's plans to leave for England with her parents, he naturally would soon stop writing. When Huxley finally had his Nettie with him, there was obviously little need to rely on Mrs. Busk for counsel, and there is no evidence to suggest that he did to any great degree.

Marriage

On 6 May 1855 Huxley's close friend, John Tyndall, wrote in his journal: "Called on Huxley and spent two or three hours ... with him. He expects his wife daily."[99] The Heathorns did arrive a few days later. Nettie's extremely poor health was an immediate concern. Indeed, one doctor to whom Huxley took her gave her only six months to live, but another doctor was more encouraging. Regardless of the uncertainty, the wedding plans remained unchanged, and they were married on 21 July, at All Saints Church. As Nettie wrote late in life, their "wanderings in the wilderness were over—& we had reached the Promised Land."[100] After a small reception at George Huxley's home in Regent's Park, the happy newlyweds set out on a leisurely trip through Shakespeare country, and eventually reached Tenby, South Wales, where they stayed for two weeks with Huxley's friends, Dr. and Mrs. Frederick Daniel Dyster, and later were joined by the Busk family. In April and June, Huxley had written to Dyster telling of the coming wedding and of the plans to go to Tenby.[101] The Huxleys stayed at Tenby through September, as he had his Geological Survey duties to perform, and then they returned to London on their way to forty years of happy wedded life.

Nettie and Ellen apparently did not become the warm friends that Huxley had so hoped and anticipated. Tension was revealed between the two women in an exchange of letters between Huxley and Nettie in October 1856. When he was in South Wales on his Geological Survey work, and reporting on a visit from Ellen, Nettie was unusually quick to accuse Ellen of being hypocritical and lacking in frankness. "She was very gentle & kind & even called me 'dear' once which was more than she ever did before. She doesn't know how I'd love her if she were only straightforward about you."[102] Huxley was greatly upset, and immediately wrote to his wife, scolding her and explaining the facts of the situation that had irritated Nettie,[103] whereupon Nettie immediately repented, and wrote to him: "I feel as if I could go & put my arms around her neck & ask her to forgive me, & worse than all I have grieved you."[104]

Fortunately we do have an interesting comparison of the two, given by Thomas Archer Hirst, who became a close friend of both families, in his journal, 4 December 1859.

On Tuesday evening I dined at Huxley's. The party consisted of Mr. and Mrs. Busk, a Mr. Dennis Macdonald (a Naval surgeon) and myself. I enjoyed the evening very much and after the wine had a long talk with Mrs. Huxley and Mrs. Busk. The latter is a tall thin lady with a face not prepossessing at first. She is however quick and intelligent and has a self-possessed rather blunt but honest manner. Compared with Mrs. Huxley however, her mind is not of so high an order, she has not Mrs. Huxley's depth and warmth, she is more purely intellectual and material. The current of her thoughts is clearly more towards the appearances than deeper realities. We were speaking of the influence of physical pain on humanity, of the compensation due to those whose life here is but a succession of tortures. Mrs. Busk *admitted* the difficulty of the subject but Mrs. Huxley *felt* it. Mrs. B[usk] insisted that compensation must be sought in another life but evaded my question as to what she would consider compensation.[105]

The Busk and Huxley families remained close friends until death took George in 1887 and Ellen in 1890. George Busk, Huxley, and

Hirst were members of the "X Club," which will be discussed in a later chapter. At the death of Ellen, Hirst spoke for many of their circle of friends when he wrote in his journal; "More intelligent, courageous and high minded lady I never knew."[106]

The Huxleys built a lifetime of close affection. After three and a half years of marriage, Nettie wrote to Lizzie, "You Lizzie, who love and know him so well, will not think me egotistical when I say how good & earnest & true hearted he is. I am very blest in possessing him—and—I know it."[107] Having only moderate income, having eight children, and supporting some of Huxley's relatives, meant that economically, as Nettie expressed it in her widowhood (she outlived him by nineteen years), "Life was indeed a struggle—but we came out winners, helped thereto by the happiness and sympathy of a great sustaining love."[108] She also reminisced, "It was the rich brightness of his great enfolding love for me, that for our forty years of wedded life knew no shadow of change, save increase of love, that brought about something of the divine light into our house. The eternal goodness in him drew me on unconsciously to better things."[109]

It is clear, then, that until the age of twenty-two, Huxley looked for intimate counsel and support mainly from his eldest sister, Lizzie; from the ages of twenty-two to twenty-five (1847–50) from his fiancée, Nettie; and from twenty-five until his marriage at thirty (1850–55), from his surrogate older sister, Mrs. Ellen Busk. Lizzie remained important in a secondary role after 1847, and Nettie's "presence" was always close while he was in London after 1850. Serving as listeners, as sources of advice, comfort, encouragement, reinforcement, and challenge, the influence of these confidantes is unmistakably clear.

There were of course, a few close male advisers. William Fanning, nine years older than Huxley, gave some limited counsel in Australia and for one and a half years in London. The advice of Huxley's closest friends and patrons in science was limited for the most part to professional concerns, and these men also were considerably older than he: Busk was eighteen years older, Dr. W. B. Carpenter was twelve, and Prof. Edward Forbes was ten. In 1851 Huxley began to develop a close bond with Joseph Hooker and John Tyndall, scientists more his own age with whom he could discuss personal as well as professional matters. Their lifelong friendship will be discussed in a later chapter on the "X Club," when I will again explore the importance of private interpersonal communication in the life of the public rhetorician.

2

Maiden Public Address, 1852

In February 1852 Huxley could write the good news to Nettie that he had just been invited by the secretary of the Royal Institution, at the suggestion of Prof. Edward Forbes,[1] "to give one of the Friday evening lectures there after Easter. Of course I was only too happy to consent as it is considered a 'crack' thing . . . it is fixed for the 30th of April."[2] This would be Huxley's first significant public lecture, and it would help enormously in setting him on his course toward becoming an influential scientific orator. Utilizing the basic oral communication elements of speaker, occasion, audience, message, delivery, and effect, this chapter will analyze this important rhetorical event in the life of the young Huxley.

Speaker

During this period in Huxley's life, he was inexperienced but potentially talented as a lecturer, increasingly experienced and effective as a writer, highly confident in his scientific qualifications, independent and courageous, considerably combative, and grief-stricken due to his mother's recent death.

Although certainly talkative and not averse to expressing himself in person-to-person or group contexts, Huxley had had very little experience in, and a great deal of anxiety about, formal public speaking. In a letter to Lizzie immediately following the lecture he termed it "my first appearance,"[3] which meant his first public lecture. In his autobiography written at the age of sixty-four, he called this 1852 lecture at the Royal Institution "the first important audience I ever addressed."[4] Julian Huxley has cautiously stated that the speech was "probably" his grandfather's "first public lecture,"[5] but we can more confidently assert that it definitely was. In his autobiography, Huxley stated that early in his life he "disliked public speaking, and had a firm conviction that I should break down every time I opened my mouth."[6]

His first experience in speaking in a public setting had occurred the previous July at the twenty-first annual meeting of the British Association for the Advancement of Science, held at Ipswich. His first and only prior attendance at a meeting of the British Association had been in 1846, at Southampton, while waiting for the *Rattlesnake* to sail from Portsmouth, and he had been duly awed by it all. Now, at the age of twenty-six and with his *Rattlesnake* experience behind him, he was considerably more confident, but still thoroughly apprehensive about his ability to speak in public. He confided to Nettie that anyone who thought he went to Ipswich "from any especial interest in the progress of science makes a great mistake. My journey was altogether a matter of policy, partly for the purpose of doing a little necessary trumpeting, and partly to get the assistance of the Association in influencing the Government"[7] for a grant to enable him to work on his *Rattlesnake* materials. In a letter to a close friend, Huxley repeated that he went to Ipswich "not by any means to advance science, but to be 'advanced' myself—by getting the Association as a body to recommend Govt. to publish my work."[8] Thus, eager mainly to further Huxley, he was highly motivated to make himself seen and heard. He attended the sessions of his Section, "Natural History" (Section D), and it is there that Huxley first faced a public speaking situation. He described his speech in a letter to Nettie.

> On the first day there was rather a dearth of matter in our section. People had not arrived with their papers. So by way of finding out whether I could speak in public or not—I got up and talked to them for about twenty minutes. I was considerably surprised to find that when once I had made the plunge, my tongue went glibly enough. On the following day I read a long paper which I had prepared and illustrated with a lot of big diagrams—to an audience of about 20 people![9]

Still another day he "made a speechification of some length in the Section about a new animal."[10] On another day in a meeting of a different group he was caught by surprise and was called on to make an impromptu "vote of thanks."[11] These episodes, together with other informal situations, such as the meeting of the "Red Lion" social club,[12] gave him some initial opportunities at speaking, but to small homogenous audiences. The experience of delivering a formal, prepared public lecture before a large and heterogeneous audience was yet to come.

It was recognized that at this early age Huxley possessed considerable potential talent for effective public speaking. When writing a testimonial letter in behalf of Huxley's candidacy for the natural Science professorship at the University of Toronto, Dr. William B. Carpenter wrote, after discussing Huxley's competence in the subject matter, "It is right that I should add, that Mr. Huxley possesses a remarkable power of expressing himself clearly and emphatically,—qualities which are most important to the success of a public speaker."[13] In his testimonial, Prof. Edward Forbes wrote that Huxley "possesses in a remarkable degree the power ... of expounding his views orally with perspicuity, readiness and eloquence."[14] Early in 1852 Huxley wrote to his friend, Dr. John Tyndall, then a promising young physicist, who was anxious to secure a position in London and hopefully at the Royal Institution (and who soon did get a professorship there and eventually succeeded Faraday as resident professor):

> What they [the Royal Institution] want and what they have are *clear powers of exposition*—so clear that people may think they understand even if they don't. That is the secret to Faraday's success, for not a tithe of the people who go to hear him really understand him.[15]

It takes a master of clear oral prose to recognize another, and Huxley could have been ascribing that same talent to himself. His forcefulness of expression, such a fundamental part of his communicative style, is present even in his letters to Nettie.

Although inexperienced as a public lecturer, Huxley had accumulated considerable experience as a writer. He had sent to London numerous papers from Sydney based on his experiments on sea specimens secured in his towing net.[16] As he later wrote in his autobiography.

> I sent home communication after communication to the "Linnean Society," with the same result as that obtained by Noah when he sent the raven out of his ark. Tired at last of hearing nothing about them, I determined to do or die, and in 1849 I drew up a more elaborate paper and forwarded it to the Royal Society. This was my dove, if I had only known it. But owing to the movements of the ship, I heard nothing of that either until my return to England in the latter end of the year 1850, when I found that it was printed and published, and that a huge packet of separate copies awaited me.[17]

This paper was entitled, "On the Anatomy and the Affinities of the Family of the Medusae," and as he wrote in his ship journal in February 1848, it was to be a turning point. If I hear well of it when we return from our long cruise, I shall consider that I am fit for such occupations and shall go on accordingly. If on the other hand, it goes badly (and I am often troubled with great misgivings) I will give these things up and try some other channel towards happiness for dear Menen and myself.[18]

In March 1848 he wrote to Lizzie that his chances for professional advancement and marriage hinged on his writing accomplishments.[19] Writing from Sydney to his mother in February 1850, he confessed, "I find myself getting horribly selfish, looking at everything [sending papers to London] with regard to the influence it may have on my grand objects."[20] By the end of 1851 he had published fourteen scientific memoirs[21] as well as magazine articles and some translating. Writing did not come easily, but through diligence he was gradually making his mark.

Clear and effective writing rests to a considerable degree on setting forth objectives, which was an early habit of his, revealed even in his teenage journal, "Thoughts and Doings," in which he set down his reading objectives for a given period, and later indicated what he had accomplished. In December 1846, while waiting at Plymouth for the *Rattlesnake* to sail, he enunciated in his ship journal his personal objectives for the voyage. Although he admitted that he may not adhere to any projected plan, nevertheless "it is well to have such a guiding thread—be it but the purpose of fixing the thoughts steadily on the main points and not allowing the mind to be frittered away on whatever falls across it."[22]

At the dawn of 1852, although Huxley lacked confidence in his public speaking ability, he was quite convinced that he could hold his own in the world of science. In November 1850 he wrote to Lizzie, "I don't know and I don't care whether I shall ever be what is called a great man. I will leave my mark somewhere, and it shall be clear and distinct."[23] Knowing that mastery of subject matter came only from hard work, he drove himself with great intensity. Early in 1852 he wrote to Nettie about his busy work schedule.

All these things take a world of time and labour. ... I am beginning to learn what *work* means ... how much may be done by steady unceasing and well directed effort. I thrive upon it too. I am as well as I ever was in my life. ... Hard work always agrees with me—it lets off the spare steam which otherwise threatens to blow up the engine. Pray do not make yourself unhappy about any such nonsense, my darling [relatives had written Henrietta that Huxley worked too hard and looked ill]—people don't understand my habits and therefore fancy they must be injurious.[24]

In February 1852 he confidently asserted to Nettie that although he would admit that he feels inferior to the contemporary leaders in science, "I feel myself, I may tell you privately, ready to go in with any of them."[25]

This confidence stemmed not only from his own self-estimate, but from praise he received from highly respected scientists, and from general recognition from the scientific world. Whatever doubts he had on the *Rattlesnake* as to the merit of the work he was doing, were swept away when upon arrival in London he received favorable treatment from the elite of science.[26] He received a letter from Prof. Forbes who had helped to get Huxley's *Rattlesnake* papers published.

> I have had very great pleasure in examining your drawings of animals observed during the voyage of the *Rattlesnake*, and have also fully availed myself of the opportunity of going over the collections made during the course of the survey upon which you have been engaged. I can say without exaggeration that more important or more complete zoological researches have never been conducted during any voyage of discovery in the southern hemisphere.[27]

In March 1851, one of his papers was read at the Royal Society, and in June he was one of fifteen selected out of the thirty-eight candidates to become a Fellow of the Royal Society. To have the prestigious "FRS" after one's name at the age of twenty-six was indeed an accomplishment. In the same year, he only narrowly missed receiving the Royal Medal, one of the highest possible scientific honors, and in fact he did win it the following year.[28] At the meeting of the British association in 1851, Huxley's *Rattlesnake* work was praised,[29] and the president of the association, Colonel Sabine, later personally advised Huxley not to despair in his efforts to secure a scientific position; he had no doubt that Huxley would be successful eventually.[30] Thus, at the end of 1851 he wrote to Nettie of the great encouragement he had received from the scientific world.

> Obstinate and self-willed as I am ... there are times when grave doubts over-shadow my mind [as to continuing in science with no prospects of a position], and then such testimony as this [being considered for the Royal Medal] restores my self-confidence. ... If this were from personal friends only, I should disregard it; but it comes from men to whose approbation it would be foolish affectation to deny the highest value. I find myself treated on a footing of equality ("my proud self," as you may suppose, would not put up with any other) by men whose names and works have been long before the world. My opinions are treated with a

respect altogether unaccountable to me, and what I have done is quoted as having full authority. . . . I have at last tasted what it is to mingle with my fellows—to take my place in that society for which nature has fitted me.[31]

Huxley had already developed an unusually strong sense of intellectual independence, which was to become a familiar Huxley trademark. His biologist-grandson, Julian Huxley, admirably summarized the point.

Throughout his life he made it a practice to verify an anatomical or zoological fact for himself before utilizing it in book or lecture. This may have been time-consuming, but it gave him and his scientific utterances an unprecedented weight. I should be pretty certain that the foundation for this practice of his was laid aboard the *Rattlesnake*, in the necessity for depending on his own resources, and in the discovery that his own observations often showed that accepted zoological authority was wrong . . . he early learnt the secret of true self-reliance, without undue diffidence on the one hand or too easy confidence on the other. More than that, he was driven in on himself and his own reasoning powers.[32]

Upon his return from his voyage, in his papers at the British Association meeting in Ipswich, in his papers read at the Royal Society, and in other situations, he challenged many accepted scientific ideas.[33] He took pride in originality. In fact, even when only about eighteen years old, Huxley had the boldness to go to the great Faraday with a scheme for perpetual motion.[34] In March 1852 he wrote to Nettie that a paper he had just finished for the Royal Society was "very original."[35] This was entitled, "On the Morphology of the Cephalous Mollusca," the originality of which was fortunately well attested to by Professor Forbes in his referee's report to the Royal Society.

It is a memoir of very great interest, full of original observations and also of theoretical considerations of great general interest. I believe it will contribute an important step in advance of our knowledge of the section of the animal kingdom to which it is devoted. I therefore strongly recommend the publication of this paper in the "Philosophical Transactions."[36]

His independent search for truth was likewise beginning in the area of religion as well as science. In February 1851 he expressed to Nettie his central concern for the intellectual search for truth, indicating that he often questioned just what he really did believe, but admitting that "it is not always that one has courage for such scrutiny."[37] Along with the formulation of independent views, both scientific and religious, he was also developing confidence in his ability to publicly express his views.

Not only did he seek independence in his ideas, but also independence from undue help from anyone. He insisted on securing honor and position only on his merit, rather than on any personal "connections." Upon his return to London from the South Seas, he wrote a letter to Lizzie in which, after mentioning some of the leading scientists who had treated him kindly, he wrote a veritable "declaration of independence."

> I am under no one's *patronage*, nor do I ever mean to be. I have never asked, and I never will ask, any man for his help from mere motives of friendship. If any man thinks that I am capable of forwarding the great cause in ever so small a way, let him just give me a helping hand and I will thank him, but if not, he is doing both himself and me harm in offering it, and if it should be necessary for me to find public expression to my thoughts on any matter, I have clearly made up my mind to do so, without allowing myself to be influenced by hope of gain or weight of authority.[38]

He was proud that he had been elected into the Royal Society "without canvassing a soul or making use of any influence,"[39] and he insisted that whatever advantageous contacts all his labors gave him, he fully intended to maintain his own independence.

It is, of course, not very far from "independence," "self-confidence," and "forcefulness of expression" to a spirit that many would term *combativeness.* This willingness, indeed eagerness, to confront ideas and men—in the cause of "true science"—was already becoming quite manifest in this young man who was soon to be labeled "Darwin's bulldog." It isn't until after 1860 that his combativeness becomes directed against theologians. In these early years he is unusually ready to stand his ground against the older conservative scientists, like Prof. Richard Owen, for example. Although Owen actually had been helpful up to this time,[40] Huxley knew thir views and personalities clashed, and carefully stepped through the dangerous political minefield. In November 1851 he wrote to W. Macleay, the famous naturalist whose acquaintance Huxley had made in Sydney, that Owen "has . . . been very civil to me and I am as grateful as it is possible to be towards a man with whom I feel it necessary to be always on my guard."[41] In March 1852 Huxley wrote to Nettie that he wasn't certain whether or not his recently completed paper to be read at the Royal Society would be published.

> That will require care and a little maneuvering on my part—You have no notion of the intrigues that go on in this blessed world of science. Science is, I fear, no purer than any other region of human activity—though it should be. ... For instance I know that the paper I have just sent in is very original and of some importance and I am equally sure that if it is referred to the judgment of my "particular friend" Prof. Owen that it will *not* be published. He won't be able to say much against it but he will pooh-pooh it to a dead certainty. You will ask with some wonderment, why? Because for the last twenty years Owen has been regarded as the great authority on these matters—and has had no one to tread on his heels—until at last I think he has come to look upon the natural world as his special preserve and "no poachers allowed." So I must maneuvre a little to get my poor memoir kept out of his hands.[42]

In a letter to Lizzie in November 1850, Huxley claimed to "hate the incessant struggle and toil to cut one another's throat among us men"[43] in the public world. But he managed to hold his own rather well.

He was, for all practical purposes, unemployed, and this burdened him throughout these early years. He had no desire to remain in the navy, for it offered him "nothing . . . except [an] irretrievable waste of time."[44] He was unsuccessful in obtaining a grant from the Royal Society or from the government to facilitate the publication of his *Rattlesnake* materials. He was unsuccessful in securing a professorship or other scientific employment. This proded him to be original in his lectures, so as to attract attention and thus to increase the possibility of a position. But he could not afford to be too mcuh of a maverick, for then he could endanger his chances of employment—and marriage. In mid-1852 he disconsolately wrote to Lizzie, "Science in England does everything—but *pay*. You may earn praise but not pudding. I have helping hands held out to me on all sides but there is nothing to help one to."[45]

Finally, as if all of the factors already discussed and his loneliness in being separated from his fiancée were not enough, the sudden death of Huxley's mother two weeks before the Royal Institution lecture left him grief-stricken. At the end of his letter in which he told Nettie of his mother's death, he revealed his deep sadness.

> I cannot tell you how strangely all this has affected me. I feel shaken like a man who has had a hideous dream. On the 30th my lecture is to take place. I cannot put it off,—and yet I feel unable properly to collect my

faculties to finish it. She was very proud of my going to lecture at the Royal Institution and took greatest possible interest in the event. I am very very sad Menen ... this has opened the floodgates and the whole weariness of existence has ... drowned all other feelings. For me there is neither certainly of faith nor any consolation—but only a stern summoning of all my courage to bear what is inevitable—Belief and Happiness seem to be beyond the reach of thinking men in these days— but Courage and Silence are left.[46]

Two days later he wrote a lengthy account of the sad news to Lizzie.[47] While not really close to his mother, Huxley nevertheless respected and honored her.[48] Immediately after finishing his lecture Huxley wrote to Nettie, "I had got very nervous about it [the lecture]—and my poor mother's death—how she would have entered into my success!—had greatly upset my plans for working it out."[49]

Thus, on the eve of his twenty-seventh birthday, Huxley was facing his first major opportunity, that would allow him to show what he could do in a public speaking situation. He was a promising speaker but he was inexperienced. These were some of the ingredients that were operating as he strode into the famous Lecture Theatre of the Royal Institution one evening in April 1852.

Occasion

Ever since its foundation in 1799 by Count Rumford, the Royal Institution of Great Britain has played a major role in the scientific world. Located in Albemarle Street, not far from Piccadilly Circus, the institution with its laboratory and lecture theater and its dedication to the discovery and dissemination of scientific knowledge, has continued to the present day to be a focal point for the promotion of science. The names of such famous nineteenth-century resident professors as Sir Humphry Davy, Michael Faraday, and John Tyndall, are universally recognized and honored. As expressed by one writer, "The Institution has become known throughout the world as a scientific and cultural centre, in which man's age-long search for truth, his questioning of the universe in which he exists, can find outlet and expression."[50] Lectures were intended to interest as well as to instruct, to appeal to the layman as well as to satisfy the scientist, to honor scientific probing as well as to emphasize the practical application of science.

Under the impetus of the great Faraday, the famous Friday Evening Discourses were started in 1825, the Christmas Juvenile

Lectures for schoolchildren in 1826. Both series continue to this day. The twenty annual Friday Evening Lectures in Huxley's time,[51] were (and continue to be) major scientific and social events, where the elite of both society and science hear a distinguished scientist deliver a lecture on a recent experiment, observation, speculation, application, or reminiscence, utilizing various illustrative aids. The lectures are published in the *Proceedings of the Royal Institution*, and thus reach a world-wide audience. Many would agree with the judgment that "In maintaining the high standard of its Friday Evening Discourses the Institution has performed one of its most valuable services to science."[52]

Thus, it is understandable that young Huxley would write excitedly to Nettie in February 1852: "A great deal may come of this lecture—a success may do me a world of service."[53] When he wrote to her in March he said he was working diligently on the lecture, "as it is a great opportunity."[54] This might be the very breakthrough he was looking for.

Audience

The unique combination of London's high society and the elite of science made the audience of the Friday Evening Discourses one of the most significant and awesome for anyone, and much more so for a young middle-class scientist, inexperienced in public speaking. In a letter to Lizzie, Huxley called it "the best audience in London,"[55] and indeed thirty years later in a letter to an American friend, Huxley termed it "the best audience in the country."[56] Royal Institution audiences were even described as "probably the most aristocratic and intellectual audiences in the world."[57] Huxley wrote to Nettie that

> the audience is a most peculiar one—at once the best and the worst in London. The best, because you have all the first scientific men there—the worst, because you have a great number of fashionable ladies—The only plan is to take a profound subject—and play at battle and shuttle-cock with it—so as to suit both.[58]

Faraday emphasized that science "and nature will have charms innumerable in every dress, yet I am sorry to say that the generality of mankind cannot accompany us one short hour unless the path is strewed with flowers."[59]

Huxley's audience that night included Faraday, Profs. Edward Forbes and Wharton Jones, Lord Overstone, and a "whole lot of 'nobs',"[60] that is, people of wealth or social standing. His brother George and his wife Polly[61] and the Fannings were also in attendance. Huxley received some admission tickets to give to whomever he wished.[62] Nettie was of course present in his thoughts, especially since he had received a letter from her that very morning. Back in February he had written her:

> I hardly know whether I should like you to be there or not. I should like you to rejoice in my success—but you are the very last person in the world I would have witness my failure—if I do fail. So I think my sweet one, you are best away.[63]

The record shows that 323 were in attendance at the lecture,[64] which for that year was considerably below average. Of the twenty lectures, seventeen drew larger audiences, but it is understandable that the young Huxley in his first attempt could hardly compete with such lecturers as Faraday, Forbes, Sir Charles Lyell, Prof. Baden Powell, Dr. W. B. Carpenter, and Dr. Lyon Playfair! The attendance was no doubt related mainly to the lecturer, but there were other contributing factors as well, for instance, the time of year, the subject, the weather, and other competing meetings in the city. Since the attendance was recorded, each lecturer must have been very sensitive to how many people he drew compared to the other lecturers. This no doubt stimulated lecturers to be as interesting as possible, in order to be asked again. Probably about seven hundred people could squeeze into the Lecture Theatre. When the attendance exceeded that, people had to wait in the ante-room and library, and settle for mingling with the people after the lecture. (Today a smaller second auditorium with closed circuit television helps to handle any overflow audience.)

Speakers were expected to prepare a brief abstract of their lecture, which would be made available to the audience, making it easier for them to follow the presentation. Thus, for instance, a week before Huxley's lecture, the secretary of the Royal Institution asked him "for an abstract of your discourse to be printed for use of our Members. All, especially the foreigners, value these sketches."[65]

Message

Huxley's manuscript copy of his lecture, "On Animal Individuality," and a brief rough draft are in the Imperial College Archives.[66] A five-page abstract is published in the *Proceedings of the Royal Institution*.[67]

In his introduction, Huxley utilized his *Rattlesnake* experiences and Coleridge's poem, "The Rime of the Ancient Mariner," to create an interesting narrative.

> I imagine that there must be very few among my present auditory, who know what a tropical calm is.
>
> There must be few if any, who have looked above, into that hot and copper sky [68]—and below into the deep blue, but still hot and glaring, sea—with its long, low, ——— just sufficient to cause a lazy shivering of the pendent sails, and cheat one with the hope of a breeze aloft.
>
> But many may have imagined such a scene.[69]

Then, referring to, and quoting briefly from, Coleridge's familiar poem, Huxley took issue with the poet's depiction of the sea as evil, dead, and unfriendly, and led into the purpose of his lecture.

> I must protest against such a libel upon the delicate and peaceful inhabitants of the Ocean: creatures which have been to me sources of occupation and of delight, for many an otherwise weary hour.
>
> It will be my endeavour in the course of the present hour—not only to claim your admiration—for the exquisite symmetry and delicacy of form—: for the brilliancy of colour: for the wonderful simplicity and yet completeness for the end of their being, of my old favourites—: but, to shew also, that the attentive consideration of their pecularities may lead us into difficult and abstract speculations:—whence I trust, we may emerge with clearer ideas on some of the most important fundamental points of Zoology—than as it seems to me, are now prevalent.[70]

Drawing an analogy with a pendulum, he developed the kind of individuality, which, as he phrased it in his abstract,

> is constituted and defined by a fact or law of succession. Phenomena which occur in a definite cycle are considered as one in consequence of the law which connects them.
>
> As a simple instance we may take the individuality of the beat of a pendulum. An individual beat is the sum of the successive places of the bob of the pendulum as it passes, from a state of rest to a state of rest again.
>
> Such is the individuality of living, organized beings. Every organized being *has* been formless and will again be formless; the individual animal or plant is the *sum* of the incessant changes, which succeed one another between these two periods of rest.
>
> The individual animal is one beat of the pendulum of life, birth and death are the two points of rest, and the vital force is like the velocity of the pendulum, a constantly varying quantity between these two zero

points. The different forms which an animal may assume correspond with the successive places of the pendulum.

In man himself, the individual, zoologically speaking, is not a state of man at any particular moment as infant, child, youth or man; but the sum of all these, with the implied fact of their definite succession. . . .

[In conclusion] The individual animal is the sum of the phenomena presented by a single life: in other words, it is, all those animal forms which proceed from a single egg, taken together.[71]

His biologist-grandson, Julian Huxley, has commented on the substance of the lecture.

The beginning of the cycle he fixed in the act of fertilization of the egg setting aside the budding and other asexual processes of reproduction as in some way less fundamental. In this last point we now know that he was wrong: there is no biological reason for dating the birth of an individual by the act of fertilization rather than by an asexual act: if it were so, we should have to say that a pair of identical twins were not two individuals but one individual. . . . But he was right in perceiving that a biological individual is a process, a cycle, and that individuality must be defined in dynamic, not merely in static terms. He was right also in assigning special significance to the sexual process of fertilization—merely wrong in linking this significance with the quite distinct significance of individuality. . . . His ideas forced men to ask themselves what they really did mean by an individual, and were a real stimulus to later advance: and his method of cutting the Gordian knot by introducing one definite fact—the cycle from one fertilization to the next—as the differential of individuality, is characteristic.[72]

Toward the end of his lecture, Huxley made clear his independence of view on the subject just discussed.

I should now be very glad to leave these views of Animal Individuality—to your consideration without further comment.

But I am unfortunate enough to stand almost alone, as their advocate. With the exception of one distinguished Physiologist—Dr. Carpenter—, Men of Science, at the present day—take precisely the opposite view of the subject.[73]

"The Theatre of this Institution is no place for controversy,"[74] he said, but, in characteristic Huxley manner he went on to label other views as absurd. The lecture thus clearly revealed his combative spirit, his bold independence of view, his thorough command of a difficult subject, clarity of organization, and effective utilization of figurative language and literary allusions.

It was a subject to which he had given considerable thought during recent years. As Julian Huxley put it, "We can assume with a good deal of probability that his first philosophizings on the subject floated through his mind as he paced the *Rattlesnake*'s deck on fine tropic nights before turning in to sleep."[75] In November 1851, Huxley wrote to W. Macleay, the Sydney naturalist:

> I have been working in all things with a reference to wide views of zoological philosophy, and the report upon the Echinoderms is intended in common with the mem[oir] on the Salpae to explain my views of Individuality among the lower animals—views which I mean to illustrate still further and enunciate still more clearly in my book that is to be.[76]

The Royal Institution lecture gave him an excellent opportunity to crystallize his ideas on the subject. So when he wrote to Nettie in February 1852, "Not a thing written or thought about it yet,"[77] he was referring to the specific lecture preparation, not to the general subject itself. In the same letter Huxley mentioned that when Faraday inquired at a social gathering as to what the subject was to be, Huxley told him, "I meant to introduce some peculiar speculation of my own—which must considerably modify the theory of zoology—he said—Well—I suppose, if you are going to oppose anybody, you have thought well over it."[78] In March he *was* working diligently on the lecture, "which I want to make striking and original,"[79] and after the lecture he wrote to Lizzie that his discourse was "on a difficult subject, requiring a good deal of thought" so that for some time he had had to "abstract my thoughts from everything else."[80] In his letter to Nettie immediately following the lecture, Huxley wrote, "I had chosen a very difficult abstract point, in my view of which I stand almost alone."[81] The importance and complexity of the subject and his independent position, no doubt contributed greatly to his already high nervous tension.

Delivery

Within an hour and a half following the lecture, Huxley was back in his room sharing his euphoria with Nettie.

> I have just returned from giving my lecture at the Royal Institution. . . . I had got very nervous about it. . . . This morning there came a letter from you, my dearest,—that I took to be a good omen—but I was nevertheless more anxious and nervous tonight, than I think I ever have been in life—.

When I took a glimpse into the theatre and saw it full of faces—I did feel most amazingly uncomfortable—I can now quite understand what it is to be going to be hanged, and nothing but the necessity of the case prevented me from running away. However when the hour struck, in I marched—and began to deliver my discourse[82]—For ten minutes I did not quite know where I was—but by degrees—I got into it, and gradually gained perfect command of myself and of my subject.[83]

A week later in a letter to Nettie he revealed how closely linked were tension and ecstasy in his professional and personal life.

My state on last Friday week was only comparable to one other condition in my life—I mean the three days which preceded October 4th, 1847—Do you remember that day darling?—[the day of their engagement][84]

On 3 May he wrote to Lizzie that because of the difficult subject, the elite audience, and it being his first public lecture,

you may imagine how anxious and nervous I was. . . . I had made up my mind all day to break down, and then go and hang myself privately. And so you may imagine that I entered the theatre with a very pale face, and a heart beating like a sledge-hammer nineteen to the dozen.[85] For the first five minutes I did not know very clearly what I was about, but by degrees I got possession of myself and of my subject, and did not care for anybody.[86]

Huxley's son, Leonard, in his biography, writes that the lecture "was very different in manner and delivery from the clear and even flow of his later style, with the voice not loud but distinct,[87] the utterance never hurried beyond the point of immediate comprehension.[88] In his autobiography Huxley wrote about that first lecture, "I believe I had every fault a speaker could have (except talking at random or indulging in rhetoric)."[89] This is probably slightly exaggerated, written from the secure vantage point of being able to look back on a life of a successful speaker. No doubt his delivery was not as effective as it later became, but certainly it was impressive enough to launch him on a successful career as a public speaker.

Effects

The immediate reaction to the lecture seemed to be highly favorable. In his biography Leonard Huxley asserted that the lecture was successful in "carrying the attention of the audience with it, eager to the end."[90] Later that same night Huxley wrote to Nettie:

> I believe I continued to interest my audience, and upon the whole I think I may say that this essay was completely successful. Thank Heaven I *can* say so. . . . I had a long supplementary discussion with Faraday and Lord Overstone & some others who came asking questions. All seemed pleased & satisfied.[91]

Three days later Huxley wrote to Lizzie, "I have had 'golden opinions from all sorts of men' about it [the lecture], so I suppose I may tell you I have succeeded."[92]

The lecture understandably left him completely exhausted. He concluded his immediate report to Nettie that night. "I am very very tired and used, my darling; and I must go and have a long sleep—my Frau Professorin."[94] On 9 May he continued his letter to Nettie.

> The foolish state of excitement into which I allowed myself to get the other day, completely did me, my dearest Menen, and I have hardly done anything since, except sleep a great deal. It is a strange thing that will all my will—I cannot control my physical organization.[95]

But he eventually recovered, for on 13 June he wrote to her, "I have been very busy—busy writing and reading and thinking—"[96]

The lecture brought him to the attention of a broader London audience and increased his stature among men of science. It was a most significant breakthrough for securing an eventual professorship, even though he had to wait two more years. To obtain a professorship, it was essential to demonstrate proficiency in public lecturing. For instance, Huxley wrote to his job-seeking friend, John Tyndall, that one could not expect a professorship at the Royal Institution "until you have given a course of lectures there."[97] To be invited back to lecture is a recognized sign of success in almost any situation, and Huxley was asked to lecture again the following April at the Royal Institution. In fact, he delivered a Friday Evening Lecture every year through 1862, and delivered a total of twenty-two, his last being in 1883. In 1876 and 1877 he set new Royal Institution records when 1,068 and 1,104 were in attendance, respectively.[98] He also, of course, delivered many other lectures at the Royal Institution.

Of major significance at the moment is that as a result of the Friday Evening Lecture in 1852, there was no doubt in his mind but that he could effectively speak in public. Immediately following the lecture he wrote to Nettie, "[The lecture] has put me completely at my ease with regard to all future Lecturings. After the Royal Institution there is no audience I shall ever fear."[99] Three days later he wrote to Lizzie, "There is one comfort, I shall never be nervous again about any audience. But at one's first attempt to stand in the place of Faraday and such bigwigs, might excuse a little weakness."[100]

These were not idle predictions made in the flush of victory. His increased confidence was readily apparent, for instance, at the meeting of the British Association at Belfast in September of that year. As he wrote to Nettie, he was again attending primarily to further Huxley rather than science. He reported to her:

We have had an excellent meeting of the British Association, I might almost say a brilliant one. More than a thousand persons attended the meetings of the sections which were held in the rooms of the New (Queen's) College— ... I had not time to attend the meetings of any Section but my own (D) as I had undertaken to report it for the Literary Gazette— ... the room was always well filled—In the chief communication I had to make[101] I spoke for about three quarters of an hour—without book—and there was a good discussion afterwards. *After that Royal Institution Lecture—I don't mind before whom I speak—it was my baptism into oratory.*[102]

That he had indeed acquired considerable confidence became apparent in another speaking engagement in November 1852. He had won the coveted Royal Medal and had to make the usual acceptance speech at the award ceremonies at the anniversary dinner of the Royal Society. Briefly and nonchalantly he included a sentence in the letter to Nettie, "The day after to-morrow I go to have my medal presented and to dine and make a speech."[103] The day after the occasion, he wrote to Professor Forbes, "When it came to my turn to return thanks, I believe I made a very tolerable speechification, at least everyone says so."[104] Two months later he wrote to Lizzie:

In the speech I had to make at the Anniversary Dinner I grew quite eloquent on that point [sending the memoir from the *Rattlesnake*], and talked of the dove I had sent from my ark, returning, not with the olive branch, but with a sprig of the bay and a fruit from the garden of the Hesperides—a simile which I thought decidedly clever, but which the audience—distinguished audience I ought to have said—probably didn't, as they did not applaud that, while they did some things I said which were incomparably more stupid.[105]

These remarks prior to and after such an important event reveal a relaxed, confident speaker in sharp contrast to the initiate in April.

Furthermore, two days after he delivered his second Friday Evening Lecture at the Royal Institution (20 April 1853), he wrote to Lizzie only that he "was so ill with influenza I could hardly stand or speak."[106] What a brief and off-hand comment compared to his lengthy discussion about his anxiety a year earlier!

It is clear, then, that Huxley's maiden lecture at the Royal Institution on 30 April 1852 was a highly significant rhetorical event in his personal and professional life. It was a wonderful opportunity to crystallize and publicize his developing views before a large and prestigious audience. Thoroughly confident in his scientific credentials, mildly confident and experienced in composition, but lacking in confidence and experience in public speaking, he approached the lecture with both anticipation and anxiety. Independence, courage, combativeness, and desire for success pushed him forward, but his mother's sudden death unnerved him. Success would greatly enhance his possibility for some position in science, which in turn would give him the income necessary to ask his fiancée in Australia to come to England to wed. His successful performance in this "baptism into oratory" brought him an enormous increase in confidence, and set him on his course toward becoming one of the most eloquent of Victorian spokesmen for science.

Eight years later another significant rhetorical event brought him even more to center stage in the eyes of the public as one who could not only clearly communicate the findings of science, but as one who could effectively defend science from its detractors, including those entrenched in the dogmas of orthodox theology.

3

"Debate" with Bishop Wilberforce, 1860

During the years between his maiden public address and the Oxford "debate," Huxley had become happily married and had become the proud father of a son and two daughters. He was becoming thoroughly immersed in the life of science. His position at the Royal School of Mines meant a very heavy lecture schedule, which was considerably expanded by his lectures at the Working Men's College, and at the Royal Institution including specifically his lectures there as Fullerian Professor of Physiology. His 1858 Croonian Lecture increased his visibility. His labors at the Museum of Practical Geology in Jermyn Street increased his interests and efforts in using museums as teaching instruments. As naturalist to the Geological Survey he was studying coastal areas. He continued his research and published scientific memoirs, monographs, reports, reviews, and translations. He became a Fellow of the Linnean Society, Fellow of the Zoological Society, and Fellow and Secretary of the Geological Society. He read papers at those learned societies and at the meetings of the British Association. He became an examiner in physiology and comparative anatomy at the London University. He was accepted into membership of the prestigious Athenaeum Club. He was on the move. At that stage, Darwin's publication and the Oxford rhetorical confrontation with Bishop Wiberforce thrust Huxley into the public eye sooner and more dramatically than would have otherwise been the case.

In June 1860 in Oxford a relatively brief impromptu verbal exchange at the annual meeting of the British association occurred, which is still vividy remembered in and out of academia. This so-called "debate" between the bishop of Oxford, Samuel Wilberforce, and Huxley, a simple and concrete episode, has continued to symbolize dramatically the complex and abstract phenomenon of the conflict between science and religion in the late nineteenth century. While that symbol may be somewhat inaccurate, or its relevance may have shifted from a century ago,[1] it still is a powerful image, one that continues to be an important part of the scientific, religious, and rhetorical history of the late Victorian era. The debate has been called "one of the most important events of nineteenth-century biological science,"[2] and Moore has asserted that "no battle of the nineteenth century, save Waterloo, is better known."[3] It is, as Altholz has recently written, "one of those historical events the substance and significance of which are clear, but whose specifics are decidedly fuzzy around the edges."[4] It is the purpose of this chapter to present a detailed and balanced view of the specific ingredients of this important rhetorical event in the life of Huxley, permitting a better insight into Huxley's role and into the event's symbolism and significance.

Background

Compiling, synthesizing, and writing about evolution through two decades, Darwin did not put his material into publishable form until the work of Alfred Russel Wallace in Malaya stimulated the coauthored Darwin-Wallace paper to be presented at the Linnean Society in July 1858 and Darwin's *The Origin of Species* to be published in November 1859.[5] Darwin later wrote in his *Autobiography* that

> Had I published on the scale in which I began to write in 1856, the book would have been four or fives times as large as the *Origin*, and very few would have had the patience to read it. I gained much by my delay in publishing from about 1839, when the theory was clearly conceived, to 1859; and I lost nothing by it, for I cared very little whether men attributed most originality to me or Wallace.[6]

The idea of evolution was by no means new, as Darwin himself briefly sketched in the beginning of his book.[7] The importance of Darwin's work lay in the accumulation of an abundance of data from many sources that he analyzed with scholarly insight, and that served as overwhelming evidence against the idea of fixed species.

> Although much remains obscure, and will long remain obscure, I can entertain no doubt, after the most deliberate study and dispassionate judgment of which I am capable, that the view which most naturalists until recently entertained, and which I formerly entertained—namely, that such species have been independently created—is erroneous.[8]

His unique contribution to the theory of evolution was his hypothesis of "natural selection," which tried to explain the manner by which evolution operates. He did not insist that it was the only method, but that it was "the most important ... means of modification."[9] Observing that many more living creatures are born than could possibly exist, Darwin demonstrated that a struggle for existence takes place among them, with the fittest, those who can best adjust to their environment, surviving. Since this natural selective process, he optimistically claimed, "Works solely by and for the good of each being, all corporeal and mental endowments will tend to progress towards perfection."[10] He also claimed, "I see no good reason why the views given in this volume should shock the religious feelings of any one,"[11] and that to the contrary, "There is grandeur in this view of life, with its several powers, having been orginally breathed by the Creator into a few forms or into one."[12] Darwin's work did not initially apply to human beings but its implications were clear, and in subsequent years he, Huxley, and others included humans in the evolutionary theory.

Huxley had conversed often with Darwin during the late 1850s about the latter's work, but what he knew of it he was noncommittal on the claims involved. He and his other contemporaries who had thought much about the general subject, had up until Darwin's publications, not been impressed with previous writings on evolution any more than with the biblical account of creation. As Huxley wrote in 1887, the publication of the *Origin* was for him a highly dramatic event. It was to him like a

Flash of light, which to a man who has lost himself in a dark night, suddenly reveals a road which, whether it takes him straight home or not, certainly goes his way. That which [I was] looking for, and could not find, was a hypothesis respecting the origin of known organic forms, which assumed the operation of no causes but such as could be proved to be actually at work. [I] wanted not to pin [my] faith to that or any other speculation, but to get hold of clear and definite conceptions which could be brought face to face with facts and have their validity tested. The "Origin" provided [me] with the working hypotesis [I] sought. ... My reflection, when I first made myself master of the central idea of the "Origin" was, "How extremely stupid not to have thought of that! ... The facts of variability, of the struggle for existence, of adaptation to conditions, were notorious enough; but [I had not] suspected that the road to the heart of the species problem lay through them, until Darwin and Wallace dispelled the darkness, and the beacon-fire of the "Origin" guided the benighted. ... The only rational course for those who had no other object than the attainment of truth was to accept "Darwinism" as a working hypothesis, and see what could be made of it.[13]

Early in September 1858 Huxley wrote to Hooker that

> Wallace's impetus seems to have set Darwin going in earnest, and I am rejoiced to hear we shall learn his views in full, at last. I look forward to a great revolution being affected. Depend upon it, in natural history, as in everything else.[14]

In November 1859, Darwin's *Origin* was published in London by John Murray and its 1,250 copies were immediately sold. In January 1860, 3,000 more were published, 2,000 in April 1861; within a decade five editions had been published, and by 1876, 16,000 had been sold.[15] Darwin later in his *Autobiography* called it "no doubt the chief work of my life,"[16] and it is still today being called arguably "the most influential book . . . of the last 150 years."[17] By 1 December 1859 one Oxford scientist wrote, "We are all reading Darwin."[18] On 23 November Huxley wrote to Darwin:

> I finished your book yesterday. . . . I am ready to go to the stake, if requisite, in support of [most of it]. . . . and as to the curs which will bark and yelp, you must recollect that some of your friends . . . are endowed with an amount of combativeness which . . . may stand you in good stead. I am sharpening my claws and beak in readiness.[19]

His beak would be used at Oxford and elsewhere, and his claws were soon employed in writing an article for the December 1859 *Macmillan's Magazine*, in which he wrote very favorably about Darwin's book.

> I observe that already the hastier sort of critics have begun, not to review my friend's book, but to howl over it in a manner which must tend greatly to distract the public mind. No one will be better satisfied than I to see Mr. Darwin's book refuted, if any person be competent to perform that feat; but I would suggest that refutation is retarded, not aided, by mere sarcastic misrepresentation.[20]

That would also be his essential message the following June in Oxford, that is, that incompetent critics were distracting the public through sarcasm. Darwin immediately wrote to Huxley, "You have explained my leading idea with admirable clearness. What a gift you have of writing (or more properly) thinking clearly."[21]

By chance Huxley was asked to review the book for *The Times*.[22] His lengthy, highly complimentary anonymous review appeared in the 26 December issue. Amazed that *The Times* would devote three and a half columns to the review of a science book, and ecstatic over such a favorable review, Darwin wrote immediately to Huxley, assuming with confidence that he was the author.

There [is] only one man in England who could have written this essay, and ... *you* [are] the man. ... Well, whoever the man is, he has done great service to the cause, far more than a dozen reviews in common periodicals. The grand way he soars above the common religious prejudices, and the admission of such views into the Times, I look at as of the highest importance.[23]

Eleven months later, Darwin wrote to Huxley, "I shall always think those early reviews, almost entirely yours, did the subject an *enormous* service."[24] Darwin's son and biographer, Francis Darwin, wrote years later, "There can be no doubt that this powerful essay, appearing as it did in the leading daily Journal, must have had a strong influence on the reading public."[25]

The months in 1860 prior to Oxford saw much controversy over Darwin's book. Reviews, articles, and lectures reacting to it poured forth. Early in January Charles Lyell, the famous geologist and close friend of Darwin, wrote to an American correspondent that Darwin's book was stirring up much discussion in scientific, literary, and theological circles.[26] Early in February Huxley delivered a lecture at the Royal Institution, which Francis Darwin later called "one of the most eloquent of [Huxley's] utterances in support of the 'Origin of Species'."[27] By February Darwin had heard that Bishop Wilberforce, who had earlier expressed dissatisfaction with Huxley's *Times* review, had said that the *Origin* was "the most unphilosophical work he ever read."[28] Rev. Adam Sedgwick, Darwin's former geology professor at Cambridge, wrote a strongly worded anti-Darwin article in the March issue of *The Spectator*, and another conservative, Richard Owen, Superintendent of the Natural History Department of the British Museum, perhaps the leading anatomist in England, wrote a bitter criticism of the *Origin* in the *Edinburgh Review*.[29] Huxley wrote a counteressay in the April *Westminster Review*,[30] which Darwin called "*brilliant*."[31] Early in May, Darwin's work was strongly attacked at the Cambridge Philosophical Society by such conservatives as Owen and Sedgwick. Darwin reacted in a letter to his close friend Hooker. "As for the old fogies in Cambridge, it really signifies nothing. I look at their attack as a proof that our work is worth the doing."[32] Throughout this period and later, Darwin was deeply appreciative for the support given him by Huxley, Hooker, Lyell, and a few others. He was sorry for the trouble he was causing them, and as long as they did not waver in their support, he was not too concerned about hostile reactions.[33]

Conference Prelude

It is, then, with a background of mounting confrontation generated by Darwin's book that the British Association for the Advancement of Science held its thirtieth annual conference in Oxford, 27 June to 4 July 1860, with about seventeen hundred in attendance.[34] Some business meetings, exhibits, and lectures were held in the Town Hall, the Clarendon Building, and Convocation House, and some general sessions in the Sheldonian Theatre, but most sectional meetings were in the new University Museum. The reporter covering the convention for *The Press*, a London weekly, wrote at the end of the gathering, "The theory of Dr. Darwin . . . on the origin of the species by natural selection, gave rise to the hottest of all debates."[35]

The conference began on 27 June, in the Sheldonian Theatre, where a "large and brilliant assembly [gathered]. The Chancellor, Vice-Chancellor, and all the heads of the University were present, as well as the men of science from all parts of Europe."[36] The Prince Consort, finishing his year as president, turned the proceedings over to the incoming president, the famous astronomer, Lord Wrottesley, who delivered the annual President's Address.

The next day in Section D (Botany and Zoology, including Physiology) a not unexpected sharp exchange between Huxley and Owen occurred. The Owen-Huxley clash grew out of a decade of smoldering professional and personal tension between the two. First introduced to Owen in 1846 by Capt. Owen Stanley before the *Rattlesnake* sailed,[37] young Huxley soon became convinced that Owen, despite some early kindness, was a likely roadblock. In 1852 Huxley wrote to Nettie that he felt Owen was "determined not to let either me or any one else rise if he can help it. Let him beware. On my own subjects I am master, and am quite ready to fight half a dozen dragons. And although he has a bitter pen, I flatter myself that on occasion I can match him in that department also."[38] Strong words about a famous established scholar twenty-one years one's senior! In 1857 Huxley's ire was raised when Owen unwarrantably listed himself as professor of comparative anatomy and palaeontology at the Government School of Mines, which Huxley took as a usurpation of his title.[39] In 1858 Huxley wrote to Lizzie, "An internecine feud rages between Owen and myself,"[40] and Huxley's Croonian Lecture, "On the Theory of the Vertebrate

Skull,'' sharply challenged Owen's views. Looking forward to the British Association meeting in Leeds in 1858, Huxley wrote to Hooker, "The interesting question arises, Shall I have a row with the Great O. there?"[41] Apparently not. The following year at the British Association meeting at Aberdeen, the relationship was even rather mellow. Huxley reported to Tyndall that

> he [Owen] read a very good and important paper, and I got up afterwards and spoke exactly as I thought about it, and praising many parts of it strongly. In his reply he was uncommonly civil and complimentary, so that the people who had come in hopes of a row were (as I intended they should be) disappointed.[42]

Indeed two days earlier Huxley had written to his wife that Owen's address as the out-going president was very good, and said that "I have never heard him do better."[43] But the animosity between the two was deeply rooted,[44] and Owen's jealousy that Huxley perceived was also felt by Darwin, who wrote later in his *Autobiography*, "After the publication of the *Origin of Species* he became my bitter enemy, not owing to any quarrel between us, but as far as I could judge out of jealousy at its success."[45]

At the Section D meeting at Oxford a paper was read that touched on Darwin's book and a tense discussion ensued. Owen strongly asserted that the brain of a gorilla differed more from the brain of man than from the brain of the very lowest animal life. This of course was an attack on Huxley, who for some time had been suggesting that the brain differences between gorillas and humans were not very great. Even though Huxley had earlier in the meeting refused to give his opinions, feeling "that a general audience, in which sentiment would unduly interfere with intellect, was not the public before which such a discussion should be carried on,"[46] he was now stimulated to reply to Owen's comments, and "somewhat facetiously remarked that they [conservative scientists and churchmen] had nothing to fear even should it be shown that apes were their ancestors."[47] This sharp exchange with Owen was a prelude for what was to occur on Saturday, 30 June, in another meeting of the same section, following the presentation of paper. This impromptu exchange in the discussion period is the so-called "debate" between Wilberforce and Huxley.

Part of the excitement was stimulated by the very building in which the rhetorical event took place. The new museum had just been completed, and indeed was only partly furnished, with the British Association being "the first organization to use the new building before it was to be opened to the University in October."[48] The museum was the culmination of a decade of effort on the part of those who had felt that science should be more prominently highlighted at Oxford, and indeed, Bishop Wilberforce, who possessed considerable ability as an ornithologist and mathematician, had been one of the movement's supporters.[49] One eyewitness-observer later recaptured the excitement. "The lovely Museum rose before us [during the late 1850s] like an exhalation. . . . "[50] The completed museum in 1860 stood as a symbol of "Oxford's concession to the claims of physical science."[51] With pride a local Oxford newspaper stated, "Few places in England ... possess a building so admirably adapted for such gatherings as the New Museum."[52] Today a plaque outside an entrance to the room where the meeting took place commemorates the occasion. "A meeting of the British Association held 30 June 1860 within this door was the scene of the memorable debate on evolution between Samuel Wilberforce, Bishop of Oxford, and Thomas Henry Huxley."

Audience

The audience was a very important part of the rhetorical event. The unusually large number of people who arrived at the Section D meeting necessitated moving it from the originally scheduled lecture room to the long west room, which was to become the library.[53] *The Athenaeum* reported that the audience was "immense,"[54] and other reports put the number between 400 and 1,000, with about 700 being likely.[55] The audience was a mixture of scientists, theologians, Oxford dons and students, and women, and thus was an audience that was considerably broader than a specialized gathering of scientists. The clergy were grouped in the middle of the room; behind them in the northwest corner was a small group of undergraduates.[56] Most of the audience were predisposed against Darwin's views,[57] though Wilberforce was unpopular with many at the university and in some segments of the church.[58] Some people came expecting and hoping "to hear the oratory of the bold Bishop"[59] in the discussion period, but one observer later wrote, "Though a few persons on each side knew of the intention of the Bishop to speak at the meeting, this was not generally known."[60] The cheers and laughter that the bishop's remarks elicited in turn stimulated him to say things he otherwise might not have said. One eyewitness later wrote, "The Bishop ... [said] he did not mean to hurt the Professor's feelings; it was our fault—we had laughed, and that made him pursue the joke. We laughed again, and Huxley was not appeased."[61] Indeed, one historian has concluded that "it was the audience, not the participants who created the event."[62]

Speakers

But the participants surely were central. The great attraction was Prof. John William Draper from New York, a famous chemist, who was scheduled to present a paper dealing with Darwin's views.[63] After six individuals had given brief reports, Professor Draper read his one to one and a half hour long paper,[64] which "gave rise to a long and very animated discussion."[65] Two people in the audience made anti-Darwin comments and Huxley declined the chair's invitation to make a statement. According to Tuckwell, Huxley made a "sarcastic response that he certainly held a brief for Science, but had not yet heard it assailed."[66] The chair then called on Bishop Wilberforce. As one of the vice-presidents of the British Association and as the local bishop, he was seated on the platform.[67] No doubt buoyed by his well-received presentation the day before in the Geography Section,[68] he now rose to speak for about thirty minutes,[69] with "great power and eloquence."[70] *The Athenaeum* summarized his remarks, reporting that he

> stated that the Darwinian theory, when tried by the principles of inductive science, broke down. The facts brought forward did not warrant the theory. . . . The line between man and the lower animals was distinct; there was no tendency on the part of the lower animals to become the self-conscious intelligent being, man; or in man to degenerate and lose the high characteristics of his mind and intelligence. . . . Mr. Darwin's conclusions were an hypothesis, raised most unphilosophically to the dignity of a causal theory.[71]

It is reasonable to assume that Wilberforce's remarks were to a large extent the same as his review of *Origin*, which he had finished in May and that would appear in the July issue of *The Quarterly Review*.[72] Resting perhaps too heavily on that assumption, Phelps and Cohen have attempted to outline what the bishop said,[73] and Lucas has developed a thorough analysis.[74]

The sarcastic question that agitated Huxley into replying was interestingly not specified by newspaper accounts, except for the London weekly, *The Press*, which reported, "The Bishop of Oxford . . . asked the Professor [Huxley] whether he would prefer a monkey for his grandfather or his grandmother."[75] Wilberforce was simply following up on Huxley's remarks at the Thursday meeting of Section D.[76] On 4 July, on the last day of the conference, Lyell gave a second-hand account in a letter to a friend, virtually identical to *The Press*. "The Bishop of Oxford asked whether Huxley was related by his grandfather's or grandmother's side to an Ape."[77] A similar version was given by eye-witnesses toward the end of the century to Francis Darwin and Leonard Huxley for their paternal biographies,[78] and by Sidgwick in a reminiscence in Macmillan's Magazine.[79] A slightly different version had the query being whether it was Huxley's mother or grandmother,[80] and another version asked whether it was Huxley's grandfather or back further.[81] Reginald Wilberforce, in his 1881 biography of his father, wrote that his father had said "that whatever certain people might believe, he would not look at the monkeys in the Zoological as connected with his ancestors."[82] Whatever the precise wording, it was in the eyes of many in the audience, "an almost incredible false step,"[83] and it stirred Huxley to respond.

Threee decades later Huxley described the situation to Francis Darwin.

> I . . . chanced to sit near old Sir Benjamin Brodie. The Bishop began his speech, and to my astonishment very soon showed that he was so ignorant that he did not know how to manage his own case. My spirits rose proportionately, and when he turned to me with his insolent question, I said to Sir Benjamin, in an undertone, "The Lord hath delivered him into mine hands". . . . The Bishop had justified the severest retort I could devise, and I made up my mind to let him have it. I was careful, however, not to rise to reply, until the meeting called for me— then I let myself go.[84]

An eyewitness who had described Wilberforce as "argumenative, rhetorical, [and] amusing" wrote that "Huxley rose, white with anger."[85] The young student, J. R. Green, strongly anti-Wilberforce, wrote to a friend that Huxley was "young, cool, quiet, sarcastic, scientific in fact and treatment."[86] *The Athenaeum* devoted almost the same amount of space to Huxley as to Wilberforce, although Huxley probably did not speak as long as the bishop.

> Prof. Huxley defended Mr. Darwin's theory from the charge of its being merely a hypothesis. He said, it was an explanation of phenomena in Natural History. . . . Darwin's theory was an explanation of facts; and his book was full of new facts, all bearing on his theory. Without asserting

that every part of the theory had been confirmed, he maintained that it was the best explanation of the origin of species which had yet been offered.[87]

One eyewitness reported that Huxley developed his contention with the following analogy: "Belated on a roadless common in a dark night, if a lantern were offered to me, should I refuse it because it shed imperfect light? I think not—I think not."[88]

In his introduction Huxley responded specifically to the Bishop's *ad hominem*. Different versions exist. The only newspaper account of the sharp retort was in *The Press*, which reported that Huxley said "he would much rather have a monkey for his grandfather than a man who could indulge in jokes on such a subject."[89] The young J. R. Green wrote excitedly on 3 July to a friend that Huxley asserted that

> a man had no reason to be ashamed of having an ape for his grandfather. If there were an ancestor whom I should feel shame in recalling, it would rather be a *man*, a man of restless and versatile intellect, who, not content with an equivocal success in his own sphere of activity, plunges into scientific questions with which he has no real acquaintance, only to obscure them by an aimless rhetoric, and distract the attention of his hearers from the real point at issue by eloquent digressions and skilled appeals to religious prejudices.[90]

On 4 July, Lyell wrote his second-hand account to a friend.

> Huxley replied (I heard several varying versions of this shindy), "that if he had his choice of an ancestor, whether it would be an ape, or one who having received a scholastic education, should use his logic to mislead an untutored public, and should treat not with argument but with ridicule the facts and reasoning adduced in support of a grave and serious philosophical question, he would not hesitate for a moment to prefer the ape."[91]

Huxley had immediately written a long account of the Oxford experience to Darwin but it apparently has been lost.[92] The only available version by Huxley is his letter to his friend, Dr. Dyster, written about two months after Oxford.

> I had listened with great attention to the Lord Bishop's speech but had been unable to discover either a new fact or a new argument in it—except indeed the question raised as to my personal predilections in the matter of ancestry—That it would not have occurred to me to bring forward such a topic as that for discussion myself, but that I was quite ready to

meet the Right Rev. prelate even on that ground. If then, said I, the question is put to me would I rather have a miserable ape for a grandfather or a man highly endowed by nature and possessed of great means and influence and yet who employs those faculties and that influence for the mere purpose of introducing ridicule into a grave scientific discussion—I unhesitatingly affirm my preference for the ape. . . . I assure you of this because all sorts of reports were spread about, e.g., that I had said I would rather be an ape than a bishop, etc.[93]

In the December 1860 *Macmillan's Magazine*, Henry Fawcett wrote that

the professor [Huxley] aptly replied to his assailant by remarking, that man's remote descent from an ape was not so degrading to his dignity as the employment of oratorical powers to misguide the multitude by throwing ridicule upon a scientific discussion. The retort was so justly deserved, and so inimitable in its manner, that no one who was present can ever forget the impression it made.[94]

In later years other versions were recorded and collected in the biographies of their fathers by Leonard Huxley and Francis Darwin.[95] We of course have to use with caution all such accounts gleaned from memory after many years, since the biographers understandably are anxious to put their families in the best possible light.[96]

When Huxley concluded, two or three anti-Darwin voices were heard, followed by two Darwin supporters, John Lubbock and Joseph Hooker. Some evidence suggests that Lubbock and Hooker have been inappropriately overlooked, but Lucas, seemingly anxious to downgrade Huxley, states it too strongly when he claims that their remarks were at the time "held to be far more important than anything Huxley said."[97] It is certainly unlikely in Lubbock's case. Although a neighbor and friend of Darwin, coming from an influential family and showing a promising beginning in his scientific work, he was, in 1860, only twenty-six years old and did not possess the stature of others. *The Athenaeum* summarized his comments very briefly, and other newspapers merely listed his name.[98]

But a stronger case can be made for Hooker. *The Athenaeum* devoted a whole column to a summary of his comments, which was three times the space devoted to either Wilberforce or Huxley.[99] The forty-three-year-old Hooker, assistant director of the Royal Botanic Gardens at Kew under his father, a close friend of Darwin's, and son-in-law to Professor Henslow (who was chairing the meeting), was a highly respected botanist and person. Hooker became greatly agitated and though not an experienced public speaker, notified the chair of his desire to speak.[100] Responding to calls from the audience,[101] the chairman called on Hooker "to state his views of the botanial aspect of the question."[102] Hooker's letter to Darwin during the Oxford conference suggests that his (Hooker's) comments were more easily heard and more favorably taken than Huxley's.[103] At the end of the century, Farrar wrote that "the speech which really left its mark *scientifically* on the meeting, was the short one of *Hooker*,"[104] but that Huxley "had scored a victory over Bishop Wilberforce in the question of good *manners*."[105] But that distinction was not perceived by the three reporters who clearly highlighted Huxley and not Hooker,[106] and many eyewitness accounts do not even mention Hooker.[107] The way Huxley put it in his letter to Dyster two months after the conference gives a helpful perspective. "Lubbock and Hooker spoke after me with great force and *among us* we shut up the bishop and his party."[108]

But clearly Huxley was the central *antagonist*. In his diary for 30 June Wilberforce wrote, "I spoke at length in controversy with Huxley."[109] Benjamin Peirce, an American scholar who observed the clash, wrote in his journal on 30 June that he had heard "a long and very earnest [sharp pass] between the Bishop of Oxford and Huxley.[110] "An important British political figure wrote in his diary on 4 July, "The British Association is meeting this year at Oxford, and there has been a great scene between the Bishop of Oxford and Huxley."[111] No mention of Hooker, Lubbock, or anyone else. History has appropriately kept Huxley at center stage.

Finally the lengthy and exciting session drew to a close; as one eyewitness put it, "The sacred dinner-hour drew near."[112] The chairman made some brief remarks, and then "dismissed us with an impartial benediction."[113]

The length of space given to a speaker in the local newspapers cannot necessarily be equated with the length or importance of the speech. For example, in one instance, *The Athenaeum* reported merely that "a long discussion ensued" in which six listed individuals took part, and in another instance, that "a discussion ensued" and the seven who took part were merely listed.[114] The determining factors in the newspaper accounts were as follows: which sectional meetings the reporters decided to attend, the degree of interest the reporters had in the subject, their understanding of the subject, their attitude toward the subject and speakers, and the eventual editorial condensing and cutting. The reporter for *Jackson's Oxford Journal* blamed the British Association for its shabby treatment of the press, indicating that the president of Section E (Geography and Ethnology) had complained

> that no reporters had attended this section, and that in consequence much interesting matter and many eloquent speeches had been lost to the world. It is, however, but common justice to the press to state that all connected with it are desirous of forwarding the views of the Association, but they are not met in a corresponding spirit, or treated with the courtesy shown them by all other public bodies, inasmuch as no provision is made for them in the way of accommodations, and they are compelled to get where they can and take notes under the most disadvantageous circumstances; and we are informed that it is owing to this fact that the London press has scarcely had a representative on the present occasion beyond their local correspondents.[115]

Also, in this instance the dailies devoted less attention to the British Association because Parliament was in session, which took up much of their time and space. When the British Association met in August or September when Parliament normally was not sitting, the British Association usually got better coverage.[116]

Immediate Effect

What was the effect of the Wilberforce-Huxley exchange on the immediate audience? *The Evening Star* gave a rather balanced reaction, writing that the bishop's speech "produced a marked effect upon the audience" and that Huxley's reply "was loudly applauded."[117] Since most of the versions that are available are from pro-Huxley observers, we are left with the story that Huxley and science experienced a resounding victory. The young J. R. Green, not yet the mature historian, reported that during the bishop's speech, his supporters "cheered lustily, a sort of 'Pitch it into him' cheer," but then of course Huxley proceeded to give "his lordship ... a smashing."[118] Lyell's 4 July letter said that Wilberforce started with the majority clearly on his side, that he "had been much applauded" but by the end of the session the audience "were quite turned the other way."[119] Huxley's letter to Dyster in September buoyantly asserted, "I believe I was the most popular man in Oxford for full four and twenty hours afterwards."[120] In her 1900 reminiscence, Sidgwick says, "The effect was tremendous. One lady fainted and had to be carried out;[121] I, for one, jumped out of my seat."[122] As Farrar wrote at the end of the century, "The impression distinctly was, that the

Bishop's party, as they left the room, felt abashed, and recognised that the Bishop had forgotten to behave like a gentleman."[123] At the end of the century Sir Michael Foster told Leonard Huxley

> that when Huxley rose he was received coldly, just a cheer of encouragement from his friends, the audience as a whole not joining in it. But as he made his points the applause grew and widened, until, when he sat down, the cheering was not very much less than that given to the Bishop. To that extent he carried an unwilling audience with him by the force of his speech.[124]

The Reverend Freemantle's version three decades after Oxford says that at the close of the meeting, the impression was left that "those most capable of estimating the arguments of Darwin in detail saw their way to accept his conclusions."[125]

Not surprisingly, Wilberforce and others saw it differently. An eyewitness to the clash, the eminent physicist Balfour Stewart, appointed director of the Kew Observatory in 1859, concluded, "I think the Bishop had the best of it."[126] Benjamin Peirce, the famous Harvard mathematician and astronomer and a friend of American anti-Darwinists, on a European trip and present at the Oxford clash, wrote in his journal on 30 June his pro-Wilberforce reaction.

> The Bishop is one of the most eloquent men I have ever heard, he's known here as Soapy Sam, and the slippery character of the divine was apparent in all his argument. His power of language was wonderful and the revulsion with which he seized upon the weak points of his opponents views and exposed them to the torture was a model of logical display. . . .[127]

The bishop himself wrote to his friend Sir Charles Anderson on 3 July 1860, "Had quite a long fight with Huxley. I think I thoroughly beat him."[128] This letter in the Bodleian Library only recently made public by Altholz is a highly significant "missing link," for it helps to explain that Huxley need not have been surprised, as he expressed it later in life to Darwin's son, that the bishop "bore no malice, but was always courtesy itself when we occasionally met in after years."[129] Huxley apparently ascribed this to gentlemanly qualities of a gracious loser, but if a person has "won," it takes little effort to treat the other party with courtesy. Reginald Wilberforce wrote in his 1881 biography that his father's "eloquent" speech "made a great impression,"[130] and even the pro-Huxley Mrs. Sidgwick wrote, in 1900, that at the conclusion of the meeting Huxley supporters were still in the minority.[131] The London weekly, *John Bull*, after the Oxford conference wrote:

> The impression left *on the minds of those most competent to judge* was that this celebrated theory had been built on very slight foundations, and that a series of plausible hypotheses had been skillfully manipulated into solid facts, while a vast array of real facts on the opposite side had been completely ignored.[132]

These divergent reactions are perhaps harmonized rather well by *The Athenaeum*'s summation, which stated that the bishop and Huxley, and a few others, "have each found foemen worthy of their steel, and made their charges and countercharges very much to their own satisfaction and [to] the delight of their respective friends."[133]

Unable to attend Oxford because of ill health,[134] Darwin received immediate, strongly positive reports from Hooker and Huxley, and responded quickly with admiration and gratitude. He wrote to Hooker on 2 July:

> I should have liked to have heard you triumphing over the Bishop. I am astonished at your success and audacity. It is something unintelligible to me how any one can argue in public like orators do. I had no idea you had this power. . . . I am glad I was not in Oxford, for I should have been overwhelmed, with my [health] in its present state.[135]

Darwin wrote to Huxley on 3 July: "I honour your pluck; I would as soon have died as tried to answer the bishop in such an assembly." He went on to chide his friend. "But how durst you attack a live Bishop in that fashion? I am quite ashamed of you!"[136] In his *Autobiography* in 1876 Darwin wrote that Huxley "has been a most kind friend to me and would always take any trouble for me."[137] It should be emphasized that the traditional picutre of Darwin rather helplessly staying in the background while Huxley and others did his rhetorical battling for him should be considerably modified. Campbell has recently marshaled much evidence to show that Darwin played a strong rhetorical role in furthering his own cause.[138] Another assertion also needs to be kept in proper perspective, that is, the claim that Huxley and other close friends of Darwin defended him mainly because of their friendship. Huxley was very sensitive on this point and in 1885 objected strongly to the notion

> that the acceptance of Darwin's views was in any way influenced by the strong affection entertained for him by many of his friends. What that

affection really did was to lead those of his friends who had seen good reason for his views to take much more trouble in his defence and support, and to strike out much harder at his adversary than they would otherwise have done.[139]

Rhetorical Characteristics

At least three observations should be made about the rhetorical characteristics of the Wilberforce-Huxley "debate." First, it was an impromptu exchange, not a formal clash of prepared speeches. The latter is usually implied when the event is alluded to in twentieth-century works, often comparing it to such events as the Lincoln-Douglas debates of 1858.[140] That misleading picture is perpetuated by such erroneous phrasings as the following, "Bishop Wilberforce read a paper aimed straight at Huxley,"[141] or "The attack on Darwin's book was to be led by the Bishop of Oxford . . . and Huxley was to head the defence,"[142] or by Reginald Wilberforce twenty-seven years later placing the exchange in the Sheldonian Theatre.[143] Both speakers merely entered into the discussion following the presentation of a prepared paper by someone else, and neither spoke until called upon by members of the audience and the presiding officer. Wilberforce, for example, wrote in his diary on 30 June, ". . . At Zoological called up by Henslow on Darwinian Theory,"[144] and in his letter to Anderson on 3 July Wilberforce wrote that the chairman "called on me by name to address the Section on Darwin's Theory. So I could not escape."[145] Farrar's account insisted that "the events of the meeting unfolded" with "naturalism" and not in a planned and formal manner.[146]

Not only were Huxley's remarks impromptu, but he very nearly skipped the meeting altogether. His scheduled paper ("On the Development of Pyrosoma") had already been given, on Friday,[147] so he was planning to relax with his family a short distance from Oxford. Thirty years later he explained the situation to Francis Darwin.

> The odd part of the business is, that I should not have been present except for Robert Chambers.[148] I had heard of the Bishop's intention to utilise the occasion. I knew he had the reputation of being a first-class controversialist, and I was quite aware that if he played his cards properly, we should have little chance, with such an audience, of making an efficient defence. Moreover, I was very tired, and wanted to join my wife at her brother-in-law's country house near Reading, on the Saturday.[149] On the Friday I met

Chambers in the street, and in reply to some remark of his, about his going to the meeting, I said that I did not mean to attend it—did not see the good of giving up peace and quietness to be episcopally pounded. Chambers broke out into vehement remonstrances, and talked about my deserting them. So I said, "Oh! if you are going to take it that way, I'll come and have my share of what is going on."[150]

It is also quite clear that the rhetorical event was, and has continued to be, cast in a dramatistic format of heroes and villains, of a military contest whereby one side would win and the other lose. For example, the military metaphor was central in letters of Darwin at this time. Hearing of the strong attacks on him by conservative scientists at the Cambridge Philosophical Society in early May 1860 Darwin wrote to Hooker:

> It makes me resolve to buckle on my armour. I see plainly that it will be a long uphill fight. . . . But if we all stick to it, we shall surely gain the day. And I now see that the battle is worth fighting.[151]

Hearing of the confrontation at Oxford, Darwin wrote of the "awful battle which had raged about 'species' at Oxford."[152] During this time he was happy to learn that in the United States "the battle rages furiously,"[153] and that Asa Gray, the famous Harvard botanist, was "fighting like a Trojan" and "fighting admirably."[154] Darwin wrote to Lyell, "I am determined to fight to the last. . . . I had lots of pleasant letters about the Brit. Assoc., and our side seems to have got on very well. . . . [Our key supporters] are determined to stick to the battle and not give in."[155] Others likewise employed similar confrontational metaphors. We have already noted Wilberforce's 3 July letter to Anderson in which he reported, "Had quite a long fight with Huxley. I think I thoroughly beat him,"[156] and J. R. Green was writing at the same time of "the episcopal defeat."[157] Another eyewitness, Mrs. Sidgwick, years later reminisced to Leonard Huxley: "I never saw such a display of fierce party spirit, the looks of bitter hatred which the audience bestowed— . . . on us who were on your father's side—as we passed through the crowd we felt that we were . . . considered outcasts and detestable."[158] Huxley of course pronounced victory for his side, and he wrote to Dyster, "I think Samuel will think twice before he tries a fall with men of science again."[159] Huxley was happy to be "smiting the Amalekites."[160] The reporter for *The Press* wrote, "The men of science were the aggressors, or, if you will, the reformers, while the divines defend the ancient bulwarks."[161]

But the battle was not only between the Darwinists and the divines, but between the Darwinists, generally the younger scientists, and the older, more conservative scientists. One eyewitness at Oxford remarked that "the younger men were on the side of Darwin, the older men against him."[162] By the end of 1860 Darwin wrote to Huxley, "I can pretty plainly see that, if my view is ever to be generally adopted, it will be by young men growing up and replacing the older workers."[163] In the December 1860 *Macmillan's Magazine* Henry Fawcett began his article by asserting that Darwin's book "has for a time divided the scientific world into two great contending sections. A Darwinite and an anti-Darwinite are now the badges of opposed scientific parties."[164] At the British Association meeting in 1894 the Marquis of Salisbury looked back at the 1860 meeting and said that "in many cases religious apprehension only masked the resentment of the older learning at the appearance and claims of its younger rival."[165]

Not only were these younger scientists a minority in 1860, but they felt they were a *persecuted* minority. Certainly this was the case with Huxley. We have already seen his frustration during the early 1850s as he struggled to secure a position in the world of science. He was angry that people like him who were trying to secure a place strictly on merit, with no family name or wealth or religious credentials, were excluded from university positions.[166] Even though he had been in secure employment for five years, he was in 1860, at thirty-five, still struggling to secure justice from the scientific establishment. In contrast, the fifty-five-year-old Wilberforce, Bishop of Oxford for fifteen years, a high official in an institution with a nineteen century history that dominated university life, was at the height of his prestigious career. Science was a babe trying to creep into university curriculums. The British Association was only thirty years old. When the bishop inserted his sarcasm at Oxford, with the excess confidence of a status quo power figure toying with a newcomer, he did not fully appreciate how much the sensitive "persecuted" minority faction[167] would resent it, just as any "disadvantaged" individual or group resents so-called humor at their expense.

Biographical, rhetorical, and historical works have entrenched the two-valued battle metaphor. In his biography of his father, Francis Darwin speaks of the "pitched battles" at Oxford and that on 30 June "the battle arose with redoubled fury."[168] Leonard Huxley's biography at the end of the century contains many testimonies to the "battle,"[169] and some twentieth-century biographies of Huxley continue the message that the outcome of the battle was victory for Huxley over the villainous Wilberforce.[170] It is understandable that

Darwin's granddaughter would continue in that vein: "Samuel Wilberforce's superficial ridicule and appeals to prejudice made him an easy prey to Huxley's eloquent and famous reply."[171] A recent rhetorical study states that Huxley's counterattack "proved forensically fatal to Wilberforce."[172] One historian wrote that by the twentieth century "Darwin through his supporters, was left master of the field,"[173] and a respected church historian more recently wrote that Huxley "annihilated"[175] Wilberforce. A recent analysis has generalized that historians "popularized the warfare between Darwinism and dogma by drawing on the military metaphor popular in contemporary culture."[175] Moore has provided an excellent analysis of the deleterious role of the military metaphor.[176] The current *Oxford University Museum* pamphlet available for the general public perpetuates the hero and villain image: "In 1860 the Museum was the scene of the memorable debate on evolution between Darwin's champion Thomas Huxley and the reactionary Bishop Wilberforce."[177]

The modern medium of television has also continued the drama. The BBC programs on Darwin in December 1978 portrayed a young, handsome, heroic Huxley, and at the end of the Oxford exchange, Wilberforce sulkily made his way through the crowd to the exit, much like a nineteenth-century American melodrama, where the cruel and unsavory landlord heads for the door, twisting his handlebar moustache, and muttering, "Curses, foiled again."[178]

Finally, in all of the seriousness connected with this rhetorical clash, analysts have overlooked the dimension of the playfulness involved. One can appreciate that Wilberforce, a polished and witty speaker, would want to lighten up the atmosphere after the passage of about two hours in a crowded and hot room, and having listened to a lengthy and rather boring paper by Dr. Draper delivered in an unpleasant accent—a blend of northern England where he grew up, and three decades of living in America.[179] One eyewitness account said that the bishop had prefaced his question by stating, "I should like to ask Professor Huxley, who is sitting by me, and is about to tear me to pieces when I have sat down . . ."[180] and another eyewitness said that the bishop's question was meant "as a sort of joke."[181] *The Athenaeum* reporter mentioned the "play" that took place in the Sectional meetings.[182] Indeed, it has been said that the British Association through the years has been "a source of rational entertainment."[183] For months prior to Oxford, evolutionists had experienced taunts linking their heritage to tadpoles, mushrooms, or apes, so it was merely a continuation of an existing joke.[184] In the tradition of British parliamentary debate, hard-hitting but with a strong undercurrent of playfulness, Wilberforce's question may not appear to be so outlandish or cruel—though its appropriateness still could be seriously questioned. Huxley, in turn, was not displeased with the "inextinguishable laughter"[185] his retort created, and two months after Oxford, he could look back on it and say, "it was great fun."[186]

Long-Range Effects

What were the long-range effects of the Oxford confrontation on the participants, on the British Association, and on the general relationship between science and religion?

The effect on Huxley was very significant. He was buoyed by what he considered to be a distinct victory, that he had been able to stand up to the talented, prestigious bishop, twenty years his senior,[187] who would now think more carefully before ridiculing science. Letters of praise, such as the following one from a friend in Edinburgh shortly after Oxford, no doubt kept Huxley's spirits high: "I hear you pitched into the Bishop of Oxford in grand style. I should have rejoiced to have been [there]."[188] The confrontation stayed vividly in his mind as a triumphant episode throughout his life. For example, when he gave the Romanes Lecture in Oxford two years before his death, he wrote to friends mentioning that the last time he spoke in Oxford was when "the great 'Sammy' fight came off" and when "the great row with Samuel came off."[189] Oxford helped Huxley to see even more clearly the importance of public speaking and planned to cultivate it in the future,[190] which he indeed did right up until his death in 1895. The debate brought him before a wide general public,[191] and gave him a "respectful hearing which might otherwise have been denied."[192] As has recently been expressed, "Huxley ceased to be simply a technical scientist and began his evolution into the great Victorian sage, as a popular educationist, essayist, and public speaker."[193]

The effect on Wilberforce is less clear. The event and its impact have not received much attention from his side, and for him it was not such a central experience. His terse forty-four-word diary entry for 30 June left an unfilled space,[194] suggesting a minimal concern with the encounter. As has been noted, he felt he had won, and he simply went about his multifaceted work. He had other subjects on his mind. For instance, on 4 July, the bishop was in the chair at the annual meeting of Queen's College, London,[195] and two days later was in the House of Lords urging that the Bible should be introduced into the government schools in India.[196] His son's biography two decades later mentions the event only very briefly and favorably,[197] as does a modern biography.[198]

The relationship between Huxley and Wilberforce remained civil, perhaps because both men believed they had won the debate. Six months after Oxford, Huxley pursued the subject in a letter to Wilberforce.

> Professor Huxley presents his compliments to the Lord Bishop of Oxford. Believing that his lordship has as great an interest in the ascertainment of the truth as himself, Prof. Huxley ventures to draw the attention of the Bishop to a paper [by Huxley] in the accompanying number of the *"Natural History Review"*[199] "On the zoological relation of Man with the lower animals." The Bishop of Oxford will find therein full justification for the diametrical contradiction with which he heard Professor Huxley meet certain anatomical statements [by Owen] put forth ... during the late session of the British Association at Oxford.[200]

Huxley and Wilberforce were together in a small group with John Bright after the Royal Academy Banquet of 1868,[201] and in 1871 Wilberforce thanked Huxley for calling his attention to an article recently published.[202] In 1887, however, Huxley and the bishop's son had a very sharp exchange of letters in *The Times*, which revealed that the tension was still very much alive. Reginald Wilberforce wrote, "Did the lash of Bishop Wilberforce's eloquence sting so sharply that, though 27 years have passed, the recollection of the castigation then received is as fresh as ever?" Huxley quickly responded:

> Those who were present at the famous meeting in Oxford ... will doubtless agree with him [R. Wilberforce] that an effectual castigation was received by somebody. But I have too much respect for filial piety, however indiscreet its manifestations, to trouble you with evidence as to who was the agent and who the patient in that operation.[203]

The Oxford confrontation affected the British Association in a number of ways. During the 1860 meeting the reporter for *The Evening Star* concluded that "so far as we could judge, the new Darwinian theory, whatever may be its real merits in a scientific point of view, has no small number of supporters amongst the members of the Association."[204] A decade later that number had grown dramatically, as Tuckwell reported.

> Ten years later I encountered him [Huxley] ... at the Exeter meeting of the Association. Again there was a bitter assault on Darwinism, this time

by a Scottish doctor of divinity; with smiling serenity Huxley smote him hip and thigh, the audience, hostile or cold at Oxford, here ecstatically acquisecent. The decade had worked its changes.[205]

The Oxford confrontation "Signalled a growing division between the older, often clerical Gentleman of Science, who believed in a voluntarism nourished by their financial independence, and those newer career-dependent scientists such as Huxley, who saw entrenched ecclesiastical power as a barrier to their own professional ambitions."[206] Originally created by and for "amateurs," the Association now moved toward being a "closed shop."[207] Furthermore, the clash at Oxford "revealed the resentment felt by the practitioners of the older reflective sciences against the new empirical ones."[208] It showed "party spirit in action, with science manifestly unable to provide that neutral ground"[209] so hoped for by many of the leaders of the Association.

The general relationship between religion and science was significantly affected by the Oxford clash. It

transformed . . . the whole nature of the conflict over Darwin's theory. Before, it had been . . . essentially the old battle within science between idealism and empiricism. . . . The Bishop of Oxford . . . made the conflict appear in the eyes of the world as one between religion and science.[210]

Gilley and Loades have appropriately noted that "Darwinism intruded upon a complex debate within Christendom itself between liberal and conservative theologies."[211] It put a great strain on natural theology and on those attempting to harmonize religion and science, whereby scientific study was viewed as discovering more about God's creation and drawing closer to God as a result. The president of the association in 1860, Lord Wrottesley, had, for instance, concluded his opening address with these words: "Let us ever apply ourselves seriously to the task [of scientific inquiry] feeling assured that the more we thus exercise, and by exercising improve, our intellectual faculties, the more worthy shall we be, the better shall we be fitted, to come nearer to our God."[212] It is interesting to note that above the main entrance to the Oxford Museum is a figure of an angel. The Oxford clash generated great interest in Darwinism,[213] and greatly emboldened the Darwinists. Shortly after the conference Darwin wrote to Huxley that "It seems that Oxford did the subject great good. It is of enormous importance the showing the world that a few first-rate men are not afraid of expressing their opinion."[214] As one of the foremost of those first-rate men, Huxley became a leading symbol of the rising assertiveness and militant spirit of the younger scientists in their insistence on freedom from scientific traditionalism and ecclesiastical dogma. Leonard Huxley's conclusion still seems to be on target. "The importance of the Oxford meeting lay in the open resistance that was made to authority, at a moment when even a drawn battle was hardly less effectual than acknowledged victory."[215]

Just as Huxley's Royal Institution lecture in 1852 helped greatly to propel him into visibility in scientific circles, and his Oxford debate in 1860 propelled him into broader public view, so did a third significant rhetorical experience in the next decade help to propel him into the English-speaking world outside of Great Britain. His seven-week lecture tour of the United States in 1876 firmly linked him to the American scene. He entrenched his reputation as an advocate of Darwinism, a spokesman for science education, and a talented lecturer working for greater freedom from constraints of academic and ecclesiastical traditionalism. The following chapter will trace in detail this important trans-Atlantic rhetorical venture in behalf of science.

4

Lecture Tour of the United States, 1876

The fame and influence of T. H. Huxley were not long in going beyond Great Britain; the European Continent and the United States soon knew him well, and indeed the English-speaking world and other areas also came to know of his works.

He was no stranger to the Continent. Mountain climbing in Switzerland and visits to France and Italy in search of improved health and relaxation as well as in connection with scientific purposes, were important aspects of his life. He developed firm associations and friendships with many key scientists in Germany, France, and Italy. For example, Ernst Haeckel, a German biologist and outspoken agnostic and supporter of Darwinism, was a close friend and devotee of Huxley. The German biologist, Anton Dohrn, founder of the significant Naples Marine Biological Research Station, was likewise Huxley's close friend and frequent correspondent. Huxley became an honorary member of academic societies in Austria-Hungary, Belgium, Denmark, France, Germany, Holland, Italy, Portugal, Sweden, Russia, as well as in Egypt, Brazil, Australia, and New Zealand. He received honorary degrees from Breslau, Würzburg, Bologna, and Erlangen.[1]

Some fragmentary selections of Huxley's works were translated into Chinese before 1898, but the first significant introduction of Darwinism into China was the translation of Huxley's *Evolution and Ethics* in 1899 by the famous scholar and translator of Western works, Yen Fu (1853–1921).[2] Partially through former students, Huxley's influence found its way to Australia, New Zealand, and South and Southeast Asia. At his death in 1895 laudatory obituaries appeared in newspapers and periodicals throughout the world.[3]

But outside of Great Britain it was in the United States where Huxley's influence and rhetorical talents came to be most fully recognized.

Background

Since the early 1860s, Huxley had developed close working ties with the American publisher, D. Appleton and Company, founded by Daniel Appleton and his son William Henry (1814–99), and with other science publishers like Edward Youmans. Sales of Huxley's books initially were discouraging, for when he asked if they would be interested in a forthcoming book, he received the following reply in April 1864:

> The restricted sale that your books have thus far met and the present doubt of their paying expenses somewhat dampens the ardor of the publishers and further disinclines them to negotiate arrangements by which the author will be led to expect a dividend while there are so many chances of disappointment. ... I have no doubt but that in the end the sales will prove remunerative. ... I trust time will improve affairs. The fact is that while your books met with thorough appreciation from the few earnest progressive thinkers, they were shamefully abused by the majority of the papers in which they were noticed. Agassiz the scientific autocrat of this Continent led off in his organ, the "Atlantic Monthly" about naturalists amusing themselves with tracing their geneology, and the signal being thus given from the Cambridge watchtower the clergy echoed and reechoed it in various notes from one end of the land to the other.[4]

Is it any wonder that Huxley's ire was stirred against the clergy and the older conservative scientists? In 1866 Appleton was willing to publish an American edition of Huxley's *Physiology*, but only reluctantly, for "the book business [is] very flat."[5] In late 1868 Youmans was dining with Huxley in London where they talked over "the American book plan,"[6] and the following year William Appleton was meeting with Huxley and others.[7]

During the 1860s and 1870s, then, American scientists, students, and the interested general reading public were becoming familiar with Huxley's work.[8] In 1869 the readers of the New York *Tribune* were informed of his busy lecture schedule in Britain, and a medical scholar in Philadelphia wrote to Huxley asking for advice on the history of the cell doctrine, as the American was preparing a paper to be used by medical students. "I believe that most of your published works are accessible to us in Philadelphia," but he thought Huxley may have something more recent to add.[9] In 1870 the reviewer in the *Nation* magazine, when discussing Huxley's new book, *Lay Sermons, Addresses, and Reviews*, remarked that many of the items in that collection were already familiar to many Americans.[10]

A group of thirteen Antioch College students wrote to Huxley in 1871 indicating that they were interested in the "subject of Sexual Physiology and Pathology," but knew of no good work for a scientific person and wondered if he could write a series of popular lectures on the subject. They assured him, "We know of no scientific author whose writings are so popular and widely read in this country as yours."[11] In 1873 W. S. Ward, the editor of the scientific department of *Appleton's Journal,* wrote to Huxley indicating that Appleton was sponsoring a project whereby they were setting up a free public aquarium in Central Park, New York City, and were anxious for words of commendation from scientists that could be published and thus attract sizable donations from the wealthy. He had heard that Huxley favored the idea and thus requested that Huxley send "for publication any such letter as you may deem best."[12] Huxley had established strong relationships with advocates of progressive science, like Prof. Othniel C. Marsh (1831–99) of Yale, holder of the nation's first chair in paleontology; and John Fiske, a Harvard librarian, philosopher, and historian, who "though no scientist himself, had done more than any other American, perhaps, to popularize the new findings in science and to consider their implications for religion and ethics."[13] In 1873 and 1874 Fiske, seventeen years younger than Huxley, visited London and the Huxley home.[14] In 1875 Huxley was sent a copy of the reports of the "Second Geological Survey of Pennsylvania," compliments of the state commission and the director of the survey.[15] By 1876 Huxley had become an honorary member of such academic societies as the Academy of the Natural Sciences in Philadelphia (1859), the Odontographic Society of Pennsylvania (1865), the American Philosophical Society of Philadelphia (1869), the Buffalo Society of Natural Sciences (1873), and the New York Academy of Science (1876).[16]

In 1876 Darwin was writing in his *Autobiography* that Huxley

has been the mainstay in England of the principle of the gradual evolution of organic beings. Much splendid work as he has done in zoology, he would have done far more if his time had not been so largely consumed by official and literary work, and by his efforts to improve the education of the country. ... He is a splendid man and has worked well for the good of mankind.[17]

It is at this stage in his life, then, at a high point in his distinguished career, that the fifty-one-year-old Huxley, with nineteen years of active labor yet to come, set out on his only trip to the United States,[18] a seven-week lecture tour.

During this period the public lecture was an important medium of cultural relations between Britain and the United States. Motivated by the desire to improve relations after the Civil War, to propagate some cause, or to secure funds for a cause or for one's self, many Britons came to America and many Americans went to Britain to speak. Minnick, who has comprehensively studied British speaking in America from 1866 to 1900, concluded that the considerable number of British speakers were mainly middle-class professionals, who tended to lecture in the larger cities in the northeastern quarter of the country, and who had considerable influence on American life.[19] In 1869 the New York *Tribune* proclaimed:

> When the historian of a later day comes to search out the intellectual antecedents of his modern society, he will devote an interesting chapter to the rise and progress of ideas as illustrated in the institution of the public lecture. He will record that at one time ... a great many ... awakeners of American intelligence, were lecturers; that philosophers and scientists were persuaded out of their studies and laboratories to take a stand on the platform.[20]

The astute English observer, James Bryce, commented in 1888 that in the United States the public lecture was "far more frequent and more valuable as a means of interesting people in literary, scientific and political questions than anywhere in Europe, except probably in Edinburgh."[21]

Motivation

Multiple motivations operated to draw the extremely busy Huxley to undertake the time-consuming trip to the United States. His letter to a young colleague on 20 April 1876 is the first available indication of his definite intention to go to America.[22] The foremost impetus was the long-standing desire to visit his sister Lizzie, who with her family had been living in the South since 1850. Their regular correspondence since then had kept firm the family bond. His letter to Lizzie in June 1876, from Edinburgh where he was lecturing, makes it clear that plans had been made for the trip.[23] He indicated that he and his wife would be sailing on the *Germanic* on 27 July, and that he would have to put off "travelling south as late as possible in order to spare the wife as much heat as possible. ... So you may look for us about the middle of September or a little earlier." He asked if she could possibly meet them at her daughter and son-in-law's home in Nashville, rather than at her home in Montgomery, Alabama, to reduce the length of the train ride and lessen the possibility of extreme heat. He then reminisced that it was thirty years ago that he had last seen her. He was just "a boy beginning life. Now I am a grey man. . . . You and I are the only two [of our family] who seemed to be capable of fraternal love. . . . It will be something so strange to see anyone of my own blood who has any love for me. I have written a horrible blasphemy for my children are of my own blood—and they love me well. I wonder how you look." Looking forward to seeing his favorite sibling again, his nephews and nieces for the first time, and having Lizzie finally meet Nettie was a major motivation to sail the Atlantic. Back in 1853 when Lizzie gave birth to a son, Huxley wrote: "First let me congratulate you on being safe over your troubles and in possession of another possible President. I think it may be worth coming over twenty years hence on the possibility of picking up something or other from one of my nephews at Washington."[24] Twenty-three years later he did come.

Not surprisingly, economic motivation was also present. Early in 1874 Huxley had written to Darwin: "I have had an *awfully* tempting offer to go to Yankee-land on a lecturing expedition, and I am seriously thinking of making an experiment next spring. The chance of clearing two or three thousand pounds in as many months is not to be sneezed at by a *pere de famille.*"[25] His interest was no doubt stimulated in part by his friend John Tyndall's highly successful four-month lecture tour of the United States in 1872–73, in which he cleared over $13,000.[26] D. Appleton and Company, aggressive book publishers that they were, had been hoping for some time to arrange a Huxley lecture tour in order to increase book sales. Also in on the planning was Edward Youmans, creator of the *Popular Science Monthly* in 1872, author of many science textbooks, and the driving force behind the International Scientific Series of books, which introduced Americans to leading world scientists, including Huxley. Publishers and author both stood likely to gain financially from a Huxley lecture tour.

Intertwined with economics was the commitment to spreading views on science, especially Darwinism. Science teachers at all educational levels stood to benefit from such a lecture tour. Huxley looked forward to visiting such science popularizers as Youman and Fiske, who had previously visited him in London, and to firming up associations with scientists, such as O. C. Marsh at Yale. In October 1874 Youmans wrote to Fiske of the possibility of a Huxley visit, and in January 1875 and March 1876 Fiske wrote to Huxley indicating that he was eagerly looking forward to Huxley's coming, and extended the invitation to use the Fiske home freely, just as Huxley had so warmly opened his home to Fiske.

A desire for a vacation from his hectic schedule was an important motivation. In March 1874 he had written to Darwin of the possibility of lecturing in America and added, "I am getting sick of the state of things here."[28] Upon arrival in New York he apparently told a reporter that he intended "to make a brief visit for health and recreation. . . . I was overburdened with work at home and hoped to make this a mere pleasure-trip." Then in a rather familiar Huxley feigned reluctance, he apparently told the reporter, "When first invited by my friends here to deliver lectures I protested vehemently against it, but I have been forced to succumb. . . . I am forced into it in spite of myself."[29]

The fact that the Huxley children were now old enough to be left alone for such a long period under the care of a trusted friend, permitted the Huxleys to consider such a trip. The ages of the seven surviving children were now between eighteen and ten, and Sir William and Lady Armstrong offered to have the children stay with them at Cragside, their estate in Northumberland. As Leonard Huxley, who was sixteen at the time, later wrote in his biography of his father, "My father sometimes would refer, half jestingly, to the trip as his second honeymoon, when, for the first time in twenty years, he and my mother set forth by themselves, free from all family cares."[30] Mrs. Huxley wrote to Lizzie shortly after arriving in the United States:

> You may fancy how my heart ached in bidding "good bye" to my seven darlings. They all came down to the little station at Rothbury in Northumberland & saw us off. . . . I had a very hard time for some weeks before leaving home—in getting everything arranged for two months absence. To put the clothes in order—for that time for seven—& our two selves—is no small matter. . . . Lady Armstrong had been so kind as to insist that we should all be together till Hal & I left. So we spent five days together—Hal joined us—from Edinburgh [on] the Saturday very tired & worn out with his lectures & Royal Commission business.[31]

If any additional motivation were needed, it was provided by an invitation to lecture at Johns Hopkins University in Baltimore, an educational institution newly created by a generous bequest from Johns Hopkins, a wealthy bachelor Quaker merchant who had died in 1873. On 14 March 1876, Daniel Coit Gilman, the president of the university, who had heard Huxley lecture at South Kensington a year earlier and who had asked Huxley for a recommendation for someone to fill the chair in biology, now informed Huxley that

Henry Newell Martin, Huxley's laboratory assistant, had indeed secured the post. Gilman went on to inquire whether Huxley would be interested in giving a special lecture if he were ever to come to the United States.[32] In June 1876, while up in Edinburgh giving three months of lectures, Huxley received the official invitation forwarded to him from London by his wife, and he wrote to her on 23 June:

> Did you read Gilman's note asking me to give the inaugural discourse at the Johns Hopkins University, and offering £100 [about $480] on the part of the trustees? I am minded to do it on our way back from the south, but don't much like taking money for the performance. Tell me what you think about this at once, as I must reply.[33]

Mrs. Huxley no doubt gave an affirmative reply, for Baltimore was soon put on their itinerary. Thus his trip to the States was planned prior to getting the John Hopkins invitation, and financial reward was not as high on his motivation list as some have implied. The lecture was to inaugurate a special lecture series by distinguished scientists, not the inauguration of the university, which is sometimes assumed, for President Gilman had given the official inaugural address on Washington's Birthday, 22 February, in which he outlined the thrust of the new institution.

Itinerary

Early in 1876 Huxley received a message from an American devotee. "The whole nation is electrified by the announcement that Professor Huxley is to visit us next fall. We will make infinitely more of him than we did of the Prince of Wales and his retinue of lords and dukes."[34] Apparently Americans were quick to identify Englishmen with nobility, for when the Huxleys arrived in New York, a local newspaper, Huxley later mentioned, "was good enough to announce my coming, accompanied by my 'titled bride'—which was rather hard upon plain folk, married twenty-one years, and blessed with seven children to boot."[35]

They arrived in New York on 5 August, having left Queenstown on the *Germanic* on 27 July as scheduled—a seven-day, nineteen-hour trip. A fellow passenger, George W. Smalley, the New York *Tribune*'s correspondent in London, later reported that as they approached New York City, Huxley

> asked what were the tall tower and tall building with a cupola, then the two most conspicuous objects. I told him the Tribune and the Western

Union Telegraph buildings. "Ah," he said, "that is interesting; that is American. In the Old World the first things you see as you approach a great city are steeples; here you see, first, centres of intelligence."[36]

Newspaper reporters interviewed him immediately and throughout the trip, thus giving considerable publicity to his tour. Met by Youmans, William Appleton and his son, and Prof. O. C. Marsh, the Huxleys immediately were taken to the Appleton residence at Riverdale for a dinner party.[37]

The Huxleys saw some sights and visited friends in New York City, then went on an excursion to West Point. Mrs. Huxley was taken by members of the Appleton family to Saratoga where she stayed while Huxley went by train to New Haven where he was thoroughly impressed by Professor Marsh's fossil collections. Huxley's subsequent "promotion of Marsh's achievements constituted some of the earliest serious European recognition of fundamental American science."[38] Marsh's wealthy Peabody relatives provided a lovely apartment accommodation for Huxley, and he greatly enjoyed his stay there. In a letter to his wife, he summarized a typical day's routine with Professor Marsh.

> We are hard at work still. Breakfast at 8:30—go over to the Museum with Marsh between 9 & 10—work till 1:30. Dine, go back to museum & work till 6. Mr. Marsh takes me [for] a drive to see the view about the town and back to tea about half past eight. He is a wonderful fellow full of fun and stories about his western adventures.[39]

Mrs. Huxley joined her husband at New Haven and they went to Newport, Rhode Island, where they spent a few days with Alexander Agassiz, who had succeeded his father, Louis Agassiz, who had died three years earlier, as curator of Harvard University's museum. Unlike his father, Alexander was sympathetic to Darwinism. The Huxleys next went to Boston, and at Cambridge Huxley visited with the famous botanist, Asa Gray, the strongest American voice in behalf of Darwin's work, who had long corresponded with Darwin. The Huxleys next spent two days with John Fiske and his family at their summer residence in Petersham, in north central Massachusetts, where a number of distinguished guests were assembled to meet them, and they had time to relax, see the countryside, and visit with the Fiskes. Five months later Fiske wrote to Herbert Spencer:

> We had a very delightful visit from the Huxleys at Petersham in August. They thought the country there somewhat like Cumberland or some parts

of Scotland. We had a great houseful of Cambridge people there, with a good deal of music and fun of one sort and another. For my part I have seldom spent two happier days. ... [40]

The American Association for the Advancement of Science (AAAS) was holding its twenty-fifth annual convention in Buffalo, which was the next stop for the Huxleys. The local newspaper expressed the hope that Huxley would give an address, but he made only an informal presentation. The Buffalo *Express* reported, "The routine work of the morning session was relieved from tediousness by the half-humorous remarks of Prof. Huxley, who gave his impressions of American life"[41] and who spoke about evolution in general and who praised Professor Marsh's fossil collection in particular. He reportedly said: "The history of evolution as a matter of fact is now distinctly traceable. We know it has happened, and what remains is the subordinate question of how it happened."[42] The London *Times* reprinted a report from their "American Correspondent," which included Huxley's comparison of America and England.

I have visited your great Universities of Yale and Harvard, and have seen how your wealthy men contribute to scientific institutions in a way to which we are totally unaccustomed in England. The general notion of an Englishman who becomes rich is to buy an estate and found a family. The general notion of an American who becomes rich is to do something for the benefit of the people, and to found an institution whose benefits shall flow to all.[43]

Following his remarks "there was loud and long-continued applause from the audience."[44] The editor of the *Express* commented:

The distinguished scientist seems to have been somewhat surprised at the warmth of his reception in the United States, but as the feeling which prompts people to honor him is the honest tribute to his established reputation as a thorough-going and most successful scientific student he must not consider it a bit of ordinary lionizing by any means. It is a real gratification to the American Association, and to many people of Buffalo who are interested in scientific matters, to meet Professor Huxley face to face.[45]

A few days later the editor felt inclined, however, to caution his readers that evolution was by no means a proven fact. After the session, the Huxleys joined the AAAS excursion to Niagara Falls, in the company of Marsh, Youmans, President Barnard of Columbia

College, and others. Huxley collected data on the gorge below the falls, which he then was to use in subsequent lectures. His thoughts also must have at least fleetingly been drawn to nearby Toronto and to his unsuccessful application in 1851 for a position at the university there. One wonders what his life would have been like if he had successfully secured the post.

The Huxleys now were eagerly anticipating the long-awaited meeting with Lizzie and family. From Niagara Falls they made their way to Nashville, apparently via Cleveland, Cincinnati, and Louisville, arriving on 4 September. One of Lizzie's sons and two of her daughters lived in Nashville, so it made a good location for the family reunion. Given the short three-day stay in Nashville, it is surprising that Huxley permitted himself to be drawn into a heavy public schedule, but such is the price of being an international celebrity. The next day "he visited the state capitol, was shown through the state library, inspected the collections of the state historical society and the cabinets of woods and minerals in the Department of Mines and Agriculture, called on the superintendent of instruction in his office, and visited Fisk University."[46] He visited Vanderbilt University[47] (where in the library he saw a bronze bust of himself) and the Nashville College of Medicine. He delivered a public lecture at the urging of a group of local citizens who had contacted him. The editor of the Nashville *Daily American*, Col. John C. Burch, a leading Democrat in the state and an enthusiastic science buff, gave Huxley favorable publicity throughout his visit, and on the morning of the lecture wrote:

> As a whole-souled, outspoken friend of popular education, Prof. Huxley has endeared himself to millions in America and Britain, without regard to party or religious creed. In this great cause he has made a reputation, very rare, indeed, in England, for ease, grace, and fluency in off-hand speaking. He is the most distinguished extempore speaker in Britain. It is a rare good fortune which, this evening, gives our citizens a treat that very few in America will be permitted to enjoy, while all covet it.[48]

Huxley refused an honorarium, but tickets were needed to secure admission to the Masonic Hall Theatre, which could hold approximately one thousand people.[49] Introduced as "the great apostle of modern science,"[50] Huxley chose as his lecture topic, "A Sermon of Stone," in which he discussed the geology of Tennessee in a hastily prepared speech lasting approximately thirty minutes.[51] Upon arrival in Nashville he had been shown two books, a history of Tennessee and one on the resources of the state, so he compared

Tennessee and England, similar in size, resources, and geological structure. He discussed histories by humans with history as taught by geology, emphasizing the greater dependability of the latter. He drew on his recent geological observations at Niagara. He emphasized the importance of understanding the history of the earth and of appreciating man's place in nature, stressing the importance of science education.

After the brief Nashville visit, the Huxleys left for Baltimore via Cincinnati. In Baltimore they stayed at the country estate of John W. Garrett, the president of the Baltimore & Ohio Railroad and a member of the Johns Hopkins board of trustees.

Johns Hopkins Address

Some years after the occasion President Gilman explained his rationale in selecting Huxley to deliver the address at Johns Hopkins.

> As the day drew near for the opening of our doors and the beginning of instruction the word reached us that Professor Huxley of London was coming to this country. We had already decided that, in view of the attention which was to be given to medicine, biology should receive a large amount of attention, more than ever before in America. ... His [Huxley's] repute as an investigator was very high, and as the popular interpreter and defender of biological investigations he was without a peer. His acquaintance with the problems of medical education was also well-known. As a public speaker upon scientific subjects there was no superior. ... The moment was opportune for informing the public through the speech of this master, in respect to the requirements of modern medicine and the value of biological research.[52]

Huxley's "Address on University Education," as he later entitled it for publication, was delivered at Johns Hopkins on 12 September, in the Academy of Music before a distinguished audience of over two thousand. Included were

> Governor John Lee Carroll, Baltimore's mayor Latrobe, the Hopkins trustees, official representatives from Annapolis and St. Johns, the Surgeon General and the Paymaster-General of the United States Army, the Japanese minister, the British consul at Baltimore, Professor Marsh of Yale and several university presidents.[53]

Gilman recollected Huxley's presentation.

I sat very near the orator as he delivered the address . . . and noticed that, although he kept looking at the pile of manuscripts on the desk before him, he did not turn the pages over. The speech was appropriate and well received, but it had no glow, and the orator did not equal his reputation for charm and persuasiveness. When the applause was over, . . . [he said] "I have been in distress. The reporters brought me, according to their promise, the copy of their notes. It was on thin translucent paper, and to make it legible, they put clean white sheets between the leaves. That made such bulk that I removed the intermediate leaves, and when I stood up at the desk I found I could not read a sentence. So I have been in a dilemma—not daring to speak freely, and trying to recall what I dictated yesterday and allowed the reporters to send to New York." . . . Those of us who wanted guidance and encouragement for a leading adovcate of biological studies were rewarded and gratified by the address, and have often referred to it.[54]

Twelve years later Huxley gave a similar account of this uncomfortable experience, citing it as one of two instances in his public speaking career where he was so unnerved by his notes.[55]

In his speech he stressed the need for educational systems from elementary school through the university level to acquire a firm command of the English language, physical sciences, mathematics, psychology, logic, music, and drawing. The university level would expand on these basic elements, adding to English a command of ancient and modern foreign languages, history expanding into archaeology, anthropology, and geography, with facilities such as libraries, museums, and laboratories. He emphasized improving the education of doctors, even though Johns Hopkins had to defer on that temporarily, due to lack of finances.

Up to this point I have considered only the teaching aspect of your great foundation, that function of the university in virtue of which it plays the part of a reservoir of ascertained truth, so far as our symbols can ever interpret nature. All can learn; all can drink of this lake. It is given to few to add to the store of knowledge, to strike new springs of thought, or to shape new forms of beauty. But so sure as it is that men live not by bread, but by ideas, so sure is it that the future of the world lies in the hands of those who are able to carry the interpretation of nature a step further than their predecessors; so certain is it that the highest function of a university is to seek out those men, cherish them, and give their ability to serve their kind full play. I rejoice to observe that the encouragement of research occupies so prominent a place in your official documents, and in the wise and liberal inaugural address of your president. . . . My own conviction is admirably summed up in the passage of your president's address, "that the best investigators are usually those who have also the reponsibilities of instruction, gaining thus the incitement of colleagues, the encouragement of pupils, and the observation of the public."[56]

But how would the educational enterprise be used? To what end would America put her great wealth and size and promising political experiment? Characteristically, Huxley expressed his concern for these overarching moral considerations.

I cannot say that I am in the slightest degree impressed by your [America's] bigness, or your material resources, as such. Size is not grandeur, and territory does not make a nation. The great issue, about which hangs a true sublimity, and the terror of overhanging fate, is what are you going to do with all these things? What is to be the end of which these are to be the means? You are making a novel experiment in politics on the greatest scale which the world has yet seen. . . . Truly America has a great future before her; great in toil, in care, and in responsibility; great in true glory if she can be guided in wisdom and righteousness; great in shame if she fail. . . . [T]he one condition of success, your sole safeguard, is the moral worth and intellectual clearness of the individual citizen. Education cannot give these, but it may cherish them and bring them to the front in whatever station of society they are to be found; and the universities ought to be, and may be, the fortresses of the higher life of the nation.[57]

In his moving peroration, he expressed the hope:

May the university which commences its practical activity tomorrow abundantly fulfil its high purposes, may its renown as a seat of true learning, a centre of free inquiry, a focus of intellectual light, increase year by year, until men wander hither from all parts of the earth, as of old they sought Bologna, or Paris, or Oxford.[58]

How prophetic can one be! He closed his address with another gaze into the future.

And it is pleasant to me to fancy that, among the English students who are drawn to you at that time, there may linger a dim tradition that a country-man of theirs was permitted to address you as he has done to-day, and to feel as if your hopes were his hopes and your success his joy.[59]

"At the end of the lecture," his biographer-son later wrote,

amid the enthusiastic applause of the crowd, he made his way to the front of the box where his hosts and their party were, and received their warm congratulations. But he missed one voice amongst them, and turning to where his wife sat in silent triumph almost beyond speech, he said, "And have you no word for me?" then, himself also deeply moved, stooped down and kissed her.[60]

At the celebration of the Johns Hopkins Centenary, his grandson, Sir Andrew Huxley, on 10 September 1976, delivered the Huxley Centenary Lecture.[61]

Although Huxley said nothing unusual to stir negative religious reaction, President Gilman soon received considerable complaints because there was no emphasis on the religious dimension of education and there was no prayer or benediction. "Huxley was bad enough; Huxley without a prayer was intolerable."[62]

The printed version of the speech reached far beyond the East. From Minneapolis, on 30 September, the president of the University of Minnesota, William Watts Folwell, wrote to his friend President Gilman:

> The reading of Professor Huxley's address at your opening makes me very desirous to have such an introduction to him as will gain me his notice and his attention to some matters relating to the organization of education which I would lay before him. Soon after planning our Secondary Department here, I had the satisfaction to learn that we had included in it just those elements of Sciences proposed by Professor Huxley. ... I saw and heard Professor Huxley at Buffalo but seeing him sorely beset by curious persons asked for no introduction.[63]

Gilman immediately followed through with a letter to Huxley on 6 October. "The writer of the enclosed note is the President of the State University of Minnesota in the far northwest. He is a man of about 40 years of age, bright and sensible. ... "[64] Gilman said he was glad to have heard of Huxley's safe arrival back in England, and he hoped that Huxley would "Retain as pleasant memories of Baltimore as we do of your visit."[65]

New York Lectures on Evolution

Leaving Baltimore a day or two after the address, the Huxleys visited the Centennial Exhibition in Philadelphia before arriving in New York City. They stayed at the Westminster Hotel in Irving Place, and Huxley visited Columbia College. Most of the weekend probably was spent on final work on his three lectures on evolution, given the overall title of "The Direct Evidence of Evolution," sponsored and publicized by D. Appleton and Company. Scheduled 18, 20, 22 September in Chickering Hall at Fifth Avenue and Eighteenth Street, these were the climax of his American tour. A reserved seat ticket for the series cost $5.00 and for one lecture $1.50; a general admission ticket for each lecture at the door cost $1.00.[66]

The audience for all three lectures was large, distinguished, and respectfully attentive. The New York *World* reporter indicated that for the first lecture "the house was filled, and the audience was of the best," and for the second "the audience was even larger" and they gave "close and respectful attention." After the third lecture the reporter wrote that the lectures had "throughout been listened to with the attention which intelligent audiences are accustomed to give to the exposition of an important doctrine by a profound man."[67] The *Times* reported that the first lecture "drew . . . a large and most intelligent audience. Every seat in the room was occupied, and many persons remained standing patiently throughout the lecture." Some late arrivals caused slight disruption at the beginning of the lecture. For the second lecture "not a vacant seat was visible anywhere within the hall. Besides being large in number the audience was also very appreciative, and the best token of this was to be seen in the careful attention shown by the auditors and the earnestness with which they seemed to follow the speaker's train of thought." The final lecture was delivered "in the presence of one of the largest and most brilliant audiences which has yet greeted him in this country.[68]

The speaker was interestingly described by reporters. The *World* said that

> Professor Huxley is a man of medium height and a "stocky build"; his eyes are deep-set under shaggy, beetling brows; his hair is abundant and dark, and his [side] whiskers iron-gray. . . . [A]t times his voice failed to fill the hall. His manner is easy and colloquial, and he emphasizes his points by a quizzical turn of the head. . . . [T]he Professor's easy unoratorical style seemed very acceptable to it [the audience]; he spoke simply as if addressing a class of intelligent men and women who had come together to learn something he had to tell them.

After the third lecture the reporter wrote that Huxley "has always spoken with gravity, though at times with some slight marks of irritation at the futile criticism which seems to be unnecessarily irksome to him, has indulged in no flights of eloquence such as popular lecturers on scientific subjects are wont to display to the gaping multitude."[69] When Huxley had arrived in New York City in early August, the *World* reporter had written, "In manner he is affable, good-humored and exceedingly unpretentious, seeming rather a type of the mercantile or commercial class. ... "[70]

Reporting on the lectures the *Times* described Huxley by comparing him to Tyndall.

> As a speaker, Prof. Huxley is of very different type to his distinguished co-laborer in the cause of science, Prof. Tyndall. He is less energetic in manner, has a voice much inferior in clearness and volume, shows less feeling, and makes no such demands on the sympathy of his hearers. He is, moreover, ... comparatively indifferent to the imaginative and poetic side of his subject, and made very few "points" for applause. ... While simple and severe in style, Prof. Huxley's lecture was in a very lively sense controversial. ... Prof. Huxley's method is slow, precise, and clear. ... He does not utter anything in the reckless fashion which conviction sometimes countenances and excuses, but rather with the deliberation which research and close inquiry foster. ...

The second lecture "was rather a difficult one to follow in thought, and imposed a constant strain on the attention of the auditors during the seventy-five minutes of its delivery."[71]

His lectures discussed the three hypotheses on the history of nature: (1) that life as we know it today has existed in largely the same condition from infinity; (2) that life as we know it today has existed for a relatively short time, and that it was created suddenly out of chaos; and (3) that life as we know it today has existed for a relatively short time, but that it was created gradually out of lower forms. His first lecture dealt with the first two hypotheses; his second lecture presented the neutral and favorable but not demonstrable evidence on the third hypothesis; and the last lecture presented the demonstrable evidence proving the soundness, as far as he was concerned, of the third hypothesis.

In his lectures Huxley revealed a two-valued orientation—a sense of partisanship, of advocacy—in a number of ways. First, he allocated a smaller portion of time to the views of his opponents, which of course is to be expected since his objective was to clarify and support the claims of evolution. In the printed volume the allocation of space (excluding the introductory overview of his subject) resulted in 3½ pages devoted to the first hypothesis, 11 pages to the second, and 63 to the theory of evolution.

Second, though he gives the impression of a serious, careful, and objective approach to all evidence for or against the hypothesis of evolution, he terminates his discussions with a strong, triumphant, dogmatic conclusion favorable to his point of view. His categorical assertions seem to come from out of nowhere and strike telling blows. For example, after a calm discussion of the first hypothesis he concludes with the following confident assertions:

> [The first hypothesis] . . . is *absolutely* incompatible with such evidence as we have; which is of so plain and so simple a character that it is *impossible* in any way to escape from the conclusions which it *forces* upon us. . . . The . . . evidence *absolutely* negatives the conception of the eternity of the present condition of things. We can say with *certainty* that the present condition of things has existed for a comparatively short period; and that, so far as animal and vegetable nature are concerned, it has been preceded by a different condition. . . . The hypothesis of the eternity of the present state of nature may therefore by *put out of court.*[72]

Following his fairly objective treatment of the second hypothesis, Huxley concludes:

> We see how *absolutely futile* are the attempts that have been made to draw a parallel between the story told by so much of the crust of the earth as is known to us and the story which Milton tells. . . . I leave you to consider how far, by an ingenuity of interpretation, by any stretching of the meaning of language, it can be brought into harmony with the Miltonic hypothesis (24, 29).

Toward the close of the last lecture, after having presented methodically and unemotionally the detailed information on the third hypothesis, he concludes:

> Thus . . . it has become evident that . . . the history of the horse-type is *exactly* and *precisely* that which could have been predicted from a knowledge of the principles of evolution. . . . the facts are shown to be in *entire* accordance [with his hypothesis]. The doctrine of evolution, at the present time, rests upon exactly as secure a foundation as the Copernican theory . . . did at the time of its promulgation. Its logical basis is precisely of the same character—the coincidence of the observed facts with theoretical requirements (89, 90).

At the end of the third lecture he triumphantly asserts that "the *whole evidence* is in favour of evolution, and there is *none* against it . . . [and he accuses opponents of engaging in] . . . obvious attempts to escape the force of demonstration" (91).

Huxley also reveals his two-valued orientation by the clever use of subtle jabs. He asserts throughout, that his point of view is shared by "anyone familiar with the facts," "the informed," "those capable of estimating the significance of these facts," "every intelligent person," "the trained intellectual," "the accurate observer," "cautious men," "candid thinkers," and "honest thinkers." The factual evidence is always "simple," "plain," or "obvious." These terms obviously suggest that one who does not agree with Huxley's interpretations is incapable of comprehending the significance of simple, plain, and obvious facts, of being an untrained and inaccurate observer, and of lacking cautiousness, candidness, and honesty in one's thinking processes. Before the opposition realizes it, it is reeling from such constant jabbing. Throughout his lectures he employs the technique of seeming not to be hostile to an idea and yet implicitly rejecting it. As the reporter for the New York *Times* put it, Huxley "has a Ciceronian way of saying that he will not denounce such and such an hypothesis, when the very negation implies that it ought, in his opinion, to be denounced."[73] It is through such indirect jabs—"side thrusts," as the editor for the *Times* called them[74]—that Huxley exhibited a considerable degree of partisanship.

Huxley cleverly entices his opponents to lower their guard. Wise to the power of connotation, he constructs new labels, which will not be offensive. For example, the second hypothesis, which suggested that the world as we know it today had existed for a relatively short time and that it was created suddenly out of chaos, he calls not the "biblical doctrine," or the "doctrine of Moses," but "Milton's hypothesis," ostensibly for reasons of accuracy. This new label thus enabled him to refute and even ridicule that view of creation without appearing to argue with the Bible.

Furthermore, he rather frequently claims incompetence on a given aspect of the subject. As the reporter for the *Times* put it, "He is seemingly very modest in declining to meddle with matters outside of his sphere."[75] For example, on the question of what the biblical view of creation actually is, Huxley states, "It . . . does not lie within my competency to say what the Hebrew text does and . . . does not signify" (19). Was Moses the author of Genesis? Huxley replies, "You will understand that I gave no judgment—it would be an impertinence upon my part to volunteer even a suggestion—upon such a subject" (20). As to the question of how much time, geologically measured, is needed for man to have evolved from lower forms, Huxley insists, "I will not pretend to say how we ought to measure this time . . . [I have] no means of arriving at any conclusion as to the amount of time which may be needed for a certain quantity of organic change" (26, 92–93). He also adopts the stance of the disinterested third person, the noncombatant, the reporter who is merely relating the facts, and who is not involved in the controversies. He frequently indicates that what he is presenting is what "the evidence," "scientific men," "scholars," and "naturalists," are saying. It is not he who is speaking; he is only the vehicle for announcing the truth.

Huxley takes away from his opponents their weapons. This is best illustrated in his handling of the material that demonstrates considerable constancy in animal forms through the centuries, which the antievolutionists felt was a most powerful weapon in their possession. Led by evidence found in Egypt, Niagara Falls, and at other localities, Huxley is frank to admit that "certain existing species of animals show no distinct sign of modification, or transformation" (37) over a period of at least thirty thousand years. Furthermore, he presents this data in climax order, beginning with the Egyptian findings, which demonstrate a constancy of forms for a four thousand-year period, followed by other evidence, which extends the time over a gradually longer period. This seems to make the information as effective as possible, but it is only building up his opponent's case so it would fall with a more resounding thud. He takes away this important argument by insisting, as we shall soon see, that it really is neutral or indifferent in relation to the theory of evolution.

Finally, Huxley exhibits his partisanship by possessing an effective defense against the argument of the opposition. As the reporter for the *Times* observed, Huxley "guards the positions which he takes with astuteness and ability."[76] Huxley is quick to place a favorable interpretation on evidence that does not necessarily support his view. for example, about the large amount of evidence that suggests that there is a constancy of species, he is quick to say that though it clearly does not advance the theory of evolution, the evidence is "capable of being interpreted in perfect consistency" (41) with evolution. He labels it as "neutral" or "indifferent" evidence. He admits that such evidence would be fatal to a theory of evolution, which held that all animal forms had to undergo continual modification, but his theory of evolution does not accept that necessity, for he holds that some things perhaps have not changed because their environment has not changed. Thus, the powerful argument of the opposition is laid to rest. Furthermore, he is quick to raise doubts about the views of the opposition. For instance, on the same issue of the constancy of species based on Cuvier's findings in Egypt, Huxley suggests that if four thousand years is too short a period and if the process of evolution is dependent upon varying surrounding conditions, then "the argument against the hypothesis of evolution based on the unchanged character of the Egyptian fauna is worthless" (34). Huxley follows this by indicating that the Egyptian monuments coeval with the mummified fauna, testify to the absence of change during those years, which effectively defends himself against a seemingly powerful hypothesis. Later he uses the same defense against the evidence that fossils of scorpions had been found, which indicated that the scorpion has existed for thousands of years without any appreciable change, he asserts that surrounding conditions had not changed, hence "the stock objection to the hypothesis of evolution, based on the long duration of certain animal and vegetable types, is no objection at all" (41).

Although making and supporting the claim that Huxley was heavily two-valued in his rhetorical orientation, it is also important to recognize that he also often had a strong strain of dialectical awareness, of being able to avoid a two-valued partisanship; of being able to demonstrate the recognition, comprehension, and sympathetic evaluation of the opposing position; and the ability to examine both points of view with a sense of objective detachment. In these New York lectures Huxley demonstrates in at least four ways this spirit of dialectial awareness.

First, he reveals the philosophical attitude of the scientist. At the outset he cautions his audience that "we must recollect that any human belief, however broad its basis, however defensible it may seem, is, after all, only a probable belief, and that our widest and safest generalizations are simply statements of the highest degree of probability" (3). He expresses a willingness to leave open those questions that at the moment have no satisfactory answers; and he couches many of his assertions with such qualifying phraseology as "so far as our present knowledge extends," or "as it appears to me at present." He claims to have no vested interest in any position, but to be willingly led by evidence, not only in the testing of his opponent's claims but also his own. He cautions against under-or over-estimating evidence. He demonstrates a hesitancy to draw conclusions favorable to his hypothesis if the evidence does not warrant it; for instance, he emphasizes that the existence of forms between groups, such as between birds and reptiles or between rhinoceroses and horses, does not necessarily mean that these are the intermediary forms through which reptiles became birds or rhinoceroses became horses. Furthermore, he places mankind in proper perspective in relation to the quest for nature's secrets. "It may be the way of Nature to be unintelligible; she is often puzzling, and I have no reason to suppose that she is bound to fit herself to our notions" (29).

Second, he demonstrates an obvious awareness and understanding of the opposing arguments. His first lecture is devoted to an investigation of the two opposing hypotheses, and in the second lecture he spends considerable time investigating the evidence supporting the idea of the constancy of the species, which was thought by many to be a strong argument against evolution. Throughout the second and third lectures he brings into his discussion the arguments of the opposition.

Third, Huxley reveals a dialectical awareness by being able to look inward upon the possible weaknesses of his own position with frankness and with a touch of humor. He recognizes that it is hopeless to secure testimonial evidence to support the theory of evolution and that one has to rely upon circumstantial evidence. He recognizes that no bridge exists between many forms (between mammals and birds for example), and frankly states that "if it could be shown that this state of things had always existed, the fact would be fatal to the doctrine of evolution" (48). He realizes the weakness of falling back upon the refuge that the geological record of time is very imperfect, and he playfully has his opponents stating, "It is all very well, but, when you get into a difficulty with your theory of evolution, you appeal to the incompleteness and the imperfection of the geological records" (43). With a touch of humor he refers to the insistence of men of science like himself to believe nothing without evidence as being a rather "awkward" (33) habit.

These instances of his demonstrating a spirit of dialectical awareness are however considerably outweighed by his spirit of partisanship, and thus the latter is clearly dominant in his rhetoric. This partisanship in turn understandably generated considerable reaction, largely negative but also positive and what might be called neutral.[77]

The day after Huxley sailed for England, the editor of the New York *World* suggested, "Now that he has left, I feel that any further communication should be on the general subject, without any reference to him personally."[78] But many if not most hostile critics were not so courteous and sophisticated, and their arrows usually struck the rhetor as well as his message. Sir John William Dawson, a scientist at McGill College in Montreal, illustrated, however, that one could render a thorough negative review of the substance and yet praise the speaker. "Huxley is an able, well-read, industrious, and conscientious biologist, and has a boldness of utterance and an instinct in favor of fair dealing and equal rights, along with a genuine hatred of humbug and superstition. . . . [His] powers of illustration and persuasion are of the highest order."[79]

The three lectures were printed in full in the New York *Tribune*, the *New York Times*, and the *Popular Science Monthly*, and condensed versions were printed in the *World* and the *Herald*. The *Tribune* prepared an extra edition of all of Huxley's American addresses—at Buffalo, Nashville, and Baltimore as well as New York, and also published a special twenty-five cent pamphlet. In 1877 Appleton in the United States, and Macmillan in England, published a volume entitled *American Addresses*, a collection of Huxley's three New York lectures, his Baltimore address, and a December 1876 lecture on biology at South Kensington. The anonymous reviewer of this volume in the *Westminster Review* said the following:

> Professor Huxley's American addresses will be widely read on both sides of the Atlantic. ... It is a popular book, dealing in a simple way with great subjects, treating them in English wonderfully clear and rich. ... The construction of the lecture is masterly, and the author has evidently put into them his best powers of exposition, and most characteristic forms of clear thought. Like so much of Professor Huxley's literary work, the mission of this volume is to carry the doctrine of evolution to the house, so that unlearned people may understand the place that it holds in the distinguished author's mind among the factors of scientific thought. ... [His work] is that of a literary man whose art requires him to put the case strongly to make it clear. ... For the general reader, the book is the best and briefest exposition of the geological aspect of evolution that we possess. ... [80]

Thus, Huxley's American lectures eventually reached a considerably wide audience.

His stay in the United States generated considerable attention,[81] and praise from supporters surrounded him. Autograph seekers had pursued him during his tour,[82] and citizens in various cities requested that he give a lecture.[83] Just before he was to leave for England, an admirer left a note for him at Huxley's hotel. "You have created a profound impression, the interest in which will certainly wax rather than wane from the moment of your departure."[84] Leonard Huxley in his biography later wrote that his father's

> reception in America may be said to emphasize his definite establishment in the first rank of English thinkers. It was a signal testimony to the wide extent of his influence ... an influence due above all to the fact that he did not allow his studies to stand apart from the moving problems of existence, but brought the new and regenerating ideas into contact with life at every point.[85]

Minnick asserted that Huxley "precipitated a heated collision of opinion in the American press ... [and] contributed to the widespread dissemination of Darwin's ideas in America."[86] Randel concluded that perhaps Huxley's greatest contribution to the American scene was that he gave "to some Americans, those committed to the advancement of knowledge, a sense that they were not, as they had so often been made to feel, second-class citizens."[87]

On Saturday morning, 23 September, the Youmans, Appletons, Marsh and his sister, and Professor Martin of Johns Hopkins saw the Huxleys off on the *Celtic*. Huxley "thanked them for their hospitality and should his labors at home permit he would be happy to repeat, but this he hardly dared hope for. He left in excellent spirits though a little worn from the exertion."[88] After twelve days of a very unpleasant voyage the Huxleys were back in England. The London *Times* duly reported his arrival from "delivering lectures in the United States on 'Evolution'."[89]

Posttour

Huxley was pleased with his American tour and was soon incorporating his scientific information and general experiences gained in the United States into his writing and lectures.[90] In October he submitted an "amended and corrected version" of the Baltimore address to the editor of *Nature* for consideration to be published.[91] He continued to be read and honored in the United States. Many of his essays and reviews of his books were printed in the *Popular Science Monthly* and in the *North American Review*. His brief *Lessons on Elementary Physiology* was widely used as a text; by 1898 it had passed through four editions and had been reprinted thirty-one times.[92] Honorary memberships in American organizations continued to come: the Boston Society of Natural History (1877), the National Academy of Sciences of the U.S.A. (1883), and the American Anthropological Society of Washington (1883).[93] Even the American Society for the Study and Cure of Inebriety, headquartered in Boston, in 1894 sought his membership.[94]

Admiring Americans made requests and offers. The colorful political figure, Ignatius Donnelly, in 1882 saw fit to send a gift copy of his just published book, *Atlantis—the Antediluvian World*, to Huxley and hoped that the latter would express "what your view is as to the theory propounded in it, should you find time to read it."[95] In 1889 the wife of the American ambassador in London, on the eve of their return to the United States, requested signed photographs of Professor and Mrs. Huxley. "I should prize them highly, and they would have a special interest for Prof. Huxley's many admirers in America."[96] In 1890 a lawyer in Tacoma sent Huxley a "skeleton sketch of certain views I entertain. I would be pleased to have you look them over and favor me with your criticism thereof."[97] The *North American Review* invited him in 1892 to write an article on the "Man of the Future,"[98] and in 1894 he was invited to speak at the American Association for the Advancement of Science meeting in Brooklyn. They would pay his round trip expenses and he would be their guest during the sessions. Also there no doubt would be many opportunities to lecture to "scientific bodies and educational institutions . . . in such number as to indicate the great respect that is held for you on this side of the Atlantic . . . there are many thousands of our fellow-citizens in this country who would be glad to have the privilege of listening to you again."[99] He was unable to accept. His death in 1895 prompted numerous tributes to be published in the American press.[100]

5

Rhetorical Combatant, 1860–1895

Huxley contributed an enormous amount of written and oral works in behalf of science and against theological orthodoxy from the Oxford clash in 1860 up until his death in 1895. He drove himself unmercifully, seeking to further his domain of science. As Loren Eiseley has put it, Huxley had "a kind of professional duelist's fury"[1] which propelled him, and despite his protestations to the contrary he relished the confrontation. The chapter will survey his more controversial and significant rhetorical efforts relevant to the conflict between science and theology during these thirty-five years, with special attention to the last decade of his life when with some time available following his retirement, he became heavily involved in a running debate with advocates of orthodox theology. This broad overarching chronological sweep will show his prolific public rhetoric in action.

During the 1860s Huxley revealed his great energy and versatility in engaging in original research, in publishing his findings by lecture and pen, and in skirmishing with theologians and conservative scientists. Already in 1861 his friends were warning him not to spread his effort over too many things. Hooker, for instance, wrote, "You may make a very good naturalist, or a very good metaphysician . . . but you have neither time nor place for both."[2] Somehow, Huxley found time and place for both. Early in the 1860s he published his experimental findings revealing the close relationship of man to animals, which had far-reaching theological implications. In 1861 he publicized his views in a lecture at the Royal Institution and in his regular six lectures to London workingmen,[3] the latter series being published in the *Natural History Review*, a periodical he had helped to initiate that year. Early in January 1862 he delivered two lectures at the Philosophical Institute of Edinburgh, on the "Relation of Man to the Lower Animals." The immediate response seemed so favorable that Huxley jubilantly wrote to Darwin: "Everybody prophesied I should be stoned and cast out of the city gate, but, on the contrary, I met with unmitigated applause!! Three cheers for the progress of liberal opinion!!'"[4] Later in January Huxley wrote to Darwin: "By about this time next year I expect to have shot past you, and to find you pitching into me for being more Darwinian than yourself. However, you have set me going, and must just take the consequences."[5] Violent opposition soon appeared in the Scottish press and brought journalistic retorts from Huxley.[6] Despite friendly warnings,[7] Huxley published his views in book form, *Evidence as to Man's Place in Nature*, in January 1863. This, his first book, was an immediate success, was republished in America, and eventually was translated into many languages.[8] This extension of Darwinism to include man obviously was highly controversial and it met with vigorous opposition even from otherwise friendly scientists, such as Lyell.[9]

With fellow scientists, churchmen, and the general public as audiences, Huxley supported the cause of Darwin.[10] In his six lectures to London workingmen in the winter of 1862 and 1863 he chose to simplify and defend the findings of Darwin, which, being taken down by a student in shorthand, were subsequently published in Britain and in the United States.[11] After reading Huxley's lectures, Darwin wrote to him that his reaction had been as follows: "'What is the good of my writing a thundering big book, when everything is in this green little book so despicable for its size?' In the name of all that is good and bad I may as well shut up shop altogether."[12] But the middle of 1863, Huxley was being "pestered to death in public and private because," as he wrote in jest to Darwin, "I am supposed to be what they call a 'Darwinian'."[13] His time was being consumed in "Colensoism and botheration about Moses."[14] In the spring of 1864 he summarized his activities in a letter to Lizzie.

> I believe I have won myself a pretty fair place in science, but in addition to that I have the reputation (of which, I fear, you will not approve) of being a great heretic and a savage controversialist always in rows. To the accusation of heresy I fear I must plead guilty; but the second charge proceeds only, I assure you, from a certain unconquered hatred of lies and humbug which I cannot get over.[15]

In a December 1864 issue of *The Reader*, a relatively new literary and scientific weekly, he wrote the lead article on "Science and Church Policy," which he playfully called his "encyclical."[16]

On Sunday, 7 January 1866, he delivered an important public lecture, "On the Advisableness of Improving Natural Knowledge," in St. Martin's Hall, which was subsequently published in the

Fortnightly Review.[17] In this lay sermon, as it was called, Huxley discussed the wonderful advances in the life of mankind due to the improvement of natural knowledge. He emphasized that most important were nonmaterial advances, such as new concepts about man and his universe, higher forms of religion and ethics, and a better methodology for discovering truth. It was the first instance in which he crystallized at length, the conflict between the method of science and the method of theology. In November 1867 Huxley addressed a gathering of clergymen at Sion College on the bearing of recent findings in science on orthodox dogma.[18] In reference to that occasion, he wrote to a friend in Germany, "I am over head and ears, as we say, in work, lecturing, giving addresses to the working men and (figurez vous!) to the clergy."[19] Huxley's lecture, "On the Physical Basis of Life," delivered in November 1868 at Edinburgh, and later printed by John Morley in the *Fortnightly Review*, created an excited reaction, for in it Huxley seemed to be presenting a materialistic philosophy of life. Morley later wrote that "no article that has appeared in any periodical for a generation back . . . excited so profound a sensation as Huxley's memorable paper 'On the Physical Basis of Life'."[20] In 1868 Huxley enthusiastically predicted to Darwin, "You will have the rare happiness to see your ideas triumphant during your lifetime."[21] It was during the late 1860s that Huxley first mentioned his interest in comparative religion.[22]

The year 1869 was particularly memorable. "The fighting itself is not particularly objectionable," Huxley wrote to Darwin in March, "but it's the waste of time"[23] that irked him. After attending the meeting of the Britsh Association in September in Exeter, Huxley wrote to Darwin:

> As usual, your abominable heresies were the means of getting me into all sorts of hot water at the Association. Three parsons set upon you. . . . They got considerably chaffed, and that was all they were worth.[24]

During this year he delivered his presidential address to the Geological Society, gave twelve special lectures on elementary science for secondary schoolchildren, published five scientific papers, and delivered an important after-dinner speech in Liverpool on scientific education. But 1869 is perhaps best remembered as the year in which Huxley coined the term *agnostic*. As a member of the newly formed Metaphysical Society, which brought together men of diverse views with the hope that personal discussion would bring a rapprochment, which was impossible through written debate, Huxley felt frustrated because he, unlike most others, had no label to attach to his ideas. As a result, he created the term *a-gnostic*. "It came into my head," he explained shortly before his death, "as suggestively antithetic to the 'gnostic' of Church history, who professed to know so much about the very things of which I was ignorant."[25] In 1883 he responded to an inquirer that he had "invented the word 'agnostic' to describe people, who like myself, confess themselves to be hopelessly ignorant concerning a variety of matters about which Metaphysicians & Theologians"[26] seemed to be so certain. He went on to write:

> Agnosticism is the essence of science, whether modern or ancient. It simply means that a man shall not say he knows or believes that which he has not scientific ground for profession to know or believe. . . . It puts aside popular theology, but also the great part of popular antitheology. It declines to have anything to do with supernaturalism.[27]

Also in 1883 he strongly insisted to another correspondent that he invented only the term *agnosticism*, not the concept.[28] The term first appeared in public print in a January 1870 issue of the *Spectator*,[29] and it became the label that most freethinkers preferred for themselves.

In the early 1870s Huxley's views were further developed and publicized. In March 1870, before the Cambridge YMCA, Huxley used Descartes as his subject to give a lecture on the value of doubt,[30] which, in the summer of 1870, was included in his second book, *Lay Sermons, Addresses, and Reviews*. In November, in a paper entitled "Has a Frog a Soul?" delivered in the Metaphysical Society, Huxley developed his agnosticism by suggesting that the presence of a soul in animals (and by implication, in humans) was unsolvable. A year earlier in his first address before the Society he had contended that the idea of immortality of the soul in humans had no reasonable base.[31] Huxley need not have been so surprised and indignant that "those confounded parsons"[32] bullied him as they did.

In 1871 Darwin published his *Descent of Man*, which brought man into his evolutionary theory and thus created more controversy than the *Origin of Species*. In the November 1871 *Contemporary Review*, in an article entitled, "Mr. Darwin's Critics,"[33] Huxley attacked St. George Mivart, a leading Catholic biologist, and A. R. Wallace, for their recent review[34] and books that were highly critical of Darwin. Mivart replied in the January 1872 issue of *Contemporary Review* and Huxley briefly recapitulated in the preface of his *Critiques and Addresses* (1873), a collection of speeches and essays of the last decade. Mivart and Huxley were estranged for years as a result of this exchange.[35]

During the mid-1870s some important rhetorical events for Huxley had their setting outside of London. In February 1874 he delivered his inaugural address as Lord Rector of the University of Aberdeen, dwelling on "Universities, Actual and Ideal," in which he urged more natural science in the curriculum and a reform of medical education. The fact that a heretic like himself had been chosen for that position over a "Scotch peer at his own gates in the most orthodox of Scotch cities," Huxley thought to be a "curious sign of the times."[36] While there he agreed to attend Sunday service in the College Chapel, which was the first time he had endured "the pain and penalties of a Presbyterian service," and "May it be the last!" he wrote to his wife.[37] In Birmingham, early in August 1874, Huxley delivered a tribute to Joseph Priestley on the occasion of the unveiling of a statue of the latter.[38] A few days before the address, Huxley wrote to Tyndall that he thought the planners of the occasion

> deserved to be encouraged for having asked a man of science to do the job instead of some noble swell; and, moreover, Satan whispered that it would be a good opportunity for a little ventilation of wickedness. I cannot say, however, that I can work myself up into such enthusiasm for the dry old Unitarian who did not go very deep into anything. But I think I may make him a good peg whereon to hand a discourse on the tendencies of modern thought.[39]

Later in August, at the meeting of the British Association in Belfast, Huxley delivered his highly controversial lecture, "On the Hypothesis that Animals are Automata and Its History."[40] During 1875–76 Huxley delivered a course of 54 lectures in natural history at the University of Edinburgh (he was granted leave from South Kensington) to a very large class of about 350.[41] In 1876 of course he had his important trip to the United States.

But Huxley was also as busy as ever in London. Earlier in 1876 he had read his third and final paper, "Evidence of the Miracle of the Resurrection," before the Metaphysical Society. Both he and Morley agreed that Huxley's position, that there was no valid evidence available to substantiate the idea of resurrection, was too unorthodox to be published.[42] In December 1876 he delivered a public lecture in London on the wisdom of studying biology, and it was published in *American Addresses*. In 1877 Huxley wrote the article on "Evolution"[43] for the *Encyclopedia Britannica*, and he gave an after-dinner response as the proxy for the absent Darwin on the occasion of the latter's receiving an honorary degree from Cambridge University. In January 1878, Huxley delivered an address at the Royal Institution on the scientist Harvey, in commemoration of the tercentenary of the latter's birth, and it was published in *Nature* and in the *Fortnightly Review*. Later in 1878 Huxley wrote a small volume on *Hume*[44] for John Morley's Great Men series, in which Huxley could propagate his own agnosticism, and in 1879 he wrote the foreword for Haeckel's book, *Freedom in Science and Teaching*. In 1880 Huxley delivered three important public lectures: "The Coming of Age of 'The Origin of Species',"[45] "On the Method of Zadig,"[46] and "Science and Culture."[47] At the death of Darwin, on 19 April 1882, Huxley wrote a brief obituary for *Nature*.[48] Darwin's son, Francis, after writing of his father's death to Huxley, concluded the letter: "I hope you will not mind my saying how often I have heard him express his affectionate regard for you. We all feel your friendship was an unvarying cause of real happiness to my father."[49]

With the failure of his health in 1884 Huxley had to abandon his teaching, and in the leisure time his retirement afforded him, he turned ever more fully to the study of philosophy and religion. His most active direct clash with theology was yet to come. With a quarter of a century of battling behind him, with numerous scars therefrom, and with a confidence that the theory of evolution and his agnostic views had been vindicated through the decades, he was quick to attack ecclesiasticism at the least opportunity. The next decade was filled with much heated controversy lasting to the very end of his active life with much of it being in the *Nineteenth Century*, a new periodical edited by his close friend James Knowles.[50]

Huxley was stirred from his retirement doldrums by an article by Gladstone in the November 1885 issue of the *Nineteenth Century*, in which Gladstone claimed that geology had shown the account of creation in Genesis to be scientifically correct. Strongly objecting to the grand old man posing as an authority in science and religion, Huxley wrote an article ("The Interpreters of Genesis and the Interpreters of Nature") for the December issue of the *Nineteenth Century*, in which he demonstrated the irreconcilability of the geological and Genesis accounts of creation.[51] Gladstone replied in the January issue, and Huxley responded with an article, "Mr. Gladstone and Genesis,"[52] in the February issue. Throughout, Huxley's fundamental object had been to demonstrate that the existence and authority of historical religions such as Judaism and Christianity depended upon their ability to show evidence for the occurrence of claimed historical events. He asserted that satisfactory evidence had not as yet been presented. He wrote a summary of his position in an article entitled, "The Evolution of Theology: An Anthropological Study,"[53] which appeared in the March and April 1886, issues of the *Nineteenth Century*.

Toward the end of 1886 Huxley became involved in an exchange in the *Fortnightly Review* with the able rhetorician William Samuel Lilly, president of the British Roman Catholic Union. In the November issue, Lilly accused Huxley, Spencer, and Clifford of advocating materialism, which brought an inevitable degrading influence in mortality. Spencer prodded Huxley:

> I have no doubt your combative instincts have been stirred within you as you read Mr. Lilly's article, "Materialism and Mortality,". . . . I should not be sorry if you yielded to those promptings of your combative instincts. Now that you are a man of leisure there is no reason why you should not undertake any amount of fighting, providing always that you find foemen worthy of your steel . . . I remember that last year you found intellectual warfare good for your health, so I have no qualms of conscience in making the suggestion.[54]

Huxley replied to Spencer on 7 November: "Your stimulation of my combative instincts is downright wicked, I will not look at the *Fortnightly* article lest I succumb to temptation."[55] But Huxley wrote to him on 25 November:

> Your diabolical plot against Lilly has succeeded—*vide* the next number of the *Fortnightly*. I was fool enough to read his article, and the rest followed. But I do not think I should have troubled myself if the opportunity had not been good for clearing off a lot of old scores.[56]

In his article, "Science and Morals," Huxley denied being a materialist and denied that materialism had a degrading effect on morals.[57] In December Huxley received a letter from Spencer "chuckling over the success of his setting me on Lilly,"[58] and the next day Huxley wrote to Spencer, "I am glad you liked my treatment of Mr. Lilly. . . ."[59]

In 1887 and 1888 another controversy for Huxley began in the *Nineteenth Century*, and eventually ended in *Nature*. The basic issue was whether lower and higher laws exist and whether miracles are the suspension of lower laws by higher laws. A printed sermon of Canon Liddon, one of the most effective preachers of that time, greatly irritated Huxley, as he wrote to Spencer, "The nonsense these great divines talk when they venture to meddle with science is really appalling."[60] Huxley strongly asserted in the February 1887 issue of

Nineteenth Century that there were no lower and higher laws, hence no miracles.[61] Liddon did not reply, but the Duke of Argyll, an influential conservative Scottish nobleman known for his oratory, activity in public affairs, and interest in science, responded for him in the March issue with the article, "Prof Huxley on Canon Liddon." Huxley sharply answered the duke in April,[62] which prompted an admirer to assure Huxley, "Your pen lacketh not its splendid energy and grace."[63] The duke replied in September, and Huxley added a response to the end of another article he had prepared for the November issue.[64] Meanwhile, a third party came to the support of Huxley's position in the 10 November issue of *Nature*. Argyll replied in letters in the 17 November 1887 and 12 January 1888 issues of *Nature*, and Huxley responded in a letter in the 9 February issue. Since Argyll would not retract his statements, Huxley dropped the matter.[65]

In 1889 the *Nineteenth Century* was the medium for a bitter rhetorical battle between Huxley on the one side, and Rev. Henry Wace, principal of King's College, London, and Dr. W. C. Magee, Bishop of Peterborough, on the other. At the annual Church Congress, held in Manchester in October 1888, Wace had attacked the term *agnostic* as a cowardly cloak for "infidel." Upon reading the official report of the Congress, Huxley became greatly agitated, and wrote to James Knowles, his friend and editor of the *Nineteenth Century*:

> I think I must have a stag among my recent ancestors, for I get mischievous late in the year—not however for the stag's reason I beg to remark. But I have been stirred up to the boiling pitch by Wace, Laing, and Harrison *in re* Agnosticism—and I really cannot keep the lid down any longer. Are you minded to admit a goring article in the February XIX?[66]

Now that Huxley's health had momentarily greatly improved, he exuded a spirit quite different from seven months earlier, when, in ill health, he did not succumb to Knowles's temptation to submit an article on another controversy. "Your invitation is tantalizing. I wish I could accept it ... [but] I have neither brains nor nerves, and the very thought of controversy puts me in a blue funk!"[67] As 1889 dawned, he relished the fray, as he wrote to his daughter Ethel, "Luckily the bishops and clergy won't let me alone, so I have been able to keep myself pretty well amused in replying."[68] Huxley's February article, "Agnosticism," defended the term and himself, and insisted that the New Testament was too unreliable for Christianity to be founded on it.[69] Hirst recorded in his journal:

finished reading Huxley's article on Agnosticism in the Nineteenth Century. It displays great biblical knowledge, and is written in his brightest style. Nevertheless, he hits hard, both Harrison and Wace, whose address to the recent Church Congress drew forth Huxley's present utterances. But notwithstanding its ability, Huxley's treatment of this subject lacks earnestness in my estimation. It displays too much self-conscious word fencing—too little depth of conviction.[70]

Wace and Magee replied in the March issue, and in the same issue Huxley had an article entitled, "The Value of Witness to the Miraculous,"[71] in which he emphasized that since there was a lack of evidence for miracles, an honest person was forced to be an agnostic. Again, Hirst's journal entry is interesting.

I finished reading Wace's reply to Huxley. Although far inferior in ability to the latter, it is not badly written. The controversy between the two writers, however, is a vain and wordy one. Their shafts glide past their antagonists, and leave no mark. They do not fight on the same ground, nor under like conditions. Huxley attacks without exposing himself more than is absolutely necessary; Wace defends a position which he has inherited, rather than one at which he has arrived after free and frank enquiry and thought; In what else can such a controversy result than in pure word-fence,—vain, futile, word-fence?[72]

Huxley, however, was confident of the importance of the exchange. "I find people are watching the game with great interest, and if it should be possible for me to give a little shove to the 'new Reformation' I shall think the fag end of my life well spent."[73]

In preparing another article for the April issue, Huxley was buoyant. "I am possessed by a writing demon, and have pretty well finished in the rough another article for Knowles, whose mouth is wide open for the . . . [and a week later] . . . I sent off another article to Knowles last night—a regular facer for the clericals. You can't think how I enjoy writing now for the first time in my life."[74] Huxley felt he had toned down his aggressiveness admirably, and he wrote to Knowles:

The pith of my article is the proposition that Christ was not a Christian. I have not ventured to state my thesis exactly in that form—fearing the Editor—but, in a mild and proper way, I flatter myself I have demonstrated it.[75]

Huxley's April essay replied particularly to Wace's article, and Huxley proudly predicted to Knowles, "All the King's horses and all the King's men won't put the orthodox Humpty-Dumpty where he was before."[76] His friend Hirst was less ecstatic. "I finished reading Huxley's second article on Agnosticism yesterday. It betrays grand erudition; but for this I care little, since long ago I arrived otherwise (directly) at all his convictions."[77] The Bishop of Peterborough responded in the May issue, but, according to Hirst, it was a "lame reply to Huxley."[78] Huxley was glad for his opponent's article, for it gave him "the opportunity of putting the case once more as a connected argument."[79]

Thus, in his June article, "Agnosticism and Christianity,"[80] Huxley summarized much of what he had written previously. He wrote to Hooker, "I want you to enjoy my wind-up with Wace in this month's *Nineteenth* in the reading as much as I have in the writing."[81] In the article Huxley defined agnosticism and defended it against various charges. He deprecated the demonology of the Bible and the Church, asserted that the evidence for miracles was an inadequate source for the actual sayings and teachings of Jesus. He emphasized the inevitable conflict between agnosticism and ecclesiasticism, and challenged the attempt of reconcilers to allegorize certain portions of the Bible. He contended that he was trying to free theology so that scholarly seekers after the theological truth, those pioneers in higher criticism, could work in greater freedom. After reading the article, his friend Hirst ho-hummed, "To tell the truth I became weary of it."[82] Huxley was prompted to omit a lively portion due to his chance meeting with the Bishop of Peterborough.

> Such a waste! I shall have to omit a paragraph that was really a masterpiece. For who should I come upon ... but the Bishop! As we shook hands he asked whether that was before the fight or after; and I answered "a little of both." Then we spoke our minds pretty plainly; and then we agreed to bury the hatchet. So yesterday I tore up *the* paragraph. It was so appropriate I could not even save it up for somebody else![83]

Huxley felt he had not been very harsh, and wrote to Knowles: "I am astonished at its [the article's] meekness. Being reviled, I revile not."[84] Huxley wrote further to Knowles, "I don't mind how long it [this running exchange] goes on so long as I have the last word, but you must expect nothing from me for the next three of four months,"[85] for he would be in Switzerland and occupied with other things. As he wrote to Hooker, Huxley was now hoping "for peace and quietness till after the next Church Congress!"[86]

According to Huxley, his central objective throughout his lengthy exchange was not to attack personalities but "to rouse people to think."[87] He elaborated on his objectives to Hooker.

I am very glad that you see the importance of doing battle with the clericals. I am astounded at the narrowness of view of many of our colleagues on this point. They shut their eyes to the obstacles which clericalism raises in every direction against scientific ways of thinking, which are even more important than scientific discoveries. I desire that the next generation may be less fettered by the gross and stupid superstitions of orthodoxy than mine has been. And I shall be well satisfied if I can succeed to however small an extent in bringing about the result.[88]

Huxley's contributions indeed did stimulate much discussion and thought, and not only in Britain but also in the United States.[89] Egged on by friends[90] and Knowles, Huxley was by no means done. Editors, Hooker put it, "feed like maggots on controversial articles,"[91] and hence are not to be trusted.

In 1890 and 1891 Huxley and Gladstone again crossed swords. Stimulated by Canon Liddon's defense of the divine authority and accuracy of the Old Testament, Huxley in the July 1890 issue of the *Nineteenth Century* retorted with "The Lights of the Church and the Light of Science,"[92] which one biographer called "one of his best polemical efforts."[93] In this article Huxley accepted the premise of the orthodox theologians that "Christian theology must stand or fall with the historical trustworthiness of the Jewish Scriptures,"[94] and he proceeded to determine whether the Old Testament, like other historical works, contained any fiction. He chose to analyze intensively the story of the flood, concluded that all available data demonstrate that it is merely a fictional story of Babylonian origin, suggested that other biblical stories are probably similarly fictional, and thus concluded that Christianity rests on an extremely shaky foundation. He insisted that the methods of scientific inquiry and the assumption that the Bible is divinely inspired are irreconcilable, and he strongly attacked those who attempted to allegorize much of the Old Testament and who said that the flood was a *partial*, not a *universal* deluge. This article served to summarize Huxley's previous controversy with Gladstone, Wace, and Magee.

In the meantime, Gladstone had gathered some of his magazine articles and published them in 1890 in book form under the title, *The Impregnable Rock of Holy Scripture*, which meant that once again arguments were publicized that Huxley had already refuted. Huxley replied with "The Keepers of the Herd of Swine"[95] in the *Nineteenth Century* in December 1890, in which he denied that he had attacked Christ's character as Gladstone had charged, but had merely maintained that insufficient evidence was available to determine the validity of this biblical story. Gladstone responded in the *Nineteenth Century* in February 1891, in an article entitled, "Professor Huxley and the Swine Miracle,"[96] to which Huxley replied in the March issue with his "Illustrations of Mr. Gladstone's Controversial Methods."[97] In this article, Huxley's main purpose was to put the opposition in the dilemma of admitting either that demonology was an essential part of Christianity or that much of the gospels was fictional. Hirst was not impressed.

> Huxley's last utterances about the Gadarene Pig-miracle (19th Century for this month) were hardly up to his usual standard. They were too "wordy"; in fact, too much after the fashion of his antagonist Gladstone.[98]

Toward the end of the decade, a source friendly to Huxley glowingly summed up the bitter exchange. "[It] was not so much a battle as a massacre, for Gladstone had nothing but a bundle of antiquated prejudices wherewith to encounter [Huxley's] luminous thought and exact knowledge."[99]

In the winter of 1890–91 the "bulldog" spirit in Huxley was briefly sidetracked into tangling in *The Times* with what he felt was the dangerously authoritarian structure and financially irresponsible governance of General William Booth's Salvation Army. In December 1890 Huxley wrote to his son Leonard:

> Attacking the Salvation Army may look like the advance of a forlorn hope, but this old dog has never yet let go after fixing his teeth into anything or anybody, and he is not going to begin now. And it is only a question of holding.[100]

In January 1891 he wrote to Hooker:

> I trust I have done with Booth and Co. at last. What an ass a man is to try to prevent his fellow-creatures from being humbugged! Surely I am old enough to know better. I have not been so well abused for an age. It's quite like old times. And now I have to settle accounts with the duke and the G. O. M.[101]

The years 1891 and 1892 were spent in summarizing the controversies of the last six years. In June 1891 Huxley published the article, "Hasisadra's Adventure,"[102] in the *Nineteenth Century*, in which he continued his claims of fiction in the Bible. Published in the *Agnostic Annual* in 1892 was his article entitled, "Possibilities and Impossibilities,"[103] in which he summarized his view that lack of evidence caused him to disbelieve miracles. Also appearing in 1892 was Huxley's book, *Essays Upon Some Controverted Questions*, in which was reprinted his important antitheological articles published since 1885. In a prologue [104] for this volume, he summarized the basic issue of whether the Bible was to be regarded as wholly true or as a mixture of truth and fiction. He restated at some length the historical struggle between naturalism and supernaturalism, and traced the conflict from the sixteenth to the nineteenth centuries. He again defined and defended agnosticism, and discussed twelve findings associated with the theory of evolution to which theology would have to accommodate itself. He concluded on a conciliatory note by expressing his appreciation for portions of the Bible. Finally, having read in *The Times* early in 1892 a debate over the old question of divine authority of the book of Genesis, he wrote four letters to that newspaper that formed a careful and final summary of his position on that issue.

Although 1893 was one of the more tranquil years for him, he nevertheless stirred much controversy with his Romanes Lecture delivered at Oxford on 18 May, on the subject of "Evolution and Ethics."[105] George John Romanes, young biologist and man of wealth, established a fund at Oxford in 1892 for an annual lecture on some general subject, as long as religion and politics were excluded. Interestingly enough, Gladstone delivered the first and Huxley the second lecture. Three days before the lecture, Huxley wrote to his old friend Tyndall:

Who would have thought 33 years ago, when the great "Sammy" fight came off, that the next time I should speak at Oxford would be in succession to Gladstone, on "Evolution and Ethics," as an invited lecturer? There was something so quaint about the affair that I really could not resist.[106]

In this lecture the aged Huxley carefully traced the battle between self-assertion (evolution) and altruism (ethics), and insisted that the latter should not submit to, or avoid, the former, but should combat it, just as a gardener combats elements which attempt to destroy his garden.[107] In short, evolution and ethics are enemies. The lecture stirred much controversy and led many to think that Huxley had abandoned his earlier views. To clarify his position, he wrote in 1894 a "Prolegomena" in volume nine of his *Collected Essays*, in which "Evolution and Ethics" appeared, in which he defended the consistency of his belief in evolution as biological process and his disbelief in an ethical system based on that process.

Huxley remained rhetorically active until his death in 1895. Late in 1893 Tyndall wrote to Spencer: "Huxley has been much in evidence of late. His activity rather daunts me, and adds to my desire for rest."[108] During 1893 and the first half of 1894 Huxley was, among other things, writing prefaces for the publication of his nine volumes of *Collected Essays*. In the November 1894 issue of *Nature*, in connection with the commemoration of the twenty-fifth anniversary of that now famous scientific periodical that he had helped to establish in 1869, he traced the ascendency of the natural over the supernatural, in an article entitled "Past and Present." He had given the substance of the article in a brief speech at the British Association at Oxford in August 1894. Arthur J. Balfour's book, *The Foundations of Belief*, published in January 1895 and reviewed in *The Times* in February, linked agnosticism with positivism and other "isms," and insisted that reason was an inadequate instrument for a firm philosophy of life. Huxley was again aroused. His repudiation of Balfour's picture of agnosticism was to be published in the March and April issues of the *Nineteenth Century*. The first part was published as scheduled but Huxley's ill health and subsequent death on 29 June 1895 (the eve of the thirty-fifth anniversary of his Oxford "debate" with Wilberforce) made it impossible for him to correct the proofs of the second article. Early in March Huxley wrote to Knowles:

> The proofs have just arrived, but I am sorry to say that (I believe for the first time in our transactions) I shall have to disappoint you. Just after I sent off this Ms., Influenza came down upon me with a swoop. I went to bed and am there still with no chance quitting it in a hurry. . . . Could you put in an excuse on account of Influenza?[109]

The article remained unpublished until Houston Peterson in 1932 included it as an appendix to his biography of Huxley.

Few would deny that Huxley had held firm to a consistent general course of thought and action throughout his life, although admirers and critics might disagree on the degree of fulfillment and the nature and extent of the effects of his accomplishments. At the age of thirty-one, anxiously waiting for his first child to be born, he had pledged in his journal "to smite all humbugs . . . [and] to give a nobler tone to science."[110] At the age of sixty-four he summarized in his brief *Autobiography* what had been his guiding objectives in life.

> To promote the increase of natural knowledge and to forward the application of scientific methods of investigation to all the problems of

life ... to the popularisation of science; to the development and organization of scientific education; to the endless series of battles and skirmishes over evolution; and to untiring opposition to that ecclesiastical spirit, that clericalism, which in England, as everywhere else, and to whatever denomination it may belong, is the deadly enemy of science. . . . [He hoped that he had] somewhat helped that movement of opinion which had been called the New Reformation.[111]

A year before his death he said he had contributed "thirty odd years of pretty hard toil, partly as an investigator and teacher in one branch of natural knowledge, and partly as a half-voluntary, half compelled man-of-all-work for the scientific household in general."[112] C. K. Thomas concluded his intensive study of the rhetoric of Huxley with the observation that the latter had been "primarily concerned with moulding public opinion to accept science and validity of scientific method; and the separate lectures and essays were but tactical details in the strategy of the whole campaign."[113]

In this campaign he adopted a rhetorical stance, which was actually similar to that of his ecclesiastial foes. Rhetorically he was a secular theologian. The following chapter will analyze this contention.

6

Rhetorical Stance: Secular Theologian

The basic nature of Huxley's rhetorical contributions was the visualization of a dramatic conflict between the forces of good and the forces of evil, the former being science and the latter being theological orthodoxy. This "Manichean view of science," according to a contemporary paleontologist, harmed Huxley's efforts "by establishing boundaries to exclude natural allies and, ultimately, by encircling science as something apart from other human passions."[1] To what degree the result was harmful or helpful may be open to debate, but it is clear that Huxley's basic rhetorical stance was that of a person fighting the good fight. There was no middle position. "Between Agnosticism and Ecclesiasticism," he insisted, "there can be neither peace nor truce."[2] The alternatives were mutually exclusive, for allegiance to one side meant complete alienation from the other camp. This was war, and one is not permitted to wander from one camp to the other or claim partial allegiance to both. Even inaction or indecision was a sign of belonging to the enemy, for those who were not for you were against you.

Theology is by its very nature two-valued. That is, it thinks in terms of God and the Devil, heaven and hell, the saved and the damned, the clean and the unclean, the blessed and the cursed, good and evil, and sinner and saint. If one is not for God, one is against him. Theology claims to bring freedom from the enslaved and the imprisoned pagan mind, and claims to be the light of the world shining in the pagan darkness. It purports to civilize the barbarian and bring truth to mankind. It insists that one cannot serve both God and man. Theology creates sharply contrasting heroes and villains. It levels charges that unbelievers are guilty of sins of thought, word, and deed, and of sins of omission, and they, the ecclesiastical organizations, bring true ideas and humane acts into the life of suffering and ignorant human beings. Theology says there can be no reconciliation with the enemy—one cannot compromise with the Devil.

Although Huxley's substantive message was quite dissimilar to that of the orthodox theologians, he adopted their rhetorical stance, making him more similar to them than he would probably care to admit. This was manifested in at least three major ways. First, he created a drama in which sharply delineated heroes and villains were jousting to the death. Second, he became an inspired messenger narrating about a journey through life to a promised land. Finally, in this journey he was playing the role of a metaphorical roadblock remover, enabling human beings to continue unmolested along life's pathway. As an historian of science has recently written, Huxley's "performance was not altogether different from a preacher's in a pulpit."[3]

Heroes and Villains

Huxley created sharply delineated heroes and villains by his selection of nouns and adjectives. His heroes were "rational men" (5:43), "the best intellects" (1:25), "trained intellects" (4:56), "all thinking men" (1:28), "any serious thinker" (5:35), "a very candid thinker" (4:48), "honest thinkers" (4:49), "serious scientific inquirers" (4:215), "all serious critics" (4:212), "right-minded men" (4:236), and anyone "competent to judge" (5:33). Other adjectives employed were "cautious," "calm," "thoughtful," "mature," "patient," and "thorough." The villains—the ecclesiastics—were "uncultured men" (1:34), "depreciators of natural knowledge" (1:28), "blind leaders of the blind" (1:30), "theological dogmatists" (4:212), or "counsels for creeds" (5:358). They were ignorant, emotionally unstable, immature, uninformed, self-righteous, irrational, inconsistent, incompetent, and lacked common sense, meekness, patience, courtesy, and love. Huxley of course occasionally spoke well of those few theologians who tended to see things somewhat similarly to him as "theologians of repute" (5:330) or "Biblical scholars of repute" (4:227).

Huxley's two-valued orientation is illustrated by his vivid reactions to the beliefs and actions of his enemies and his camp. Although he retained a considerable respect for the Bible because of its ethical teachings, he heartily despised the idea that it was an infallible volume. To Huxley the stories of the Creation and the Flood were simply fiction. The latter was "a physical impossibility" (4:234) and the story of the Fall of Man was "even more monstrously improbable" (4:234). He asserted that "the evidence of the Gadarene miracle is altogether worthless" (5:36–37). He spoke of ecclesiastical "pretensions" (4:215), "dogmatism" (5:36–37), "outworn creeds" (4:233), and "old fashioned artillery" (4:236). He spoke of "the necessity of breaking in pieces the idols built up of books and traditions and fine-spun ecclesiastical cobwebs" (1:38). The supernaturalism in the Bible was "as gross as that of any primitive people" (5:36); the blind faith upon which orthodoxy was based was "an abomination" (5:314); and the idea that morality was based on religious dogma was an "absurd notion" (5:316). On the other hand, natural knowledge was a "real mother of mankind, bringing them up with kindness, and, if need be, with sternness, in the way they should go, and instructing them in all things needful for their welfare" (1:30). Natural knowledge had "found the ideas which can alone still spiritual cravings" (1:31). Huxley calls experience "the great schoolmaster" (5:5), and refers to agnostics as those individuals who "refuse to be the prey of verbal justifications" (5:312). He speaks of the "weapons of precision . . . of the advancing forces of science" (4:236), and he cites the "marvellous intellectual growth" (1:24) brought about by men of science.

Basic doctrines and premises of ecclesiasticism Huxley claimed to be false, ridiculous, and unsound. He objected to the idea of the presence of good and bad supernatural beings engaging in eternal warfare, and of the good spirit—God—who was accessible by prayers, benevolently guiding mankind or in violent judgment sending plagues and other misfortunes because of mankind's wickedness. Huxley denounced the notion that the clergy were inspired, or that the Bible was free from error and was not to be examined critically. He attacked biblical narratives and the theological doctrines derived therefrom. He attacked the idea of atonement and messiahship. The concept of eternal rewards and punishments, the Last Judgment and physical resurrection, demonology, and miracles of all types he labeled as false and unsound ideas. He attacked the notions that blind faith was virtuous, and that doubt and skepticism were sins. He branded as false the ideas that the acquisition of natural knowledge brought only material gains, and that modern science merely strengthened the authority of the Bible. Ridiculous was the notion that fossils were only special creations intended to test the faith of humans. He deprecated the importance of certain ecclesiastical ceremonies, and he lamented the claim that things of this world were despicable. He forcefully denounced the charges that agnostics were too cowardly to use their real label of "infidel" and that they were in their hearts ashamed of themselves. He attacked as unsound the attempts of reconcilers to label portions of the Bible as allegory and to insist that since miracles serve a moral or religious end they do not have to be historically accurate events.

On the other hand, the ideas of those who belonged to the camp of the scientists were true and sound. Plagues and other catastrophes had natural causes and had no relationship to the sinfulness of people, and there was no evidence of interference by a supernatural force in physical or human life. He demonstrated, to his satisfaction, that many of the stories in the Bible had pagan origins, and he emphasized that the material was further untrustworthy in that the authors, even if eye-witnesses to a reported event, were predisposed to believe in demonology or miracles or whatever was the subject of their writing. Since the Gospels were untrustworthy sources for the ideas of Jesus, one could not be accused of denying his teachings. Furthermore, death was a natural and apparently necessary aspect of life and was not to be feared. He insisted that skepticism and doubt were virtues, and believing something on inadequate evidence was a sin. As he put it in his address at the opening of Mason College, Birmingham, science "warns us that the assertion which outstrips evidence is not only a blunder but a crime."[4] Social unity and morality rested not on theological dogma but on inherited instincts and on the needs of society. Ceremonies and traditions needed to be continually altered in order to retain meaning. He emphasized the cherishing of man's most noble and humane emotions, the silent worshiping of the Unknown God, and the fruitfulness of the agnostic attitude in all areas of life. Pleasure and suffering were not moral rewards or punishments but had natural origins. The Bible should be taught in schools by laymen so that "the theology and the legend would drop more and more out of sight, while the perennially interesting historical, literary, and ethical contents would come more and more into view" (5:57). He stressed that the fundamental guide in all of life should be not whether something is consoling but whether it is true.

Huxley insisted that his side in the conflict propagated true ideas about mankind and the universe. Evolution taught that everything at present was but "the last of an immeasurable series of predecessors" (1:39). It demonstrated that development of a whole species was analogous to individual development, which begins with extremely simple anatomical structure and acquires complexities of structure and function. Probing the mystery of the origin of consciousness, it asserted that consciousness was based on the physical, that plants had no consciousness, that pleasure and pain did not appear until long after the appearance of consciousness, and that pleasure and pain increased with the higher forms of life. Evolution asserted that man had not fallen from a higher to a lower state, but had evolved from lower to higher, and it emphasized that the structure and development of mankind were very similar to that of the higher mammals. But it also indicated that "the results of the process of evolution in the case of man, and in that of his more nearly allied contemporaries, had been marvelously different" (5:51). The differences between mankind and the higher forms of mammals were the following: humans possess a more highly developed brain, a voice more capable of modulation and articulation; limbs more adept at gesturing; hands more adaptable, which makes writing possible; more curiosity; more of a tendency to imitate, stronger family affection; longer life; and more prolonged youth. Humans thus are able to store up experiences and pass them on to succeeding generations. Astronomers promulgated the heliocentric theory, made it known that the heavens were not necessarily peaceful, and demonstrated that the earth was but a small part of the universe. Geologists made it clear that the earth was infinitely old. Biologists had indicated that humans were not the center of the living world but were only one of many forms of life now existing on the globe, and that for life to exist in humans certain molecular arrangements must be present. Science had also demonstrated the orderly and unchanging causation behind all of life, the importance of gravitation, and the indestructibility of matter and force.

Huxley accused his ecclesiastical foes of committing, throughout the centuries and at present, a considerable number of inhumane and useless deeds. The formation of rigid religious frameworks had brought disunity, tension, hatred, persecution, massacre, and war to various societies. Inflicting torture, imprisonment, and death against unbelievers or against people accused of witchcraft had been a notorious historical characteristic of the Christian Church. Ecclesiasticism had encouraged the subjugation of women. If forced humans to lie—to say they believed something when really they saw no evidence for belief. If the investigation of scholars did not conform to the existing dogmas, ecclesiastics hurled the label of *infidel* or other derogatory terms at them, accused them of evil motives, and removed them from their positions. The opposition committed the sin of omission of willfully ignoring facts; and they wasted valuable time by trying to see what was above and beyond nature and by discussing the miraculous. Ecclesiasticism had stood in the way of the advancement of science, art, jurisprudence, the best political and social theories, and the highest ethics.

In sharp contrast, Huxley's camp, according to him, had performed useful and humane acts. It had discovered and stored an increasing amount of natural knowledge. It had taught the truth about humans, society, and the universe; and had made known the real causes and curse of disease, fire, and other catastrophes. Material advances in transportation, communication, industry, and agriculture had resulted, but even more important, scientific advancements had brought more comfort, wealth, and happiness, and had developed in humans better concepts of right and wrong and better modes of thinking. In short, humans had been progressively civilized and their life had been increasingly enriched by the work of scientists. Men of science had not engaged in the name-calling of their opponents, and had not wasted their time speculating over the supernatural and the miraculous. Indeed, Huxley's side was as angelic as the opposition was despicable.

Huxley's two-valued orientation was also apparent in his insistence that reconciliation between the two was impossible. Virtue can not compromise with sin, and truth can not compromise with errors. Science and ecclesiasticism could not drink from the same cup. Essentially it was a conflict in methodology.

> The improver of natural knowledge absolutely refuses to acknowledge authority as such. For him, skepticism is the highest of duties; blind faith the one unpardonable sin. And it cannot be otherwise, for every great advance in natural knowledge has involved the absolute rejection of authority, the cherishing of the keenest skepticism, the annihilation of the spirit of blind faith; and the most ardent votary of science holds his firmest convictions, not because the men he most venerates hold them; not because their verity is testified by portents and wonders; but because his experience teaches him that whenever he chooses to bring these convictions into contact with their primary source, Nature—whenever he thinks fit to test them by appealing to experiment and to observation—Nature will confirm them (1:40–41).

When Cardinal Newman, one of Huxley's antagonists, flatly asserted that evidence was not the best test of truth, Huxley replied, "This sudden relevation of the great gulf fixed between the ecclesiastial and the scientific mind is enough to take away the breath of any one unfamiliar with the clerical organon" (5:334). Huxley was prepared, and indeed anxious, to accept the challenge of churchmen that people "must be prepared to choose between the trustworthiness of scientific method and the trustworthiness of that which the Church declares to be Divine authority" (4:230). Huxley insisted that the antagonism between natural knowledge and the Pentateuch . . . arises out of contradiction upon matters of fact. The books of ecclesiastical authority declare that certain events happened in a certain fashion; the books of scientific authority say they did not (4:213).

The account in Genesis and the findings of science relative to creation were "hopelessly discordant" (5:35), and the story of the Flood was completely irreconcilable with elementary physical science. "The longer I live and the more I learn," Huxley wrote in 1863, "the more hopeless to my mind becomes the contradiction between the theory of the universe as understood and expounded by Jewish and Christian theologians, and the theory of the universe which is every year growing out of the application of scientific methods to its phenomena."[5] Science, he asserted on another occasion, had "rendered it impossible for [people] to accept the beliefs of their fathers" (1:35).

Huxley strongly attacked those who attempted to reconcile the two antagonists, for he contended that any effort in that direction could be unsound, absurd, ambiguous, and doomed to failure. He contemptuously spoke of the "would-be reconcilers" (4:224), those "queer people" (4:237) who only created "hopelessly untenable" (4:236) positions for themselves. He referred to them as those people who, "having distilled away every inconvenient matter of fact in Christian history, continue to pay divine honours to the residue" (4:237). He referred to allegory and accommodation as "those refuges for the logically destitute" (5:324). He ridiculed those who "affirm that some quite different sense may be put upon . . . words; and that this non-natural sense may, with a little trouble, be manipulated into some sort of non-contradiction of scientific truth (5:33). Huxley asserted that "it is the merest ostrich policy for contemporary ecclesiasticism to try to hide its Hexateuchal head" (5:35), that is, to suggest that some material may be legend. To attempt to harmonize geology and the biblical account of Creation was "absolutely futile" (4:68), to endeavor to reconcile science and the story of the Flood was "absurd" (4:219), and to arrive at a middle-ground between the "anthropomorphism (however refined) of theology and the passion-less impersonality of the unknown and unknowable"[6] of science was impossible. Huxley wrote to Darwin on one occasion, "I confess I have less sympathy with the half-and-half sentimental school . . . than I have with thoroughgoing orthodoxy."[7] The reconcilers, asserted Huxley, "must surrender, or fall back into a more sheltered position" (4:237).

Inspired Messenger

Throughout this unfolding drama Huxley was an "inspired" messenger, similar to a theologian. Basic to the rhetorical function of clergymen is that they are messengers, not originators. They are simply relaying to their audience a message from God, which the latter has had placed in written form in sacred Scriptures or in the works of Church Fathers, or has communicated in some mysterious fashion directly to the preacher. Clergymen claim that their message is not from them but from God, who is speaking through them. Theoretically this creates an attitude of humility, whereby the preacher retreats to the background and God takes center stage. It also means that the messenger ought not to be praised or blamed for the message. Huxley conceived of himself as being a messenger for "Nature" or "Truth." He was merely humbly gathering facts and was being led by them regardless of his personal desires or ideas. In 1860 he wrote to Kingsley:

> Science seems to me to teach in the highest and strongest manner the great truth which is embodied in the Christian conception of entire surrender to the will of God. Sit down before fact as a little child, be prepared to give up every preconceived notion, follow humbly whereever and to whatever abysses nature leads.[8]

Huxley claimed to have surrendered to a force outside of himself and over which he had no control, that is, the force of Evidence—of Truth. What Evidence revealed to him he reported. He was a messenger for a Rhetor no less grand or awesome than the God of the theologian. It was not Huxley who was speaking, but Nature, or Truth, who spoke through him. The theologian insists that the truth is available to all who, with a humble and contrite attitude, will read it in the Bible or in the writings of the Church Fathers, or listen to the quiet inner voice. Huxley claimed that the truth also was available to all who would objectively observe it in Nature. Theologians claim that their surrender to the will of God results in their being "called," "chosen," or "inspired." Huxley implied that his surrender to Nature's facts and to reason, courage, and honesty was tantamount to "inspiration." In his youthful letters to his fiancée he used to speak of science as that enterprise "for which nature has fitted me,"[9] much as a young theology student feels a calling. In his Johns Hopkins address he spoke of the *divine* impulse of the intellectual quest for knowledge,[10] in which he was a participant.

Huxley's narrative took on a familiar format. The pre-Christian (prescientific) era followed by the coming of the Savior (Science/Reason) resulted in the conversion of the disciples who for a considerable period were few in number and victims of much persecution. Even though the enemy had thrown all of its strength into the struggle, the forces of good were winning and, though much remained to be done, could be assured of ultimate victory. Portrayal of the glorious life in "heaven" once ultimate victory was secured was matched by threats, usually implied, as to what will happen to those who did not join forces with the victors.

Huxley proudly noted the decline of the opposition and increased influence of science. The authority of the Bible had been weakened, and an increasing number no longer accepted as historical fact such stories as the Creation, the Flood, the many other record-ed miraculous events, and supernaturalism in general. "The phraseology of supernaturalism may remain on men's lips," acknowledged Huxley, "but in practice they are Naturalists" (5:38). He continued, "In all practical affairs we admit that intelligent work is the only acceptable worship; and that, whether there is a Supernature or not, our business is with Nature" (5:38). More and more man was discovering and propagating realistic data about himself and his universe; organizations for the advancement of natural knowledge had grown in size, strength, and prestige; and greater freedom of inquiry and expression was now enjoyed. Huxley enthusiastically noted that more people were relying on the scientific method in their everyday activities and were adopting the agnostic attitude on a number of questions. More evidence was becoming available both in science and in biblical scholarship. The late nineteenth century was for Huxley the culmination of the Renaissance, and near the end of his life he joyfully wrote that the forces of science were "gathering strength year by year" (5:32).

Just as theologians periodically and forcefully reminded their audiences that the good things in life are a result of religion, Huxley emphatically asserted that humans had arrived at this present high station in life due to, not religion, but science. Not only were material developments such as machinery due solely to the progress of natural knowledge, but the sciences in general, the arts, jurisprudence, and the best political and social theories and structures, grew up not because of Christianity, but in spite of it and with the aid of people whose thinking concided with Huxley's. Be not deceived, it is *our* side that has advanced mankind.

Though our side has brought wonderful trophies to mankind and is winning the battle, the final victory, cautioned and acknowledged

Huxley, was not yet complete. Supernaturalism still existed and had risen its head in a number of new forms. He realized that it had "deep roots in human nature, and will undoubtedly die hard" (5:32). Bibliolatry still flourished and countless numbers of Christians still believed in, and occasionally acted upon, the primitive hypothesis of demonology. They high-church Oxford Movement, he said, unfortunately had grown greatly in power during his lifetime. He admitted that to be realistic, his side "for some generations [was not], likely to constitute a majority" (4:237). Furthermore, plagues and diseases were still present because people still did not know enough about their causes and cures. In most areas of life, man's knowledge was really very limited, and Huxley was quick to admit that humans were still children when confronted with all of the unknowns of life. Since victory was not yet complete, Huxley called on his would-be followers to recognize more fully the wisdom of improving natural knowledge and to be more obedient to that which was already known.

Although victory was not yet complete and much, therefore, remained to be done, one may rest assured that ultimately victory would result. Huxley was convinced that science was "destined . . . to be more and more firmly established as the world grows older" (1:41), and that the scientific spirit was "fated . . . to extend itself into all departments of human thought" (1:41). Supernaturalism and demonology would inevitably be rejected and when they were, orthodox Christianity would collapse. He was "tolerably confident that time will prove [evolution] to be substantially correct" (5:54). He was confident that the number of people relying on the scientific method in their everyday activities "will continually increase" (4:38). In short, the enemy is destined to fall, and our side is assured of victory. This was so because the enemy had built on sand whereas we have built on solid rock. The Christian Church, Huxley claimed, was "building their dogmatic house on the sands of early Church history" (5:331) and biblical infallibility. His side was building on evidence, reason, and honesty.

Once the final victory has been secured, once "salvation" has been won, what will "heaven" be like? Huxley seldom explicitly prophesied about the future, but his "heaven" in this world was clearly implied throughout his work. Under the reign of science, misfortunes, such as disease and famine, would be under greater control, and reason, evidence, and freedom would be revered to a greater degree. Material comforts would be more abundant; but more important, people would have healthier attitudes toward all of life and thus would live more meaningfully. Humans would be more humane and civilized. If people would live up to the agnostic principle, asserted Huxley, "a reformation would be effected such as the world has not yet seen; an approximation to the millennium, such as no supernaturalistic religion has ever yet succeeded, or seems likely ever to succeed, in effecting" (5:40).

If one is not counted among the victorious, what "hell" will be experienced? Agnostics could utilize no threat comparable to the theologian's eternal fire, but the former did hold before their audience, by implication, some powerful social threats. That is, the unsaved would be counted as ignorant, fearful, superstitious, childish, dishonest, timid, intolerant, cruel, hypocritical, and unscientific. Rather than resting content with condemning foes to such a social hell, Huxley was generally more anxious to seek to educate and rehabilitate them.

There was no central creed holding his message together. In fact, his creed was to have no creed, for he conceived agnosticism to be "not a creed, but a method" (5:245). "Science," he said on one occasion, "commits suicide when it adopts a creed."[11] Shortly after his retirement Huxley wrote to a correspondent:

> But the theologians cannot get it out of their heads, that as they have creeds to which they must stick at all hazards, so have the men of science. There is no more ridiculous delusion. We, at any rate, hold ourselves morally bound to "try all things and hold fast to that which is good"; and among public benefactors, we recken him who explodes old error as next in rank to him who discovers new truths.[12]

In short, Huxley conceived of himself as an "apostle" for science, honesty, and truth. He once wrote to a friend on the continent that he saw himself as a missionary "to convert the Christian Heathen of these islands to the true faith"[13] of science. That was the task and message of this "inspired messenger."

Roadblock Remover

In the process of developing his narrative Huxley placed himself in the rhetorical role of a roadblock remover. Next to military metaphor, which has already been discussed, the roadblock metaphor was the most central and revealing image for Huxley throughout the decades as he carried out his rhetorical controversy with orthodox theology.

Carrying valuable cargo (such as "reason," "truth," "scientific method," "honest doubt," "progress," "freedom," "honor," "justice," "happiness," and "civilization") along life's road, he felt that he was being impeded by the obstacle of ecclesiasticism, an obstacle that not only was passively blocking the way, but that was actively inflicting harm on the innocent traveller. The man of science, Huxley contended, was being impeded by "ecclesiastical barriers" (4:371). Himself a traveler in "the service of natural knowledge" (1:31), Huxley claimed that he had discovered early in life that one "could hardly follow to the end any path of inquiry without finding the way blocked by Noah and his ark, or by the first chapter of Genesis" (4:215). Orthodox theology was an "obstacle to the progress of mankind" (5:241) in that it made it extremely unpleasant and dangerous for a person to speak what he honestly believed.

Using a nautical metaphor, no doubt going back to his *Rattlesnake* experience, Huxley stressed that those opposing Darwinism were people who were seeking to turn a ship from her course.

> I was convinced as firmly as I have ever been convinced of anything in my life, that the *Origin of Species* was a ship laden with a cargo of rich value, and which, if she was permitted to pursue her course, would reach a veritable scientific Golconda, and I thought it my duty, however naturally averse I might be to fighting [to defend the ship].[14]

Nor was the use of a barrier as an image of orthodoxy accidental or fleeting. In 1893 in the preface to the volume of his collected essays looking back over a lifetime of dealing with the challenge of science to the Christian tradition, Huxley wrote, this time employing a land metaphor:

> I had set out on a journey, with no other purpose than that of exploring a certain province of natural knowledge; I strayed no hair's breadth from the course which it was my right and my duty to pursue; and yet I found that, whatever route I took, before long, I came to a tall and formidable-looking fence. Confident as I might be in the existence of an ancient and infeasible right of way, before me stood the thorny barrier with its comminatory notice-board—"No Thoroughfare. By order. Moses." There seemed no way over; nor did the prospect of creeping around, as I saw some do, attract me. ... One is apt to get very dirty going on all-fours. The only alternatives were either to give up my journey—which I was not minded to do—or to break the fence down and go through it (5:vii–viii).

To the " 'Mosaic' fences" (5:xi) Huxley in the same preface added the New Testament roadblocks. "I found the Gospels, with their miraculous stories, of which the Gadarene is a typical example, blocking my way, as heretofore, the Pentateuch had done" (5:xiii). In 1860 Huxley wrote to an Anglican clergyman with great confidence that it was "of no use to try to barricade us [scientists]";[15] and near the end of his life he asserted that "the fence turned out to be a mere heap of dry sticks and brushwood, and one might walk through it with impunity: . . . the which I did" (5:ix).

Being the man that he was, Huxley, not stopping, retreating, or going around the roadblock, used his talents and energy to remove the impediment so that it could no longer obstruct him or those later travelers who would be making their rightful journey through life. He (1) employed blunt accusations in frontal assaults, (2) attempted to associate the foe with weak allies, (3) sought to create disunity among opponents, (4) enticed the barricaders to relax their diligence, (5) launched flank attacks, and (6) concentrated his fire like a rifleman on a single vulnerable point.

First, Huxley often leveled strong frontal assaults at the roadblocks. As has already been noted, he persistently accused his enemy of propagating many false ideas. For example, in deprecating the story of the Flood, he strongly asserted:

In the face of the plainest and most commonplace of ascertained physical facts, the story of the Noachian Deluge . . . is utterly devoid of historical truth . . . [It] is merely a Bowdlerised version of one of the oldest pieces of purely fictitious literature extent; . . . the events asserted in it to have taken place assuredly never did take place (4:226, 229).

He extended that by asserting that he knew "of no reason to suspect any different origin for the rest" (4:235) of the biblical stories. He insisted that the evidence "completely and fully" (4:75) demonstrated the biblical view of Creation to be untenable. He often boldly asserted that if the opponents would only take the trouble to study the facts, they would recognize that all of the evidence supported his contentions.

Second, Huxley occasionally sought to weaken his antagonists by linking them with undesirable allies. "Ecclesiasticism," which he made synonymous with French "clericalism" (5:313), was a label that associated his opponent with Catholicism, with extreme reaction, and with an historic national enemy. References to the primitive heathen origin of many of the basic Christian doctrines were frequent, and on occasion he suggested that the orthodox religionists, especially the Catholics, ought to feel at one with the contemporary sect of Spiritualists, who were providing better evidence for their supposed miracles than the Bible or the early Church had given for theirs (5:339–43).

Third, Huxley hoped to weaken the roadblock defenders by dividing the constituents. He cited the mutual exclusiveness fundamental to all religions, which made their adherents "delight in charging each other, not merely with error, but with criminality, deserving and ensuing punishment of infinite severity" (5:6), and he exploited the cleric-laity tensions by suggesting to the clergy that some of their laymen allies (such as Gladstone) were "friends from whom [the clergy] may well pray to be delivered (5:35). Furthermore, he frequently alluded to the East-West split in Christendom, the historic animosity between Catholics and Protestants, and the general liberal-conservative split across all groups. Fanning the low-high church tensions, he on one occasion warned his countrymen that the Anglican Church under the growing influence of the Oxford Movement was becoming "a preparatory school for Papistry" (5:345). He reminded his audiences of the disagreements between the Church of England and the Nonconformists.

Fourth, Huxley enticed the barricaders to relax their diligence. He frequently exerted great care to avoid being associated with other freethinking individuals or groups. He strongly denied that he was a Materialist, a Positivist, a Deist, or an Atheist. In 1887 he wrote to a correspondent:

> To my mind, atheism is, on purely philosophical grounds, untenable. That there is no evidence of the existence of such a being as the God of the theologians is true enough, but strictly scientific reasoning can take us no further. Where we know nothing we can neither affirm or deny with propriety.[16]

He did not even want to be associated with any school of Agnostics. In 1889 he wrote: "I speak for myself alone. I am not aware that there is any sect of Agnostics; and if there be, I am not its acknowledged prophet or pope" (5:210–11).[17] He gave no support to friends of science whose claims went too far, and he was not one of those who wanted to advance science for its material ends only. He endorsed Christianity for its development of the high ethics of Israel, and he certainly did not advocate discarding the Bible from curriculums. He also was quick to mention the points on which he agreed with his antagonists, he acknowledged his incompetence in various areas, carefully used qualifying phrases, and skillfully flattered audiences at appropriate times.

Fifth, Huxley was a master at launching flank attacks through irony, understatement, and ridicule. For example, the statement "at the present time, I suppose there is no one who doubts that histories which appertain to any other people than the Jews, and their spiritual progeny in the first century" (4:205) contain fiction along with truth was an ironic thrust at the basic concept of biblical infallibility. Despite a "diligent search" (4:217), he had found no contemporary defender of the idea that the Flood was worldwide. The attempt of opponents to rest their case on the story of Balaam's ass evoked the observation that "there seems to be no end to the apologetic burden that Balaam's ass may carry" (5:347, n). Jacob, he suggested, "somewhat over-stepped the bounds of fair play" (5:338) in his wrestling match with the angel, and in general the biblical miracles "to put the case gently, are not exactly probable" (5:335). The parading of various interpretations of some biblical passage produced the coy observation that "a person who is not a Hebrew scholar can only stand aside and admire the marvelous flexibility of a language which admits of such diverse interpretation" (4:64). The embarrassing Anglian position of rejecting the Catholic doctrine of continuing miracles while accepting biblical and early Church miracles prompted the remark that the Anglicans had been able to rise to the occasion "with a little adjustment—a squeeze here and a pull there" (5:332). The concept of the Trinity met ridicule through a reference to Arius as the man who "fell short of the Athanasian power of affirming contradictories with respect to the nature of the Godhead" (5:338–9). Theology was unnecessary for a stable and moral society "even if the human race should arrive at the conclusion that, whether a bishop washes a cup or leaves it unwashed, is not a matter of the least consequence, it will get on very well" (5:316). After quoting the harsh things that a recent clerical opponent had said about him, Huxley ironically observed that it "illustrates the great truth, forced on me by long experience, that it is only from those who enjoy the blessing of a firm hold of the Christian faith that such manifestation of meekness, patience, and charity are to be expected" (5:348).

Sixth, Huxley concentrated his fire on a precise area. Singling out an episode as representative of a larger issue, he proceeded to shoot it full of holes. Thus, as a means a of establishing his contention that the Bible contained some fiction like any other historical work, he attacked the story of the flood by marshaling much evidence demonstrating its fictional character (4:213–34). In like manner he concentrated attacks on the story of Creation (4:139–200), on the narrative about the Gadarene swine (5:366–419), on demonology

(5:319–28), on miracles (5:328–47), on the general claims of scriptural and Church infallibility (5:22–32), on false ideas about the theory of evolution (4:58–74), and on false claims as to the actual sayings of Jesus (5:348–63).

The horizontal image of a roadblock remover makes it relatively easy for the challenger of the status quo to assume the role of hero. A helpful, courageous servant of his fellowmen, he seeks only to remove an unnatural, unwanted, unnecessary, unattractive, unworthy, useless, and dangerous obstruction. The vertical image of someone tearing down something, to bring to the ground the high superstructure of organized theology, slowly built over many centuries, may well put one in a less favorable light, for the demolition of historic landmarks, however outmoded, often generates nostalgic sympathies and negative feelings toward the demolition agent. In contrast, the remover of the roadblock is not negatively destructive, but rather is a positive, responsible, constructive individual engaged in creating an opening through which his fellowmen may stream into the promised land.

Conclusion

Recent scholars have lamented the tendency of some late nineteenth-century figures like Huxley and some twentieth-century commentators to generate and entrench a simplistic two-valued orientation. As Moore has put it, "There was not a polarisation of 'science' and 'religion' . . . but a large number of learned men, some scientists, some theologians, some undistinguished, and almost all of them very religious, who experienced various differences among themselves."[18] Stephen Jay Gould, a popular scientist who is no stranger to controversy, has insisted on shifting the alignment of opposing forces.

> But no battle exists between science and religion—the two most separate spheres of human need. A titanic struggle occurs, always has, always will, between questioning and authority, free inquiry and frozen dogma—but the institutions representing these poles are not science and religion. These struggles occur *within* each field, not primarily across disciplines. The general ethic of science leads to greater openness, but we have our fossils, often in positions of great power. Organized religion, as an arm of state power so frequently in history, has tended to rigidity—but theologies have also spear-headed social revolution. . . . The struggle of free inquiry against authority is so central, so pervasive that we need all the help we can get from every side. Inquiring scientists must join hands

with questioning theologians if we wish to preserve that most fragile of all needs, liberty itself. If scientists lost their natural allies by casting entire institutions as enemies, and not seeking bonds with soul mates on other paths, then we only make a difficult struggle that much harder.[19]

The conflict has indeed been distorted and exaggerated, but to one in the trenches at that time and place, such as Huxley, the atmosphere was clearly perceived to be one of dramatic scientific heroism versus unworthy theological foes.

7

Communicating with Close Friends: The X Club

People have been aided in a host of significant ways by their intimate associates with whom they comunicate regularly over a long period of time. This was surely true for Huxley. He belonged to a number of groups and clubs but none was as meaningful to him as the "X Club." From early friendships forming in the 1850s to the creation of the club in 1864 until his death in 1985, his life was closely intertwined with that small intimate network. To view only the public rhetoric of a highly visible person such as Huxley, is to catch only a portion of the person. This chapter surveys his communication with the X Club, an intimate fraternity and scientific caucus that enriched the lives of the members and helped them to marshall their efforts on behalf of science in many different directions. Huxley was at the center of the small group.

Basic Features

In November 1864, in a hotel not far from Piccadilly Circus, Huxley and seven other eminent scientists, who had long been close friends, formed a dining club in order to further the cause of science. An account of its creation is given in the journal of one of its members, Thomas Archer Hirst.

> Thursday evening, Nov. 3, an event probably of some importance occurred at St. George's Hotel, Albemarle Street. A new club was formed of eight members; viz: Tyndall, Hooker, Huxley, Busk, Frankland, Spencer, Lubbock, and myself. Besides personal friendship, the bond that united us was devotion to science, pure and free, untramelled by religious dogmas. Amongst ourselves there is perfect outspokenness, and no doubt opportunities will arise when concerted action on our part may be of service. . . . We agreed to meet on the first Thursday in every month [except July, August, and September]. . . . There is no knowing into what

this club, which counts amongst its members some of the best workers of the day, may grow, and therefore I record its foundation.[1]

Huxley's diary for 3 November merely records, "X Club 6:30 St. George's Hotel Albemarle."[2] Late in life he described the motivation. "As time went on, as the work became harder, the distractions of life more engrossing, a few of us, who had long been intimate, found we were drifing apart; and, to counteract that tendency, we agreed to dine together once a month."[3]

At the second meeting, a ninth member, William Spottiswoode, was added. The club occasionally discussed bringing in new members, especially when vacancies were created by deaths, but no new members were ever added. Spencer explained it this way: "No one was found who fulfilled the two requirements—that he should be of adequate mental calibre and that he should be on terms of intimacy with the existing members."[4]

From the oldest to the youngest, the members and their status in 1864 were as follows: George Busk (1807–86) was retired from his naval surgeon duties at Greenwich and was engrossed in his many scientific interests. Joseph D. Hooker (1817–1911) was, under his father, assistant director of the Royal Botanic Gardens at Kew. Herbert Spencer (1820–1903) had already published many philosphical works. John Tyndall (1820–93) was a Professor of Natural Philosophy at the Royal Institution of Great Britain, where Edward Frankland (1825–99) was Professor of Chemistry. Huxley (1825–95) was Professor of Natural History at the Government School of Mines in Jermyn Street and had already made his mark as Darwin's "bulldog." William Spottiswoode (1825–83) was pursuing his mathematical explorations while serving as the Queen's printer. Thomas Archer Hirst (1830–92) was a mathematics master at the University College School. The youngest of the group, John Lubbock (1834–1913), had studied privately with Darwin, his neighbor at Down, and had made significant contributions in archaeology. We have encountered most of them in previous chapters, but here we focus on them as a cohesive communication network, as an entity in itself.

Looking back on the X Club late in life, Huxley wrote:

I think originally, there was some vague notion of associating representatives of each branch of sicence; at any rate, the nine who eventually came together— ... could have managed, among us, to contribute most of the articles to a scientific Encyclopedia.[5]

The title, "X Club," was decided on only after seven months of existence. The best account is given in Spencer's *Autobiography*.

So long did our anonymous character continue, that at length it was remarked (I believe by the wife of one of the members, Mr. Busk) that we might as well name ourselves after the unknown quantity. The suggestion was approved, and we became the X Club. Beyond the advantage that it committed us to nothing, this name had the further advantage that it made possible a brief, and, to a stranger, an enigmatical, notice of our meetings.[6]

Although death gradually reduced the size of the X Club, and illness, retirement to country homes, and other factors reduced the number in attendance, the group met regularly until 1892, after which time the survivors managed only very sporadic meetings. But the club did not need regular meetings to remain alive and in a sense its spirit lived on until 1911, when with Hooker's death the flickering flame finally went out, leaving Lubbock (then Lord Avebury) the lone survivor. Hirst's suspicion, voiced in his journal entry just cited, that this club might become a significant entity, was indeed prophetic. Gaining influence due to the length of it life and eminence of its members, this dining club definitely left its mark on the late Victorian scene and also on the lives of each of the members.[7]

The fragmentary and unsystematic records of the club are contained in two small notebooks, whose whereabouts were unknown until discovered in 1969,[8] although some excerpts had been published in past volumes.[9] Most of the information about the club comes from the journals, letters, and memoirs of the members, their family and friends.

Prior to forming the club the members had been friends for a number of years. The oldest relationship was the friendship of the trio, Tyndall, Hirst, and Frankland. In 1846 the twenty-six-year-old Tyndall and the sixteen-year-old Hirst worked together in a surveyor's office in Halifax, Yorkshire. In 1847 Tyndall was teaching mathematics and Frankland chemistry at Queenwood College, Hampshire, and the next year the two went to study in Germany. Hirst joined them in 1849, and the three received their Ph.D.s from Marburg. When Tyndall left Queenwood in 1853 to go to the Royal Institution, Hirst succeeded him. After Hirst's three years of marriage left him a widower in 1857, he and the bachelor Tyndall were drawn even closer together. Tyndall and Frankland likewise kept up their early friendship and their letters have the jocular tone permitted only to intimates. Frankland was Professor at Owens College, Manchester, from 1851 to 1857, then became lecturer in chemistry at St. Bartholmew's Hospital in London, and in 1863, through the help of Tyndall, was elected Professor of Chemistry at the Royal Institution.

Huxley, Tyndall, and Hooker were another especially cohesive trio. They first met at the meeting of the British Association at Ipswich in 1851. Each of the young scientists had just returned from foreign accomplishments—Tyndall from Germany, Huxley from Australia, and Hooker from Nepal. In 1852 Tyndall was elected a Fellow of the Royal Society, in part through Huxley's assistance. A year after Tyndall came to the Royal Institution in Albemarle Street, Huxley (in 1854) began his lectureship a few blocks away in Jermyn Street at the Government School of Mines. Tyndall was one of the few invited to attend Huxley's wedding in 1857, and Mrs. Huxley reminisced late in life, "From the first, Dr. Tyndall was the most intimate [of our friends], and in a short time we were Brother John, brother Hal and sister Nettie to one another."[10] Hooker also attended the Huxley wedding in 1855, and the following year Hooker and Huxley joined Tyndall in his Swiss mountain climbing expedition. Huxley wrote to Hooker in 1858, "Why I value your and Tyndall's and Darwin's friendship so much is, among other things, that you all pitch into me when necessary."[11] In 1861 Hooker fulfilled the role of godfather at the christening of Huxley's son.

It was Tyndall who brought Huxley and Hooker together with Hirst and Frankland. In August 1856 Tyndall introduced Frankland to Huxley and Hooker on the Alpine mountain climbing expedition,[12] and the following August, Tyndall's mountain climbing in Switzerland similarly brought Hirst into the circle of friendship.[13] In July 1859 Hirst met Mrs. Huxley for the first time,[14] and late in life Mrs. Huxley noted in her memoirs, "Dr. Tyndall introduced his friend Mr. Hirst to us & he became ours."[15]

Huxley first met Spencer at the British Association in 1852, and introduced him to Tyndall in 1853.[16] Spencer soon, and constantly through the years, relied heavily on them for testimonials, ideas, and critiques of his work. As was noted in an earlier chapter, Huxley and Busk were close friends ever since 1851, and Busk and Tyndall became acquainted shortly thereafter. Considerably older than the others, not a regular Alpine companion, and less argumentative and outgoing, Busk was not at the center of activities as were some of the others, but he was one of the most respected members of the club. Spottiswoode was an early friend of Tyndall's. Lubbock first met Hooker in 1854 and two years later met Huxley, Tyndall, and Busk.

A number of Huxley letters to Lubbock in the 1850s can be found in the British Library. Lubbock soon was a member of Tyndall's Alpine expeditions, and his observations were reported in 1863 in his first Friday Evening Lecture at the Royal Institution.[17]

The X Club continued to dine at the St. George's Hotel, but occasionally used the Almond Hotel or the St. James Hotel. The main alternative to St. George's was the exclusive Athenaeum Club on the corner of Pall Mall and Waterloo Place. In the 1880s the Athenaeum became the regular meeting place, as it was much easier for the aging and ailing members to stay and play billiards or read or visit with other friends and not make an additional trip there following dinner at some hotel. The Athenaeum was a second home for the bachelor Spencer and widower Hirst,[18] and the others used its facilities frequently.

The X Club dined, at 6:00 or 6:30 P.M., usually as a prelude to other evening activities. The most common evening function were the sessions of The Royal Society, which took place at Burlington House, two blocks from St. George's. Members also attended the meetings of the Mathematical and Linnean societies, and other scholarly societies to which they belonged, most of which also were located at Burlington House. Sometimes a night at the theater, or billiards and relaxation at the Athenaeum followed the dinner.

The intimacy and small size of the club would suggest that a minimum of rules and regulations would exist, and this was indeed the case; this was a welcome relief from the elaborate and somewhat pompous regulations of some other clubs to which the men belonged. Huxley wrote late in life, "The ... proposal of some genius among us, that we should have no rules, save the unwritten law not to have any, was carried by acclamation."[19]

The perfunctory function of presiding was performed by a different member each time, in alphabetic rotation. Hirst was the treasurer the first three years, after which the job was passed among the other members until 1888 when Hooker became the final and perpetual treasurer. The duties of the treasurer were to make arrangements for the dinners, handle the club's finances, send out notices of each meeting, and record the meeting in the X Club notebook. A few days prior to each meeting the treasurer sent a notice to each member, usually expressed in a form of an algebraic equation, such as "$x = 3$," which meant that the next meeting was to be on the third of the month. Those were sometimes imbedded in a letter or in a postscript to a letter, but most often were sent on postcards, so that, as Spencer expressed it, "Doubtless many speculations and many absurd conclusions were caused in the minds

of servants who took in [the] post-cards."[20] Upon receipt of the
notice, each member was supposed to notify immediately the
treasurer as to whether or not he would attend, and if he planned to
be absent he should give some news about himself that the treasurer
would then share with the club. Attendance was taken very seriously,
and absence was justified only for such reasons as illness or
being out of the city.[21] The fragmentary records of the X Club
notebooks contain only a list of those attending, the bill of the
dinner, and occasionally a few rough notes of what was discussed.
Of the 240 recorded meetings of the club, each member attended the
following number of times: Frankland 186, Spencer 173, Huxley 171,
Hirst 170, Hooker 169, Spottiswoode 160, Tyndall 147, Busk 143, and
Lubbock 131.[22] Some of the greatest names in science and literature,
not only of Britain but also of the continent and the United States,
were included in the list of guests.

During the first decade, toward the end of June the club climaxed
each season with a weekend excursion into the country with their
wives. This outing became known as the "XX" and the proper
algebraic equation announcing its meeting was, for example, "x's +
yv's = 24." On the designated Saturday the group would go by
train, usually to Maidenhead, but occasionally would stop at
Windsor or go all the way to Oxford, and their activities included
boating on the Thames, picnicking, and dining.[23] In June 1875
Huxley confided to Spencer: "I have never held much to the country
x as you know—and perhaps it might as well come to a natural end.
New wives are new elements of frustration—and I don't particularly
admire the recent importation [Frankland's second wife]."[24]

Intimate Fraternity

The X Club played a highly significant role in the lives of its members
by being a ready reservoir of good lighthearted fellowship. Although
these men were known to the general public largely as stern, serious
individuals, quite a different side of their characters was able to
manifest itself in the intimate X Club meetings where they could,
with complete abandon, engage in dinnertime banter. Frequent
comments in members' journals and letters mention the "jolly,"
"pleasant," "jovial," or "merry" time that was had at the
meetings. As Frankland expressed it, "There was always a judicious
admixture of ordinary dinner-table talk, with a by no means sparse
sprinkling of witticisms, good stories, and perhaps occasionally,
though very rarely, a little scandal."[25] Lubbock had a storehouse of

anecdotes, and Tyndall was a vivacious conversationalist who, according to Huxley, "assuredly ... did not usually help us to be serious."[26] Quite the opposite was Spencer, who complained that despite his efforts to discuss serious subjects, "time was spent chiefly in lively talk, of which *badinage* formed a considerable element."[27] Huxley once teasingly wrote to Spencer, "In your absence, I am afraid we inclined to frivolity."[28] The two following terse statements in Hirst's journal have an implied cause and effect relationship: "All present but Spencer. A very merry meeting indeed."[29] It was like a monthly sauna bath where their overburdence spirits could be cleansed and refreshed.

But the good fellowship was not limited to the meetings of the club, for the members and their families socialized in a number of other contexts as well. They spent Sundays, weekends, and holidays at each other's homes, dined frequently at each other's homes, or dined out together. A letter from Spencer to his father on 7 April 1985, illustrates this frequent contact: "Returned on Monday from the Lubbocks with whom I had been spending five days. ... [last night was the X Club] Tonight I dine with Huxley."[30] Another illustration is an entry in Hirst's journal in which he notes that he and Spencer dined with the Busks, that on the previous day he had been at the Lubbocks's, and that he saw Tyndall "for tthe first time for nearly a week!!"[31] The Lubbocks' home was the center of many social gatherings at which one or more members of the club were frequently present, and the Spottiswoodes also entertained often. The Huxleys frequently served tea on late Sunday afternoons to which at least some X Club members (especially Spencer) came regularly, and New Year's Day dinners were traditional at the Huxleys's, with Tyndall, Spencer, and Hirst often present. The nonfamily men entertained at the Athenaeum Club. The X Club members were at the center of wedding festivities of their fraternity brothers: in 1876 Tyndall got married at the tender age of 56,[32] and Frankland remarried in 1875, Hooker in 1876, and Lubbock in 1884, after their first wives had died. Weddings of their children, birthday dinners, and other such family occasions brought many of the club members together. They and their families attended members' public lectures. Spencer tapped the club for someone to play billiards and racquets with him, and Tyndall secured hiking and mountain-climbing companions. After Tyndall's death, Huxley reminisced, "Pleasant are the recollections, for me and for others, of such hard tramps [with Tyndall], it might be in the Lake country, or in the Isle of Wight, in the Peak of Derbyshire, or in Snowdonia."[33] In short, the fellowship was an all-inclusive one.

More specifically, the X Club was a reservoir of goodwill and assistance during times of sorrow and need. At the death of a member, his wife, or other member of the immediate famly, the bereaved received much warm sympathy, appropriate aid, and continued contact from the other X Club members and their families. When a club member was ill, others were kept informed, expressed their concern, visited him, and were solicitous about his welfare. Spencer was a hopeless hypochondriac and Hirst, Huxley, and Tyndall also spent much of their life in search of health. As all grew older, health became a major concern, and they drew much comfort knowing that the brotherhood was concerned and ready to help. When Huxley's health broke down in 1873, his X Club brothers helped to raise money that enabled him to travel in search of a cure. Financial aid was also forthcoming from one or more of the brotherhood when someone had difficulty getting works published or when someone was venturing into some big expense, such as purchasing land or a house. The club thus served as a source and outlet for aid and compassion. One who knew Huxley well, and who was often at odds with him, said of him shortly after his death, "Great as he was in intellect, his goodness of heart to his friends was yet more worthy of esteem."[34]

The X Club was also a forum for exchanging information about, and advice on, personal affairs. It was common practice at their meetings to discuss their experiments, scientific observations, recent travels, and personal and professional plans. Members particularly looked forward to the October meetings when they could be brought up-to-date on each other's experiences during the summer months. They counseled each other when new job opportunities became available. For instance, they discussed "the advisability of Tyndall's acceptance of the Professorship of Physics at Oxford,"[35] and Tyndall was directly influential in convincing Hirst not to apply for the post of Professor of Mathematics in Queen's College in Ireland.[36] No doubt the very existence of the X Club was a major factor in keeping its distinguished individuals in the London area. Their encouragement helped to launch Lubbock on what became a lengthy career in Parliament. As the minutes record it, "[We] decided to give him *our* support by expressing our unanimous opinion that scientific men would regard him as a most appropriate representative in Parliament."[37]

The X Club served as a forum for exchanging expert criticism of each other's work, and as a source of general intellectual stimulation. They relied heavily on each other to evaluate preliminary drafts of their books, articles, and lectures. Praise from the brotherhood was more meaningful and significant to them (so they claimed anyway) than praise or condemnation from other quarters. The club constituted a board of standards, a source of expert evaluation, freely, fully, and privately given, which no doubt raised the quality of the published product and gave the author professional and personal satisfaction regardless of the howling of unfavorable criticism from other sources. Although the members did occasionally adversely criticize publicly some material of their fraternity brothers, as will soon be noted in the Huxley-Spencer rift, such criticism was no doubt reduced sharply in quantity and intensity from what it otherwise would have been if the X Club had not existed. After all, they were friends, and they did have to face each other once a month! Likewise, they no doubt came to each other's defense in public more quickly and with more forcefulness than would have otherwise been the case, for they were defending the club as well as the individual. It takes high-powered individuals to judge and to stimulate high-powered individuals, and the X Club provided such an opportunity. Their conversations and fellowship surely widened their intellectual horizons, made them increasingly interdisciplinary, crystallized and refined their ideas, influenced each other's views, and kept their mental and rhetorical faculties razor sharp.

The X Club fulfilled a function familiar to most fraternities. It was a source of nominators and supporters, who helped each other gain membership into, or recognition in, various clubs and organizations,[38] and that increased the likelihood of various successes. They wrote favorable referee's reports on papers submitted to the Royal Society.[39] Hirst in one instance wrote in his journal that at the last X Club meeting

> Spottiswoode told me he proposed to name me for the post of Registrar General, Earl Beaconsfield [Disraeli] having asked him in his capacity of Pres. of R[oyal] S[ociety] for advice on the matter. I allowed him to do so but reserved my acceptance, should an offer be made, for further consideration.[40]

Spottiswoode and Huxley played leading roles in getting Hirst selected as the first director of naval studies at the newly established Royal Naval College at Greenwich,[41] and Lubbock was instrumental in Hirst's application for assistant registrar of the University of London.[42] Huxley helped Lubbock to become the first president of the Anthropological Institute.[43] The rise of X Club members to positions of leadership in the Royal Society, in the British

Association for the Advancement of Science, and in the Victorian scientific world in general will be discussed later. Hooker proposed Tyndall and Lubbock for membership in the prestigious "The Club."[44] Hooker and Frankland urged Spencer not to refuse to sit for a portrait for the National Portrait Gallery,[45] and Lubbock was chairman of the Committee of the Society of Authors who nominated Spencer for the Nobel Prize for Literature in 1902.[46] It should also be remembered that it was not a case of pushing unqualified and undeserving people into responsible posts or into the limelight. In death as well as in life the fraternity took care of its own. When Spottiswoode died, some X Club members convinced the dean of Westminster to have Spottiswoode buried in Westminster Abbey,[47] and Huxley helped to create a memorial to him at the Royal Society. Eloquent bioraphical tributes to a departed X Club member, such as Huxley's on Tyndall in *The Nineteenth Century*, help to give posthumous praise.

No matter how firm and tested the bonds of friendship, however, any group of mortals is bound to experience occasional tension and ill will. Momentary clashes at meetings and between meetings were bound to occur, and feelings of ill will did occasionally build between some members. In 1883 Huxley wrote to Hooker:

> It has long been too obvious to me that the relations of some of us at the x are getting very strained. Strong men as they get old seem to me to acquire very much the nature of ... elephants—and tend to ... run amuck at everything that does not quite suit their fancy. I am conscious of the tendency myself and it is hateful to me. ... I put it down at all costs.[48]

Spencer, for one, was difficult to get along with, and Hirst in one instance complained of "Spencer's inherited habit of fault finding and criticising."[49]

The only serious instance in which ill will actually threatened the stability of the X Club was the rift between Spencer and Huxley, which erupted late in 1889. The two men had frequently crossed swords on many issues during their lifetimes, but now the ill and hypersensitive Spencer could not absorb the Huxley barbs. On 12 November Huxley's letter to *The Times* took issue with Spencer's political ethics, and a battle between the two men raged in that newspaper with a letter by Spencer on the fifteenth, by Huxley on the eighteenth, and by Spencer on the nineteenth and twenty-seventh. Hooker and other X Club members attempted to reconcile the two antagonists. On 5 December, the day of the X Club meeting, Spencer wrote to Hooker, complaining, "Huxley, besides causing me a serious relapse has done me irreparable damage by making me look like a fool to a hundred thousand readers."[50] Spencer went on to say he was thus resigning his membership in the X Club. "I shall greatly regret," he wrote, "to miss the occasions for pleasant meetings but I do not see that there is any alternative."[51] The next day Hooker wrote to Tyndall:

> You have no doubt heard from Huxley of Spencer's contemplated withdrawal from the [X Club] and his reasons for it; your absence last night was greatly deplored as Spencer's action in the matter of withdrawal did not meet with approval by Hirst, Frankland and myself, the only members present, Huxley having withdrawn.
>
> The upshot of conversation preliminary to the proposed communication of Spencer's letter of withdrawal was, that it should not be communicated, and that he should be informed that the members present viewed with much regret even the contemplated withdrawal of a member with or without sufficient grounds, that the reading of his letter was postponed in the hope that time would modify his feelings.
>
> It was further considered that there was no need at all for Spencer's making a club matter of it, requiring as this would, an entry in the club minutes, and more or less discussion on the merits of the case. He had nothing to do but to stop away and inform the members privately of his motive. Is this your opinion?
>
> Spencer could not have considered the painful position in which his withdrawal would place any member who happened to be asked, "Of whom does your club now consist?" To me and to Hirst especially the subject is most distressing. Here we are seven septuagenarians (or all but) who have met in friendship and harmony for five and twenty years, to be disunited at last, and the disunion to be impossible of concealment, if Spencer persists.[52]

On 11 December Hooker was able to write to Tyndall that Spencer "has withdrawn his resignation."[53] But the Huxley-Spencer duel continued in the pages of *The Nineteenth Century* and the *Daily Telegraph* in January and February 1890, after which the tension simmered until reconciliation finally came three years later. On 24 October 1893, Huxley wrote to Spencer:

> We are old men and ought to be old friends. Our estrangement has always been painful to me. Let there be an end to it. For my part, I am sorry if anything I have said or done has been or has seemed, unjust.[54]

Two days later Spencer replied:

> Your sympathetic letter received this morning has given me great satisfaction. We are both of us approaching our last days, ... and to which ever of us survived it would have been a sad thought had forty years of friendship ended in a permanent estrangement. Happily by your kind expressions that danger is now finally averted and cordial relations reestablished.[55]

The most serious gash in the X Club had finally been sutured.[56] In 1904 after Spencer's death, Mrs. Huxley wrote, "In spite of all [Spencer] achieved, I have a great pity for him. He never knew the happiness of a 'home,' nor, for his being so self-centered, that other happiness, of deep and fullest affectionate sympathy with his friends."[57]

Throughout the years Spencer had been something of an ugly duckling in the group and was rather frequently at odds with someone. The friction arose not only from personality clashes, for deeper differences lay in scholarly presuppositions and procedures, in investigative and communicative habits. Spencer preferred serious, abstract, philosophical discussion compared to the other members' predilection for more concrete, specific subjects springing from experiments or experiences. In a sense, it was a clash between the lover of *a priori* reasoning, and the adherents of induction. Huxley used to tease Spencer by saying that the latter would define a tragedy as the slaying of a beautiful deduction by an ugly fact. Spencer's working habits, which consisted of very little reading, much conversation,[58] limited experiences, dictating to a secretary at approximately twenty-minute intervals sometimes alternating with walking, rowing, billiards, or racquets, and revising very little, somewhat appalled and amused the other members. They depended on incredibly wide reading, varied experiences, detailed experimentation and observation; and they usually wrote careful, tedious, multidrafts before their final written version reached the world.

Scientific Caucus

Much of the discussion at the meetings of the X Club focused on the affairs of the Royal Society. By 1864 all of the X Club members were Fellows of the Royal Society except Spencer[59] who, due to principle and possibly pique, steadfastly refused to agree to be nominated.[60] Nominees for president were discussed and agreed upon. For instance, at one meeting, "Airy was spoken of as a possible future President of the Royal Society,"[61] and a year later, "Airy was agreed upon as a fit person to propose as next President of the Royal Society."[62] He became president. The X Club provided three presidents of the Royal Society. At the January 1873 meeting, the club members "communicated to Hooker that he might be nominated as the next President of the Royal Society,"[63] and the next November he became president. After serving for five years he was succeeded by Spottiswoode, and when the latter died, Hooker and others persuaded Huxley (who had been a secretary of the society from 1871 to 1880) to serve as temporary president and to stand for election to the presidency in November, which he did, and he was chosen. Thus, from 1873 to 1885, when Huxley stepped down, a member of the X Club was the president of the Royal Society: Hooker, 1873–78, Spottiswoode, 1878–83, and Huxley, 1883–85.

During the latter half of the nineteenth century the Royal Society numbered slightly over five hundred members, approximately half being bona fide men of science and others still being merely men of high social standing. Fifteen new members were elected to the Royal Society each June (which balanced the losses by death during each year), so it was common for the X Club in months preceding June to discuss the relative merits of potential candidates. The club also discussed the merits of certain candidates for the Council of the Royal Society. At least one, and often as many as four, of the members of the X Club was on the (approximately) twenty-one-member governing Council of the Royal Society, which frequently met in the afternoon preceding the X Club meeting. Thus, decisions arrived at could be immediately communicated to those at the dinner. At the very first meeting of the X Club in November 1864, Tyndall was informed that the council had voted him the Rumford medal.[64] In October 1870, Huxley wrote to Lubbock, urging him to be a candidate for the vacated treasurership of the Royal Society. "I can think of no one so proper as yourself and I wish you would turn this over in your mind so that we may talk it over at the x on Thursday."[65] At the November 1871 X Club meeting it was announced that Busk had just been awarded one of the royal medals and Hirst had been selected as a member of the new Council.[66] On 1 November 1883 Hirst wrote in his journal that at the X Club meeting that evening, "Huxley [then acting president of the Royal Society] told me that the Council of the Royal Society had just awarded to me the Royal Medal."[67] In March 1886 Mrs. Huxley wrote to Mrs. Tyndall that Huxley had gone up to London "for the

R. Soc. Council Meeting and for the X."[68] In November 1888 the X Club diners were informed that the council had awarded the Copley Medal to Huxley.[69] In May 1890 they discussed "possible Presidents of the Royal Society seeing that Stokes is about to retire."[70] The club concerned itself with a host of Royal Society issues, such as whether the colonial societies should affiliate with the Royal Society, whether the Royal Society should be the agency to administer state financial assistance to experimental research, what the role of the Royal Society should be in inspecting ships' compasses, how to reduce fees, and how to speed up the publishing of scientific papers in the Royal Society's *Philosophical Transactions*. Just how much influence this small group wielded would, of course, be difficult to pinpoint, for after all, other groups, such as the Philosophical Club, to which all of the X Club members, except Spencer, belonged,[71] were also discussing Royal Society business.

The X Club also gave much of its attention to the affairs of the British Association for the Advancement of Science (BAAS). By 1864 all of those who formed the X Club, except Spencer, had become members, and within the next few years five were to serve a year's term as president: Hooker (1868), Huxley (1870), Tyndall (1874), Spottiswoode (1878), and Lubbock (1881). Attempting to counteract the influence of nonscientific individuals, the X Club succeeded in urging their own to agree to be nominated for president.[72] Not only did they help to elevate their own members and other like-minded scientists to the presidency of the association, but also to the presidency of the individual sections in which the X Club members were extremely active. For instance, the notebooks of the X Club contain more than once such an entry as: "The presidents of sections for the next meeting of the British Association were then discussed and the list provisionally filled."[73] In 1868 Frankland was president of the Chemical Section and Tyndall was president of the Mathematics and Physical Science Section. The Zoology, Botany, and Physiology Section (the famous Section D) had Huxley as its president in 1862 and 1866, Busk in 1869, and Lubbock in 1872. When Lubbock was president of the association in 1881 he persuaded Hooker to be a sectional president. Thus it is understandable that the affairs of the British Association would be a common topic of conversation at the X Club, particularly during those periods when members held high office. The X Club members went to the annual meetings of the association with a sense of group unity. In 1870 when Huxley was president, the association met in Liverpool and Lubbock reported that "Huxley made an excellent chairman."[74] Spencer later wrote in his autobiography:

On this, as on other occasions when a member of the X Club presided, the gathering had a concomitant pleasure resulting from the quasi-domestic arrangements made. All members of the X who came, usually bringing their wives, took a suite of rooms at the chief hotel and united their forces.[75]

Spencer wrote similarly about the 1874 meeting at Belfast when Tyndall was president.[76] Tyndall earlier in that year had thought of resigning the presidency due to his heavy work load, but Huxley and other X Club members convinced him not to do so.[77] When X Club members were not at the BAAS meeting, it was worthy of noting, as Hirst one year recorded in his journal, "Tyndall was the only absent one of the 9 X."[78] Thus, with cohesiveness and energetic involvement, the X Club was near the center of the affairs of the British Association.

The members of the X Club were also active leaders in learned societies, such as the Linnean, Mathematical, Geological, Chemical, and Ethnological societies. If the X Club diners did not go to the meeting of the Royal Society, they usually went to the meeting of one of these other societies, and they supported each other in their respective scholarly organizations. Thus, it is understandable that the club would frequently discuss the general affairs of these societies and the candidates for posts of leadership in them.[79]

The Royal Institution of Great Britain was also of central interest to the X Club members. Dedicated to the search for, and the dissemination of, scientific knowledge, the Royal Institution, with its laboratory facilities, large lecture hall, and publications, had become a highly important scientific and cultural center. As has been noted in an earlier chapter, Huxley gave his first significant public lecture there in 1852, and he often attended lectures given there by Tyndall, after whose death Huxley reminisced, "[Tyndall] was one of the few orators whom I have heard to whom I could not choose but listen."[80] Tyndall became a Professor of Natural Philosophy there and succeeded Faraday as Superintendent, Huxley was for a time Professor of Physiology, and Frankland became Professor of Chemistry. With various X Cub members also giving occasional lectures there, serving as treasurer, or as one of the fifteen managers, or in other capacities, it is not surprising that the Royal Institution, just across the street from the St. George's Hotel, was a familiar subject of conversation at the dinner table of the X Club. Its central location made it easy for members to drop in to chat with Tyndall about their work, recent travels, or X Club affairs. After Tyndall retired, the X Club talked about the degeneration of the Royal Institution.[81]

Members of the X Club were deeply involved in publishing scientific information and views in scholarly and popular outlets, in the form of learned papers, essays, lectures, periodical articles, books, and letters to newspaper editors. Their contributions were simply incredible in quantity and quality, and they reached a very wide audience indeed. At the very first meeting of the X Club Spencer brought up the subject of *The Reader*, a weekly review of literature, science, and art first published in January 1863. It was "a journal in which the Young Guard of science were seeking a literary mouthpiece."[82] Huxley's lectures and writings were advertised and reviewed in *The Reader*. But it was on an insecure footing, and Hirst wrote in his journal that it "is about to change hands, and, provided a liberal editor is appointed, we agreed to give it hearty support."[83] A month later Spencer wrote to the American publisher, Edward Youmans, that "the prospects of *The Reader* about which I told you, are highly encouraging,"[84] for Huxley and Tyndall were to be two of the five editors and Lubbock and Tyndall were to give financial assistance. In January 1865 Huxley wrote to his friend, Frederic Dyster: "A lot of us have got [*The Reader*] in hand and make it a scientific organ. I published my encyclical in it in the leading article on 'Science and Church policy' in the last week of last year."[85] In April 1865, Spencer requested Darwin to write a letter supporting the project, and wrote:

> We are getting our staff of the *Reader* into better working order ... Profs. Huxley and Tyndall ... and myself, have severally agreed to write a few leading articles by way of giving the intended tone and direction.[86]

In October Darwin wrote to Huxley, "I shall regret extremely if the Reader fails as a newspaper for general science."[87] But it soon failed. Spencer, however, was immediately suggesting a similar venture, which he explained in a letter to Youmans in January 1867.

> An attempt is being made here to establish a scientific journal, to do what *The Reader* was intended to do ... I mentioned it at the X, and the notion was well received. I propose that we shall take a year or so to organize matters, before making a start.[88]

This apparently resulted in *Nature*,[89] in whose first issue on 4 November 1869 Huxley wrote the leading article and a second brief article, and Lubbock wrote a book review. The editor of *Nature*, Norman Lockyer, had been the editor of the science department of

The Reader.[90] In the issues of *Nature* up to April 1870, seven members of the X Club had written at least one article each.

X Club members were at the center of scientific writing and lecturing not only in Great Britain but also in the United States. Huxley, Tyndall, and Spencer were particularly active in establishing publishing and lecturing linkages with the United States. They served as Edward Youmans's London Advisory Committee for his projected "International Scientific Series," and they were constantly involved in negotiation with their American publisher, D. Appleton and Company.[91] On one occasion the X Club discussed "some arrangement for the publication of English scientific works in America,"[92] and when Youmans was the guest of the club, the talk no doubt involved publishing. Appleton could report to Lubbock in March 1872 that the initial sale of his *Pre-historic Man* was excellent.[93] Youmans and others assisted in setting up Tyndall's lecture tour in the United States in 1872.[94] John Fiske of Harvard, a very significant liaison,[95] was in England in 1873 meeting with Spencer, Tyndall, Huxley, and other X Club members. As was noted in the previous chapter, Fiske, Youmans, and Appleton were instrumental in arranging Huxley's 1876 lecture tour of the United States.[96] In 1879 and 1880 Huxley was helping to arrange a lecture tour for Fiske in Britain.[97] In 1882 Fiske and Youmans helped arrange for Spencer's visit to the United States,[98] and Huxley, Spencer, and Tyndall began arrangements for Fiske's lectures in 1883 in England,[99] during which time Fiske of course was dining with his X Club friends.[100] In 1893, when writing a biography of Youmans, Fiske sought advice from his X Club contacts, and Spencer characteristically advised him that if his book contained extracts from letters of Spencer, Huxley, and Tyndall, Fiske should publicize that fact, for the book would no doubt sell better.[101]

Before the X Club members published their material, portions of it had most likely first been shared with, and reacted to by, their fraternity brothers either in meetings or individually. It was common practice at their meetings to discuss their current experiments and scientific observations. For instance, the minutes indicate that the club discussed Spencer's "botanical inquiries,"[102] Tyndall's discoveries "in the reflecting of blue rays from the molecules of attenuated vapours,"[103] and Huxley's "new observations on microscopic organic forms."[104] At one meeting Hirst had a "long talk with Frankland about his experiments on illumination,"[105] and on another occasion the group talked about Huxley's controversial articles in 1889 in *The Nineteenth Century.*[106] On one occasion Huxley wrote to Tyndall:

Will you bring with you to the "x" to-morrow a little bottle full of fluid containing the Bacteria, etc., you have found developed in your infusions? I mean a good character specimen. It will be useful to you I think if I determine the forms with my own microscope and make drawings of them which you can use.[107]

Discussions at the meetings prompted follow-up letters to each other and dyadic contacts so the interaction continued beyond the actual meetings. Members, for example, expanded on the subject discussed, clarified their positions, apologized for any potentially painful comments, supplied information that they did not give at the time, and expressed their thanks for what they said.[108] Spencer was particularly reliant on Huxley, Tyndall, and others to evaluate his writings.[109] Also, it is only natural that an event like the death of Darwin generated eulogistic expressions at the next X Club meeting.[110]

One of the prime motivations governing the activities of the X Club members was the desire to ward off attacks on science by conservative theologians. The entry in Hirst's journal cited previously,[111] reporting the first meeting of the X Club, is revealing in this context when he referred to the group as outspoken men of science, "pure and free, untrammelled by religious dogmas . . . and no doubt opportunities will arise when concerted action on our part may be of service." From the outset these men, who "were of one mind on theological topics,"[112] manned the ramparts of science. Huxley especially was in the forefront of the battle, and some of his antitheological public lectures were discussed in the X Club prior to, or following, their delivery. For instance, the minutes record that "Huxley's forthcoming lecture at St. Martin's Hall [7 January 1866], and the Sunday League generally, were subjects of conversation,"[113] and on another occasion the club discussed his lecture at Sion College [12 December 1867] where he had discussed before theologians the conflicts between theology and science. The minutes also reveal that "Hirst read a letter from the Secretary of the Sunday League in reference to the suppression of the Sunday lectures by the Sabbatarians,"[114] and that "Huxley reported that the question of Sunday evening lectures had been revived independently by the Sunday League; and [he] will report further hereafter."[115] No doubt when Bishop Colenso, Prof. Robertson Smith, and others were guests at the X Club dinners, the discussion centered on the relationship between science and theology.

The devotion of the X Club to science brought them into conflict not only with theologians, but also occasionally with politicians.

Two examples will illustrate this role. Between 1870 and 1872 Hooker, as Director of Kew Gardens, became embroiled in difficulties with Mr. Ayrton, the First Commissioner of Works in Gladstone's government, who had jurisdiction over all Royal Parks. Ayrton looked on Kew Gardens as just another park rather than a center of scholarship, and treated Hooker as a minor subordinate rather than as a famous botanist. In righteous indignation the X Club members, and other leaders in science, drew up a twenty-five-page remonstrance, drafted mainly by Tyndall, which when published stirred considerable controversy, and that led to Lubbock defending the cause of science in the House of Commons.[116]

Another major episode was Gladstone's Irish Home Rule policy, which all survivors of the X Club strongly opposed. They feared that religious liberty would suffer a severe setback. They felt that the small minority of Protestants in Ireland would be at the mercy of their historic Catholic foe. Tyndall, who was born in Ireland and grew up among these Protestants, was particularly concerned for their welfare.[117] The X Club also shared the widespread views of those who felt that the economic investment by Protestants in Ireland would be in serious jeopardy, who questioned the ability of the Irish to rule themselves, and who feared that the security of England would be seriously threatened. The X Club members had by this time developed a passionate personal antipathy to Gladstone, whom they regarded as a despotic, shifty, dishonest, and untrustworthy politician. It will also be remembered that at this time Huxley was engaged in his vigorous battle in *The Ninetenth Century* and *The Times* with Gladstone on theologial issues. In November 1887, Frankland wrote to Huxley:

> At the X it was considered advisable to draw up a kind of scientific declaration in favour of the maintenance of the Union and Tyndall was deputed to draw it, strong but in moderate language, and we all agreed to sign. It was thought that nearly every scientist of note would sign it.[118]

Tyndall's initial draft stirred some apprehension in Hooker and Huxley, and the latter wrote to Tyndall:

> [We] entirely agreed with what you say about Gladstone and his policy but doubt whether it will not be objected to by many as having too much the air of a personal attack. In short, we are full of doubts and difficulties but they can be set forth best by a talk at the x to which I hope you are coming on Thursday next.[119]

Tyndall was unable to come, so he wrote immediately to Huxley:

> I entirely surrender the personal element should it be there. It is a pity, however, having such a force in reserve, not to apply it at the present crisis. I hear from various good men and true that they are tired of the professional politician (don't let Lubbock know this) and wish to hear the free and unbiased sons of science speaking out. ... I withdraw what I have written and thus leave the X carte Blanche.[102]

The X Club members did differ, of course, on some important political issues. The American Civil War found Huxley favoring the North, and Tyndall and others siding with the South, with Hooker taking a somewhat neutral position. In connection with the Eyre Affair in Jamaica in 1866, where Governor Eyre was accused of excessive force in putting down a Negro insurrection, Huxley criticized Eyre, whereas Tyndall felt that the governor had acted properly. Huxley wrote to Tyndall on the Eyre Affair:

> That you and I have fundamentally different political principles must, I think, have become obvious to both of us during the progress of the American War. ... There is nothing for ... us [but] to agree to differ each defending his position and respecting the other's.[121]

That such sharp differences could exist simply speaks all the more to the strong cohesiveness of the X Club and the respect that Huxley and the others had for the club and each other.

A host of additional miscellaneous subjects related to science were of course discussed around the table of the X Club. They discussed bolstering the cause of science at Oxford,[122] "the merits of Bacon as the originator of the method of induction in Science,"[123] atoms,[124] and on one occasion "Tyndall stated that he had a new theory of comets, which he was about to propound at the Cambridge Philosophical Society."[125] When Huxley became a candidate for the first London School Board in 1870, it was only natural that it was discussed: "The organisation for Elections to the Educational Board of the Metropolis was discussed,"[126] and "Huxley made some remarks on the approaching Election for the Metro School Bd. for which he was a candidate."[127]

Fading Away

During the late 1880s the club was beginning to weaken, due to ill health, deaths, retirements, and migration from London. In 1883

Spottiswoode had died and Hirst retired because of ill health. In 1885 Huxley, Frankland, and Hooker retired; in 1886 Busk died, and the next year Tyndall retired. Frankland moved to Reigate, Hooker to Sunningdale, Tyndall to Haslemere, and Huxley down to Eastbourne. Lubbock was at High Elms, Kent, and in 1898 Spencer moved to Brighton. The death of Hirst in February 1892 was a major blow to the continuance of regular X Club meetings, as he was one of its most devoted members.[128] The last recorded meeting in the X Club Notebook was that of March 1892 but the Club did not die, it merely faded away. In December 1892 Hooker wrote to Tyndall:

I have not seen a fraction of an X since last summer, and the dear old club is so far defunct that I see no prospect of this continuance except by a summer gathering. Huxley lives too far off, ditto Frankland, Lubbock has other gods; Spencer has been so unwell that he could not have attended this winter if he would, and I am warned by a tendency to bronchitis to avoid night air. .... Hirst's decease was the death-blow.[129]

In June 1894 Lubbock wrote to Spencer: "I never see Huxley now except at meetings occasionally and Hooker never at all. It makes me feel quite a 'survival'—not I fear 'of the fittest'."[130] When Huxley died in 1895, Hooker wrote that "the club died with him."[131]

Hooker, the last treasurer of the club, valiantly attempted to get the survivors together occasionally, but not with much success.[132] Frankland died in 1899, so only three saw the dawn of the twentieth century: Spencer, Hooker, and Lubbock. In 1901 Hooker wrote to Spencer: "You have held and still hold a big grip on my life. .... I have not seen our surviving versatile fellow x [Lubbock] for months and decline his invitations to High Elms [due to ill health]."[33] In 1903, shortly before Spencer's death, Hooker wrote to him:

The dear old X Club is rapidly with us, I fear, approaching the vanishing point. How curious it seems, that we who were, I think, considerably the oldest members, should be amongst the three survivors.[134]

During the first decade of the twentieth century, Lubbock, now Lord Avebury, made almost annual visits to Hooker's home in Sunningdale, usually in October or November, and these visits were looked on by the two as X Club meetings where over lunch they would reminisce on the past.[135] In June 1911 Lubbock again visited Hooker at Sunningdale and wrote in his journal: "Found him very well, but he will be 93 in a few days. I fear it may be the last meeting of the X Club."[136] The remark was prophetic, for six months later Lubbock recorded in his journal: "December 10th. Hooker died. A wonderful man and a most kind friend. The last of our little group.''[137] Secondary accounts dealing with the lives of these nine scientists assert or imply that the X Club died abruptly and with finality in 1892 or 1893. But the letters, journals, and memoirs of the survivors make it clear that the X Club lived on in spirit if not in actual meetings until 1911.

Impact

The club indeed left its mark on the late Victorian era. As Spencer summarized it in his *Autobiography*:

> It is not surprising that its influence was felt. Among its members were three who became Presidents of the Royal Society, and five who became Presidents of the British Association. Of the others one was for a time President of the College of Surgeons; another President of the Chemical Society; and a third of the Mathematical Society. To enumerate all their titles, and honours, and the offices they filled, would occupy too much space. Of the nine, I was the only one who was fellow of no society, and had presided over nothing.[138]

In 1885 Huxley wrote to Sir Michael Foster that among many outsiders "there was a jealousy of the x club,''[139] and in 1886 Huxley wrote to Frankland, "Nobody could have foreseen or expected twenty odd years ago when we first met, that we were destined to play the parts we have since played.''[140] Two years later Huxley wrote to Hooker, "It has happened that these cronies had developed into big-wigs of various kinds, and therefore the club has incidentally—I might say accidentally—had a good influence in the scientific world.''[141] In 1894 Huxley wrote:

> I believe that the "x" had the credit of being a sort of scientifice caucus, or ring, with some people. In fact, two distinguished scientific colleagues of mine once carried on a conversation (which I gravely ignored) across me, in the smoking room of the Athenaeum, to this effect: "I say, A, do you know anything about the x Club?" "Oh yes, B, I have heard of it. What do they do?" "Well, they govern scientific affairs; and really, on the whole, they don't do it badly.''[142]

But influence can sometime be exaggerated, and Huxley went on to suggest that if his Athenaeum colleagues "could only have been present at a few of our meetings, they would have formed a much less exalted idea of us, and would, I fear, have been much shocked at the sadly frivolous tone of our ordinary conversation."[143] Spencer also cautioned against exaggeration. "In course of time the existence of the Club became known in the scientific world, and it was, we heard, spoken of with bated breath—was indeed, I believe, supposed to exercise more power than it did."[144] The difficulty of precisely tracing the effects that the X Club had is of course considerable. As Spencer put it, "These consultations had their effects, though in what exact way I do not know."[145]

It is clear, however, that the X Club's presence was felt in the Royal Society, the British Association, various learned societies, the Royal Institution, and in publishing and lecturing in Britain and the United States. Fiske called the club "the most powerful and influential scientific coterie in England."[146] For its members, the club deepened friendships, was a reservoir of good fellowship, a source of condolence and assistance, and a forum for interacting on scholarly endeavors. The Victorian scientific scene and the lives of the club members would have been significantly different without the X Club. Furthermore, as MacLeod reasonably suggests, "Perhaps it has served as a model for other informal groups of influential scientists in Britain and abroad. Certainly, its history has a continuing appeal for those who believe that informal elites still decide the most important questions of scientific policy."[147] Moore has rightly admonished that such informal forums as the X Club deserve "detailed investigation,"[148] and I trust that this chapter has contributed to that exploration.

Clubs, however, can become time-consuming and counter-productive, and, as Huxley once put it near the end of his life, "Clubs are like hypotheses, not to be multiplied beyond necessity."[149] But the X Club was special to him and to the others. It was more than the sum of its parts, and the individual members surely were more fulfilled human beings than they would otherwise have been. Their lives and the lives of their families were deeply enriched by that remarkable communication network. That surely was true for Huxley, and his public rhetorical battles were bolstered by having this intimate sustaining network of friends backstage.

8

Rhetorical Legacy

Huxley's long active life left a rich rhetorical legacy. In his numerous written and spoken accomplishments, he demonstrated a number of characteristics that stamped him as an outstanding rhetorician, and that earned him the plaudits of contemporaries, including foes. The twentieth century has continued to honor his prowess as a premier rhetorician, perpetuating his legacy as a popular expositor of science to a general audience, as a vigorous advocate for what he felt was true, and as a skillful practitioner of extemporaneous speaking. His effectiveness stems in part from his rigorous habits of preparation, his integration of thought and word, the integrity of his individualistic style, and his high ethos in the minds of many of his auditors and readers.

Habits of Preparation

His attitude toward speaking and writing of course varied from episode to episode and from youth to old age, but in general, writing and speaking did not come easily, and his excellence resulted only through much hard work. Late in life he wrote in an unpublished manuscript: "Forty years ago there was nothing I disliked so much as the labour of writing. It was a task I desired to get over and done with as soon as possible."[1] In his autobiography he wrote that when he was a young medical student "and for many years afterwards, [he] detested the trouble of writing, and would take no pains over it."[2] But he *did* come to take pains over it. He confessed to Lizzie in 1854 that his "pen is not a very facile one, and what I write costs me a good deal of trouble"[3] in expenditure of time and energy. He wrote late in life, "Sheridan's reply to the lady who told him that his writings were such charmingly easy reading—"Easy reading, madam is damned hard writing"—has never got into the general mind; and very few of the thousands of delighted listeners, I imagine, ever had an inkling of what these facile discourses cost the lecturer."[4] In his 1888 article in the *Pall Mall Gazette*, he gave an interesting account of his speech preparation habits.

> The use, to me, of writing, sometimes of rewriting half a dozen times over, that which I threw aside when I had finished it, was to make sure that the framework of what I had to say—its logical skeleton, so to speak—was, so far as I could see, sound and competent to bear all the strain put upon it. I very early discovered that an argument in my head was one thing, and the same argument written out in dry bare propositions quite another in point of trustworthiness. In the latter case, assumptions, supposed to be certain while they lay snug in one's brain had a trick of turning out doubtful; consequences which seemed inevitable proved to be less tightly connected with the premises than was desirable; and telling metaphor showed a curious capacity for being turned to account by the other side. I have often written the greater part of an address half a dozen times over, sometimes upsetting the whole arrangement and beginning on new lines, before I felt I had got the right grip of my subject. A subordinate, but still very important use of writing, when one has to speak, is that the process brings before the mind all the collateral suggestions which are likely to arise out of the line of argument adopted. . . . [Furthermore] it is just when the strange intoxication which is begotten by the breathless stillness of a host of absorbed listeners weakens the reason and opens the floodgates to feeling that the check of the calmly considered written judgment tells, even if its exact words are forgotten.[5]

Approaching retirement he seemed to find it more difficult to prepare his major addresses, as he expressed it to a younger colleague. "I believe that getting things into shape takes me more and more trouble as I get older—whether it is a loss of faculty or an increase of fastidiousness I can't say—but at any rate it costs me more time and trouble to get things finished—and when they are done I should prefer burning to publishing them."[6]

Preparing his essays likewise took much revising and multiple drafts. He thought nothing of "writing a page four or five times over if nothing less will bring the words which express all that I mean, and nothing more than I mean."[7] In 1882 he wrote to a younger friend:

> My own way is to write and re-write things, until by some sort of instinctive process they [his articles] acquire the condensation and symmetry which satisfies me. And I really could not say how my original drafts are improved until they somehow improve themselves.[8]

To another correspondent Huxley wrote after his retirement, "When I get to a certain point of tinkering my phrases I have to put them aside for a day or two."[9] In 1889 he confessed to Knowles about a recently submitted article to the *Nineteenth Century*. "I did not take the trouble to write the article over and over again. ... I have been punished for my laziness,"[10] as critics roughed him up badly. Having completed the enormous task of cataloging the Huxley Papers at the Imperial College, Warren Dawson commented on Huxley's preparation of his written materials.

> Throughout his life he seldom wrote a dozen lines without cutting up his text—altering, deleting, or interpolating words and phrases in almost every sentence. And when at last he was sufficiently satisifed with his copy to send it to the printer, the arrival of the proofs signalized the onset of another attack on his prose. Some specimens of his corrected proof-sheets are preserved amongst his papers and these show the same process of altering, deleting, and inserting that his manuscripts display: indeed he at times almost rewrote his articles when in proof. ... [I]t cannot be said that writing was an easy and natural gift to Huxley, for his papers demonstrate quite the contrary, namely that it was painful and laborious.[11]

Even Huxley's letters often have many crossed out words, phrases, and sentences with substitutions inserted. While untidy at times, it showed his concern for saying exactly what he wanted to say. As one contemporary put it, Huxley's "clearness and careful finish" are "due not solely to an inborn gift of language, but in larger part to persistent painstaking."[12] Though he grumbled over the time and effort expended in writing and lecturing—a familiar human protestation—he had an underlying satisfaction in believing that it all was in behalf of the cause of science and the new reformation. Obviously he was willing to continue to perform despite his claimed dislike for the task. In short, Huxley has left the advice and the model to aspiring communicators that to be successful takes much hard work.

Blending of Thoughts and Words

Huxley demonstrated that if communication is to be clear and effective, then thought and expression should be closely intertwined. One's writing and speaking will not be clear if one's thoughts are not clear. Huxley's article on Darwin's *Origin of Species* in *Macmillan's Magazine* in 1859 drew from Darwin the excited reaction: "You have explained my leading idea with admirable clearness. What a gift you have of writing (or more properly) thinking clearly."[13] In his autobiography in 1876 Darwin wrote that Huxley's "mind is as quick as a flash of lightning and as sharp as a razor. He is the best talker whom I have known."[14] This talent of blending thought processes with effective expression had been noted by others very early in Huxley's life. For example, his anatomy teacher at Charing Cross Hospital, T. Wharton Jones, in writing a testimonial for Huxley's application for that position in Toronto in 1851, said that Huxley "possesses the faculty of communicating knowledge with clearness and logical precision."[15] Late in the century, Spencer told the story about his friend Huxley that when personal writing habits were being discussed at a dinner gathering,

> some describing the difficulty they had in getting into the swing of it, and others saying they found it easy at the outset. Lewes, one of the last, said—"I never hesitate. I get up the steam at once. In short, I boil at low temperatures." "Well, but," remarked Huxley, "that implies a vacuum in the upper region."[16]

Late in life Huxley wrote that "to be accurate in observation and clear in description is the first step towards good scientific work,"[17] and that "full and familiar knowledge is the condition of successful exposition."[18] He asserted that "by dint of learning and thinking" one acquires "clear and vivid conceptions" of subject matter, and then one needs to take "infinite pains to embody these conceptions in language exactly adapted to convey them to other minds."[19] Henry Sidgwick wrote of Huxley being "unrivalled in the clearness, precision, succinctness, and point of his statements, in his complete and ready grasp of his own system of philosophical thought, and the quickness and versatility with which his thought at once assumed the right attitude of defence against any argument coming from any quarter."[20] Near the end of Huxley's life his old friend Hooker wrote of the former's "grasp of mind, powerful reasoning, and admirable style."[21] George Jacob Holyoake wrote that "when Professor Huxley speaks or writes, his style seems the product of an original mind dwelling in an atmosphere of realities."[22] Early in the twentieth century William T. Thiselton-Dyer wrote that Huxley "had the gift of genius in clothing the pregnant thought with the living words that clinch it, drive it home. I do not know any writer in whom thought and expression are more completely wedded."[23] One of Huxley's recent biographers has succinctly summed it up. "One feels sure that [Huxley] found his ideas before he found his phrases.''[24] Rigor of mind and carefulness of tongue were indeed inextricably bound together.

The Style Is the Man

Huxley firmly agreed with the dictum that style is the man. Late in life he advised; ''Buffon said that a man's style is his very self, and in my judgment it ought to be so. The business of a young writer is not to ape Addison or Defoe, Hobbes or Gibbon, but to make his style himself, as they made their styles themselves. ... Nothing comes of imitation but that every man's style should express his own individuality.''[25] Reflecting *his* individuality, there was a verve and vivacity, energy and earnestness about Huxley's presentations. In 1851 Prof. Edward Forbes had testified that the young applicant's writings ''are remarkable for force of expression and clearness of language.''[26] During Huxley's midcareer, Darwin wrote that his friend ''never writes and never says anything flat,''[27] and *The Spectator* commented on a lecture by Huxley, ''so much bottled life does he infuse into the driest topic on which human beings ever contrived to prose.''[28] His admirer Holyoake exuberantly summarized Huxley's lifetime efforts, stating that the latter's ''sentences are as fresh as bunches of grapes gathered the same morning, the bloom is upon them.''[29]

Acknowledged rhetorical influences helping to mold him as a communicator were few. Late in life he indicated: ''I never had the fortune, good or evil, to receive any guidance or instruction in the art of English composition. It is possibly for that reason I have always turned a deaf ear to the common advice to 'study good models'.''[30] He did, however, acknowledge his indebtedness to his physiology teacher at Charing Cross Hospital, Thomas Wharton Jones.

> The extent and precision of his knowledge impressed me greatly, and the severe exactness of his method of lecturing was quite to my taste. I do not know that I have ever felt so much respect for anybody as a teacher before or since. I worked hard to obtain his approbation, and he was extremely kind and helpful. ... It was he who suggested the publication of my first scientific paper ... and most kindly corrected the literary faults which abounded in it. ... [31]

He greatly admired the oratory of his friend Tyndall and the great Faraday, who for many years delivered excellent public lectures at the Royal Institution.[32] The only other orator who is praised by Huxley as a potential influence is his famous contemporary, John Bright. Wilfrid Ward, Huxley's neighbor at Eastbourne records his conversation with Huxley.

> One of the subjects of his enthusiasm was John Bright—his transparent sincerity, his natural distinction, his oratorical power. . . . "His was the only oratory which ever really held me. His speeches were masterpieces. There was the sense of conviction in them, great dignity, and the purest English."[33]

What better succinct summary of Huxley's rhetorical values! Huxley was impressed with the clear and simple style of Descartes.[34] He acknowledged his indebtedness to Carlyle for the latter's emphasis on precise and clear writing and speaking, but he did not think Carlyle followed his own advice too well, and late in life he wrote, "I was rather inclined to take him [Carlyle] as a great tonic; as a source of intellectual invigoration and moral stimulus and refreshment, rather than a theoretical or practical guidance."[35] It should also not be overlooked that Huxley's wife and close friends such as Darwin, Knowles, and Hooker helped considerably in toning down some of his strong statements present in preliminary drafts.[36]

Broadly conceived, science and literature were influences on his rhetorical style. Science emphasizes singleness of purpose, careful word choice, word economy, clarity, and simplicity. Alan Paton, the distinguished midtwentieth century literary figure, once wrote that "training in the more exact sciences has a great influence on one's literary style, . . . to make it more simple and more clear. Such a training teaches the writer to avoid overembellishment and extravagance."[37] Huxley's former laboratory assistant, W. H. Flower, showed the relationship in Huxley's scientific method and rhetorical style when he wrote,

> In dissecting, as in everything else, he [Huxley] was a very rapid worker, going straight to the point he wished to ascertain with a firm and steady hand, never diverted into side issues, nor wasting any time in unnecessary polishing up for the sake of appearances.[38]

Huxley's wide reading in literature, like Darwin's,[39] gave him a literary grounding that would astound most contemporary scientists and that fed into his writing and speaking endeavors. He was firmly rooted in the Bible, Shakespeare, Milton, Descartes, Spinoza, Hobbes, Carlyle, Mill, Hume, Berkeley, and devoured an extremely wide menu of English, French, and German literature. His American friend, John Fiske, observed that Huxley "was an omnivorous reader. ... [He] seemed to read everything worth reading,—history, politics, metaphysics, poetry [and], novels. ... This reading was in various languages."[40] As Blinderman put it, Huxley "alluded with graceful erudition to Greek and Norse mythology, Persian and Indian fairy tales, Hindu and Egyptian scriptures, the Bible, to the art, music, literature, history, and philosophy of East and West."[41] When Huxley was separated from his family to teach for a term in Edinburgh in 1876, he brought quite a bit of reading material with him, and a letter to his wife gives an interesting insight into a postlecture habit. "I have been getting through an enormous quantity of reading. ... When I come back from my lecture I like to rest for an hour or two over a good story. It freshens me wonderfully."[42] One observer wrote shortly after Huxley's death, "Behind his great scientific work and colossal industry thereon, there lurked a really stronger literary taste."[43]

Behind these general and specific influences on Huxley's rhetorical style there lurked a distinct individuality, and as his protégé, E. R. Lankester, wrote, in Huxley's case "more than in that of his contemporaries it is strictly true that the style is the man."[44]

Extemporaneous Mode of Oral Presentation

Of the four modes of oral delivery—impromptu, memorized, speaking from manuscript, and extemporaneous—Huxley disliked and distrusted the first three. The impromptu speech suggested lack of thought, and he felt that "the burden of going through the process [of memorizing a speech] would be intolerable," so he "never committed the written matter to memory."[45] Likewise, he was not comfortable reading from a manuscript, and in his early speaking efforts, he confessed, he "clung to [his] copious MS. as a shipwrecked mariner to a hencoop."[46] Of course for major occasions, such as the Romanes Lecture in the Sheldonian Theatre in 1893 he spoke from a carefully prepared manuscript.[47]

Both in the classroom and on the public platform he came to be a highly effective user of the extemporaneous mode of presentation, that is, being in firm command of the ideas, having the organization clearly worked out, preparing drafts and notes, but leaving the exact words to the actual moment of delivery. Among the Huxley Papers in the Imperial College archives one can find rough notes of some of his speeches and lectures. He often enumerates items, sometimes indenting subpoints, but in a very sketchy manner. In his 1888 *Pall Mall Gazette* article he gives a description of his habits in this regard. For major addresses he at first wrote them out, then, as he became more experienced he used

> brief but still elaborate notes—not unfrequently, however, having the big MS. in my pocket to fall back upon in case of an emergency, which, by the way, never arose. Then the notes got briefer and briefer, until I have known occasions on which they came down to a paragraph. But the aid and comfort afforded by that not too legible scrawl upon a small sheet of paper was inexpressible. ... if I were put to it I could very well do without notes [but], I have never willingly been without them—at any rate in my pocket. At public dinners and ordinary public meetings they have long ceased to come out; but, on more serious occasions, I have always had them before me, though I very often forgot to look at them. I think they acted as a charm against ... physical nervousness.[48]

Nature gave him no great gift of tongue, and he had a long struggle with nervous tension when giving a public address. He jokingly blamed it on his nurse, who, at the time of his infancy, upon seeing a swarm of bees at the window, hastily shut them out, which only stopped them from settling on his lips and giving him "mellifluous eloquence."[49] He continued in his autobiography, "I disliked public speaking, and had a firm conviction that I should break down every time I opened my mouth. I believe I had every fault a speaker could have."[50] In his 1888 *Pall Mall Gazette* article he wrote, "For twenty years I never got up to speak without my tongue cleaving to the roof of the mouth."[51] He continued:

> I have never quite got over [nervousness], and the origin of which has always been a puzzle to me. With every respect for the public, I cannot say I ever felt afraid of an audience; and my cold hands and dry mouth used to annoy me when my hearers were only students of my class, as much as at other times.[52]

A year before his death he wrote that he used to suffer badly from "lecture-fever."[53] By midcareer it had ceased to be so much of a "bugbear"[54] to him, and he did succeed in gradually controlling it.[55] The first few minutes of his public addresses seemed to be the worst, but then he settled down and came to realize that by the end of a speech he could experience "the keenest of pleasures" having been substituted "for one of the greatest of the smaller miseries of life."[56] Usually, however, he continued to suffer from nervous exhaustion following lectures.

Huxley did not have a strong voice, which was most noticeable in a very large assemblage or when he was very tired or ill. It has already been noted how difficult it was for the audience to hear him during a speech at Oxford in 1860, when he was responding to Wilberforce. After his Lord Rector's address at the University of Aberdeen in 1874 to an audience of approximately two thousand, he wrote to his wife, "As the address took me an hour and half to deliver, and my voice has been very shaky ever since I have been here, I did not dare to put too much strain upon it, and I suspect that the people at the end of the hall could have heard very little."[57] In 1876 during his speech in Nashville he apparently "had scarcely any voice"[58] as he was very tired, and at Johns Hopkins he encountered the same problem.[59] During one of his addresses in New York City, some of the members of the audience actually had to call out for him to speak louder.[60] A month before he delivered the prestigious Romanes Lecture in the Sheldonian Theatre in Oxford at the age of sixty-eight and suffering from the flu, he wrote to Romanes that he was grappling with influenza and "as usual with me it affects my voice."[61] Romanes responded on 27 April, "Lest your voice should fail during the lecture, I will have the Public Orator, or some other important reader, in readiness, to take your place."[62] A week before the lecture Huxley wrote to Sir Sidney Lee, "I am but very slowly shaking off the effects of influenza, and shall be fortunate if I can make myself heard at Oxford next week,"[63] and three days before the lectures Huxley wrote to Tyndall that due to the flu he was losing his voice and was worried about the lecture. "What will happen when I try to fill the Sheldonian Theatre is very doubtful."[64] Huxley's neighbor at Eastbourne, Wilfrid Ward, later reminisced, "I saw him more than once before he went to deliver the lecture, and he was suffering both from weakness and from loss of voice—so much so, that he doubted his being able to deliver it at all."[65] Fortunately Huxley was able to read his speech, but could not be heard too well.[66] Just think of how much more effective Huxley might have been if he had had electronic loud speaking systems at his disposal. He does serve as an example, then, than one may be an excellent orator without having a bombastic voice.

Popular Expositor

Huxley's ability to make science understandable and interesting to the general public, both in his writing and in his public speaking, is one of his lasting accomplishments in his legacy as a communicator. He is traditionally spoken of as "the foremost popularizer of science in the nineteenth century,"[67] and is still praised today as one of the greatest popularizers of science of all times.[68] In 1855 he wrote to his friend Dyster:

> I enclose a perspectous of some People's Lectures (*Popular* Lectures I hold to be an abomination unto the Lord) I am about to give here. I want the working classes to understand that science and her ways are great facts for them. . . . I . . . mean to see what I can do with these hard headed fellows who live among facts.[69]

Huxley "felt a strong interest in working-men, and was much beloved by them."[70] Throughout his life he gave not only these special workingmen's lectures, but also an endless number of lectures to popular audiences of all types, spreading the message of the substance and method of science, hoping to inform, persuade, and edify his audiences.

When publishing in American in 1863 Huxley's popular scientific lectures, the D. Appleton Company enthusiastically pronounced, "The gift of translating the highest question of science into popular forms of expression, without sacrificing accuracy and introducing error, is a very rare one among scientific men, but Professor Huxley possesses it in an eminent degree; his lectures are models of their class."[71] This early publisher's promotional hype has met well the test of time. Blinderman has summarized succinctly the task of the popularizer.

> The popularizer of science is obligated to express himself in such a way that his language will be scientifically accurate and at the same time comprehensible to a lay audience. If he popularizes controversial material, he must further effect a balance between the objectivity of expository prose and the subjectivity of argumentative prose in his effort to convince a hostile public of the truth of new ideas.[72]

Huxley was fully aware of the danger of being labeled "a mere popularizer,"[73] of being thought of as one who did not have much solid substance behind one's veneer. Huxley and Hirst once discussed this problem in relation to Tyndall, and Hirst recorded in his journal: "From Tyndall's lectures one would not expect the man to be so governed by vigorous accuracy of thought as he is. The element of pleasing popularity he introduces would certainly mislead many as to his natural cast of severe thought."[74] Many no doubt thought the same about Huxley, but his close friends and many others knew the mental rigor, commitment to accuracy, abundance of data, and depth of insight behind his statements.

One year before his death, Huxley summarized his attitude toward the popular lecture.

> I have not been one of those fortunate persons who are able to regard a popular lecture as a mere *hors d'oeuvre*, unworthy of being ranked among the serious efforts of a philosopher. . . . On the contrary, I found that the task of putting the truths learned in the field, the laboratory and the museum, into language which, without bating a jot of scientific accuracy shall be generally intelligible, taxed such scientific literary faculty as I possessed to the uttermost.

Half of the justification of the popular lecture was "in the self-discipline of the lecturer" and "the other half in its effect on the auditory . . . though I venture to doubt if more than one in ten of an average audience carries away an accurate notion of what the speaker has been driving at; yet is that not equally true of the oratory of the hustings, of the House of Commons, and even of the pulpit?" He continued, "The most zealous of popular lecturers can aim at nothing more than the awakening of a sympathy for abstract truth, in those who do not really follow his arguments; and of a desire to know more and better the few who do."[75] He likewise emphasized that the lecturer should remember Faraday's admonition to assume that the audience knew very little if anything about the subject to be discussed.[76]

To Huxley, science and literature joined hands in the popularizing of science. In the Huxley Papers in the Imperial College Archives is an undated Huxley manuscript in which he expresses that there is an aspect of

> scientific work which seems to me to have an indisputable claim to the title of literature—I mean the work of the popular expositor—of the man who being a well-qualified interpreter of nature translates that interpretation out of the hieratic language of the experts into the demotic vulgar tongue of all the world. I call this literature—for it seems to me to be the essence of literature—that it embodies great emotions and great thoughts in such form that they touch the hearts and reach the apprehensions not merely of the select few but of all mankind. That is the work which lies before every man of science who is worthy of the name who addresses a popular audience. . . . [He should be mindful] that every subject is a unity and however vast it may be embraced by a single discourse; that full and familiar knowledge is the condition of successful

exposition; that every sentence should be a link in a chain of ideas; that entire good faith is the best way of showing respect for one's hearers or readers.[77]

Tributes to Huxley's effectiveness as a popularizer of science are of course endless. One observer wrote that Huxley "has no equal as an expounder, both to scientific and popular audiences, of matters difficult to comprehend. Nor perhaps is it too much to say that no one before ever wrote with such marvellous clearness, united with equal literary finish." In fact, that writer continued, "When a good speech is desired on any subject, with which a broad-minded scientist might be thought qualified to cope, an Englishman instinctively thinks of Huxley."[78] Even Huxley's antagonists praised "his truly marvelous power of popular exposition."[79] The many eulogies at Huxley's death invariably highlighted his legacy of being a popularizer of science par excellence. For example, on the other side of the world the editor of the *Rangoon* (Burma) *Gazette* wrote that to Huxley (and Tyndall) "were due the first steps taken towards popularising science," and they "showed the world that the truths of science could be taught in language as lucid and beautiful as any."[80] Huxley illustrated what a recent treatise has called "true popularisation [of science] which, when done in depth, induces the public really to meditate on science and demand an effort of attention and understanding."[81]

A number of ingredients contributed to his effectiveness as a popularizer. he wisely selected an appropriately narrow subject. Asa Gray early detected this strong point, indicating that part of Huxley's merit as a lecturer was that he would "select some good topic or point of view and make a clear exposition of it, the clearness of which very much depends upon his not scattering himself over too much ground."[82] Furthermore, Huxley was, as Blinderman put it, "always careful to keep to the mean between the incomprehensibly complex and the insultingly simple."[83] Although Huxley brought material to the level of his audience, he also made them work.[84] With his orientation toward a mechanical engineer's sense of structure and unity, Huxley developed clear organization, greatly aiding comprehension for the reader or auditor. Word economy, even in conversation,[85] was a trademark. He regarded "rhetorical verbosity as the deadliest and most degrading of literary sins,"[86] and contemporaries often spoke of his "habit of never wasting words,"[87] though of course he occasionally did not live up to that.

One of the most important ingredients was Huxley's frequent and effective use of figurative language. Metaphors, similes, and analogies abound. He is looked upon as one of those unusual people, especially among scientists, who could employ such language colorfully and yet not sacrifice the accuracy of his statements. It has been customary to warn scientists against using figurative language.[88] A number of scholars have analyzed Huxley's effective use of figurative language.[89] Huxley's heavy reliance on the military and roadblock metaphors as central motifs in his rhetoric have already been noted, as well as his employment of naval and gardening analogies, among others. It is also important to note his tendency to use animal metaphors when characterizing his opponents, much as is done in wartime rhetoric, which relegates one's foes to subhuman status, leading one to treat them more roughly. To cite just two illustrations, it has been noted how in 1859 he wrote to Darwin about "the curs which will bark and yelp"[90] about the ideas in the *Origin*, and thirty years later he wrote that "the pack give tongue just as loudly as ever"[91] in hostile reaction to Huxley's *Nineteenth Century* articles. In general, Huxley's "telling figures of speech"[92] were a prime stylistic characteristic that made his speaking and writing more appealing, and that have remained one of his important trademarks.

Two additional ingredients characterized and helped to entrench Huxley's effectiveness in his lecturing. His unusually expert use of visual aids, such as charts and artifacts, and his skillful sketches on the blackboard, often with colored chalks, enlivened his presentations.[93] Finally, he possessed an important intangible asset, which separates the outstanding from the mediocre lecturer—a sense of poetic cadence. He advised aspiring orators that they need an "artistic sense of rhythm and proportion," which give "grace to force, and, while loyal to truth, make exactness subservient to beauty."[94] Not many scientists would dare assert that. Not many lecturers could deliver that.

Advocate

Having discussed in earlier chapters his role as a foremost advocate of science, of Darwinism in particular, and as a vigorous antagonist of orthodox theology, his central rhetorical legacy as an effective practitioner of argumentation has been demonstrated. It would be well to recall his autobiographical summary of his life of advocacy written four years after his retirement.

To promote the increase of natural knowledge and to forward the application of scientific methods of investigation to all the problems of life

... to the popularisation of science; to the development and organisation of scientific education; to the endless series of battles and skirmishes over evolution; and to untiring opposition to that ecclesiastical spirit, that clericalism, which ... is the deadly enemy of science.[95]

He has been called "a savage polemicist"[96] by some, but by others "a skilled dialectician."[97] The quality is admittedly open to varying interpretations and labeling. One friendly contemporary wrote at Huxley's death: "No doubt he will pass into history as a born fighter. The combative instinct was in him, but it was very far from being merely pugnacity. He fought for that which he thought to be true and right."[98] He took great pride in "defending," whether it be the cause of science, Darwinism and Darwin, or other individuals. For instance, when he heard of the death of his close friend Tyndall, his immediate letter to Knowles included this revealing self-characterization, "You know how I stood up for him against all comers."[99] Near his retirement Huxley wrote to his friend Hooker, "I am not usually accused of unwillingness to fight (in spite of being a man of peace) when any great interest is at stake. ..."[100] His assertion that he preferred peace, is a familiar claim of many who love controversy. As a twentieth-century intellectual historian once put it, "Skilled controversialists are normally those who enjoy the exercise, however much they may protest that they do not do so."[101] Leslie Stephen summarized well Huxley's advocacy by selecting two key adjectives, that is, that Huxley was "a strenuous and honourable combatant."[102]

Huxley's contemporaries inevitably highlighted his pugnacious characteristic. Walt Whitman said that Huxley had "a fighting gift that would appall me if I was in the opposition,"[103] and the president of the Royal Academy, when introducing Huxley on one occasion, spoke of the latter's "doughty sword play when he jousts in the controversial lists."[104] Henry Sidgwick wrote to Leonard Huxley about his father's participation in the Metaphysical Society debates. "I seem to remember him as the most combative of all the speakers who took a leading part in the debates. ... I used to think that he liked fighting."[105] Likewise, James Knowles wrote to Leonard that Huxley was one of two in the Metaphysical Society who supplied the most lively verbal dueling, but "never with a touch of lost temper or lost courtesy."[106] Huxley on occasion displayed the talent to exude gentleness when in reality he was inflicting a damaging blow. For example, he once admitted to Knowles that mildness in one of his articles was not "the softness of the answer which turneth away wrath, but with that of the pillow, which smothered Desdemona."[107] His friend Spencer characterized one of

Huxley's magazine articles. "As usual [it], exemplifies the hand of iron in the glove of velvet."[108] Huxley also could have a disarming gentleness in interpersoonal communication, as illustrated by Darwin's autobiographical statement, "From his [Huxley's] conversation no one would suppose that he could cut up his opponents in so trenchant a manner as he could do and does do."[109] But Wilfrid Ward, a Catholic adherent, found his elderly Eastbourne neighbor in conversation to be "less in the spirit of philosophic inquiry than in that of a clear-headed but convinced advocate, whose ultimate positions are absolutely predetermined."[110] A more flexible Huxley was described by D. J. H. Gladstone, a member of the London School Board with Huxley, who wrote that board members "found that with all his [Huxley's] strong convictions and lofty ideals he was able and willing to enter into the views of others, and to look at a practical question from its several sides."[111] Some felt that "his bark was much worse than his bite."[112]

It is too strong to say, as one biographer has asserted, that Huxley's poor health was largely responsible for his militant, aggressive nature,"[113] but it is true that ill health acted as a sort of catalyst, stirring him to action against the foe of orthodoxy. For example, when ill health forced him to retire early from teaching and to resign his presidency of the Royal Society, he used his leisure time for reading and writing in the area of theology. Early in his retirement he wrote to a friend, "When I am ill (and consequently venomous), nothing satisfies me but gnawing at theology; it's sort of crib-biting."[114]

His combative spirit was of course only a part of his legacy as an advocate, for his impressive accumulation of evidence was acknowledged, as was his skill in reasoning. Of course, his foes challenged his evidence and his conclusions but he held up under fire, and left a legacy as one who argued cogently and courageously against strong antagonists. He became recognized as an articulate, intelligent, and courageous spokesman for a cause in which he thoroughly believed. Posthumous eulogies emphasized that he was a model for those who were committed to free and responsible expression. E. B. Poulton wrote that Huxley "stands out as the man to whom more than to any other we owe the gift of free speech and free opinion in science."[115] In America the editor of the *Nation* wrote that "hardly anyone, either in England or in America, dared to express more freely the conclusions which he reached, after honest and conscientious study,"[116] and Huxley's friend O. C. Marsh wrote that "every man of science to-day is indebted to Huxley for no small part of the intellectual freedom he enjoys."[117]

Ethos

One of the central factors in the effectiveness of rhetoricians is that they should be perceived by the audience to possess high ethos. That is, the rhetor should be seen to possess a high degree of expertise and trustworthiness. A number of ingredients were present to generate high ethos in Huxley's case, which strengthened his effectiveness despite his challenging certain aspects of the status quo, which stands as an important part of his rhetorical legacy.

For instance, although he was conspicuously out of step with, or far in advance of, his generation in religious and scientific attitudes, he clearly aligned himself with the broad political, economic, social, and cultural status quo. While many freethinkers were associated with radical ideas and movements, Huxley demonstrated that he was an integral part of the free enterprise, laissez-faire, middle-class society. He was a life long Liberal, opposed Home Rule for Ireland, and despised radical political and economic ideas, being appalled, for instance, by the ideas of Henry George. He was of the professional wing of the rising middle class, which was becoming dominant in late nineteenth-century Britain. His professional occupation, and his accomplishments and honors attendant thereto, gave him notoriety and prestige, and brought him a large listening and reading audience of the best elements in society. He was a pioneering biological experimenter, an effective teacher and administrator, a talented public lecturer, and an author of many scientific treatises, essays, books, and reviews. He was a respected member and officer of numerous learned societies and social clubs, and was associated with the leading scholars of his generation. He was the recipient of scientific medals and honorary academic degrees, and was made an honorary member of numerous scholarly societies in foreign lands. He served devotedly on ten royal commissions, was elected to the first London School Board (1870–72), and in the twilight of his life was appointed to the Privy Council.

The changes in the social order, which Huxley advocated, were changes that many church people and members of the rising middle class also supported. He publicly disavowed slavery, for he was convinced that it was bad for the master as well as for the slave. He sympathized with many of the problems of the working classes, and favored increased opportunities for women. He favored the secularization of Sunday, and he occasionally spoke out against the evils of excessive use of alcohol, though he was strongly out of harmony with the religious absolutism of the temperance movement. As a biologist he was acutely sensitive to the issue of vivisection. Although he abhorred cruelty to animals and claimed that he never dissected a living creature without first rendering it insensible to pain, he nevertheless advocated the right of scientists to engage in vivisection in the interests of physiology and in the hope of alleviating future human suffering.

Educational reforms were of course at the top of his concerns, and here again a number of church people and other foes agreed with his emphases. As early as 1858, Huxley and his friend Hooker both agreed that "the present mode of teaching is worse than useless,"[118] and Huxley labored throughout his life to improve it. His insistence on extemporaneus lecturing, laboratory instruction, and the use of museums, marked him as a leading reformer of science education. His persistent efforts to reform London University, and his active role in adult education, won him much prestige as an innovative educational reformer. During his two years on the London School Board he did much to mold the educational structure, and his advocacy to keep the Bible in the curriculum as a moral guide did much to rehabilitate him in the eyes of many of his religious foes. He advocated more governmental aid to education and less church control. A major curricular modification, of course, which he advocated throughout his life, was the inclusion of science into the curriculum to a much greater extent than it currently was, and a championing of the idea that science was really a humanistic, liberalizing, area of study, much as literature and other so-called liberal arts were. Together, the classical and the modern, and the humanities and the sciences, should join hands in the great enterprise of education.

Furthermore, Huxley imaged the values of his society by advocating and exemplifying Victorian orthodoxy in matters of morality, family, and sex. He disavowed the free love emphasis of some other free-thinking individuals. His marriage, and the happiness that was present in his large family circle, made him an example of the best type of family man. With twelve years of happy home life behind him, he wrote to Haeckel, the Huxley of Germany, upon the occasion of his friend's marriage, "The one thing for men, who like you and I stand pretty much alone, and have a good deal of fighting to do in the external world, is to have light and warmth and confidence within the four walls of home."[119] Huxley's good moral character robbed his enemies of any scandal-mongering, which was possible against some other rationalists.

Huxley possessed other personality traits that helped to make him a respected and effective partisan. Honesty and integrity were prime characteristics, and they were matched by candor and tenacity. Sincerity, earnestness, and courage were important trademarks, as were his sense of duty, his sensitivity to injustice, and his devotion to what he felt truth to be. His utter commitment to truth and honesty was illustrated in 1860 when in the depths of despair at the death of his young son, he replied to the clergyman, Charles Kingsley, "I have searched over the grounds of my belief, and if wife and child and name and fame were all to be lost to me one after the other as the penalty [for his religious views] still I will not lie."[120] It is important, however, to note Ward's observation that Huxley "tended to identify outspoken candour with love of truth, and prudent reservation or patient suspense of judgment with insincerity."[121]

Thus, Huxley mirrored many of the values of his generation, and strengthened accordingly, his ethos and rhetorical effectiveness. He chopped away at only one major root of British society, while actually being a conservative husbandman of the tree of British culture. He was able to reach and influence people who would be appalled by rationalists not possessing those virtues. Near the end of his life, he was pleased to hear that he "got named in the House of Commons last night as an example of a temperate and well-behaved blasphemer."[122] Part of Huxley's rhetorical legacy, then, is to suggest to potential advocates of change that their chances of success may be greater if they make it clear that they are hewing only one root.

Rhetorical Legacy in the United States

Huxley's rich rhetorical legacy has had, and continues to have, a notable presence in the United States. There were the usual tributes by contemporary admirers. In 1881 an observer claimed that Huxley was more influential in the United States than any other nonpolitical Englishman.[123] The controversial freethinker, Robert Ingersoll, in 1889 wrote to Huxley: "For many years I have read your books, lectures, and essays with the keenest pleasure. You are one of my mental creditors and will always remain so."[124] Ingersoll included the following tribute in one of his public lectures: "No man ever had a sharper sword—a better shield. He challenged the world. ... Huxley had intelligence, industry, genius, and the courage to express his thought. He was absolutely loyal to what he thought was truth."[125] In 1889 Huxley received fulsome praise from a Brooklyn admirer: "It seems to me that you are greater than you think— probably the greatest man of our century; indisputably the most effective (and I do not forget Darwin). The charm of your personality you can never know, whatever your greatness."[126] In 1892 he was informed that the All Souls' Universalist Church in Grand Rapids, Michigan, had included in its cornerstone, a copy of his address on the "Advance of Science in the last half century."[127] Walt Whitman ecstatically praised Huxley's rhetorical virtues.[128]

More significantly, authors of American textbooks in the field of rhetoric have, throughout the twentieth century, referred to Huxley's lectures and essays for illustrative material. He continues to be found in speech anthologies, in books on general public speaking, in textbooks specifically in argumentation and persuasion, in books on interpretive reading and interpersonal communication, in textbooks on rhetoric/composition/communication, and in general college readers.[129]

These textbooks have used Huxley as a model of courageous free expression, clear exposition, effective argumentation, skillful use of evidence, and sound inductive, deductive, and causal reasoning. His works are cited so as to teach clear defining, vivid describing, incisive analyzing, and effective drawing of concrete illustrations and examples from everyday experiences. He encourages students to make careful vocabulary selection, employ vivid figurative language, and develop rhythmical phrasing, skillful sentence constructions, and helpful outlines. His introductions are cited as good examples of how to catch attention, how to announce clearly the proposition and its main subheads, how to convey the relevance and importance of the subject, and how to demonstrate that the subject is not too difficult for the audience to grasp. Students are also directed to him for effective transitions, summaries, and tight coherence. He is used to teach refutation techniques, how to anticipate and parry opposing arguments. The historic encounter with Wilberforce is used to illustrate an effective counterattack against supposedly diversionary taunts of an opponent. Students are encouraged to use his extemporaneous mode of delivery and to learn to use notes for guidance in speaking. He is mentioned as an example of a highly talented writer and speaker who found it necessary to make numerous revisions, hence, less capable students should realize that they ought to do the same. His works are included in rhetoric textbooks, in order to give students ideas for their speeches or papers, or to provide scientific materials for class discussion.

Some of his better students and their students, secured positions at important American universities and spread his ideas and rhetorical techniques. Henry N. Martin in 1876, while teaching biology at Johns Hopkins, made commendable innovations.[130] One of Huxley's former students, Henry F. Osborn, described the everwidening influence of Huxley:

> When called to Princeton in 1880 as assistant professor of comparative anatomy, I introduced the Huxley method of extemporaneous lectures and laboratory verification to my college classes, and ten years later when called to Columbia University to lay the foundations of the department of zoology, I introduced the same method to the larger graduate and under-graduate classes. Thus ... between the years 1880 and 1908, the broad Huxleyan method had been widely extended over the United States.[131]

That Huxley remains eminently quotable in the United States at the present time may be illustrated by the twenty-five Huxley quotations in the 1980 edition of *Bartlett's Familiar Quotations*,[132] and by the fourteen Huxley quotations in George Seldes's 1985 volume, *The Great Thoughts*.[133] A recent textbook in mass communication ethics called upon Huxley to reinforce the need for honesty. "The foundation of morality is to have done, once and for all, with lying."[134]

Conclusion

Out of a small obscure village now part of greater London, a youth in a family of little material wealth, social prominence, or emotional warmth grew to become a leading biologist, educator, and rhetorician in late nineteenth-century Britain. Educated by internal curiosity, medical training, and a lengthy naval expedition, he edged slowly into the world of science, eventually establishing a professional career, and propelled himself throughout life with workaholic energy. He was to gain prominence and accumulate many honors. Early in his career he won a Royal Society Gold Medal, and eventually became president of the Royal Society and the recipient of their Copley Medal. He became president of the British Association and a leader in learned societies. He long served as a prestigious professor and dean at the Royal School of Mines, was an examiner at the University of London, a frequent lecturer at the Royal Institution, and was elected to the first London School Board and to the post of lord rector of Aberdeen University. He served on ten royal commissions and eventually became a privy councillor. Prime ministers, the highest of church officials, and prestigious scientific powers felt his rhetorical thrusts.

Until the age of thirty, communication in person or via letter with three respected confidantes, his eldest sister, Lizzie; his fiancée, Nettie; and a surrogate older sister, Mrs. Ellen Busk, was of central importance in his maintaining a career direction into science and in bringing confidence and stability to an often discouraged and distraught young man. To be able to have such trusted private confidantes with whom he could communicate his innermost personal and professional concerns, was a significant backstage factor in the life of this future public communicator.

His important maiden public lecture in 1852, on the eve of his twenty-seventh birthday, at the prestigious Royal Institution, was a wonderful opportunity to crystallize and publicize his developing independent views before London's leading scientists and socialites. It increased his stature among the powers in science, and gave him

186

great confidence in public speaking, pushing him forward toward becoming one of the most eloquent of Victorian spokesmen for science.

A second significant rhetorical event examined here was Huxley's historic sharp encounter at the age of thirty-five with the powerful Bishop Samuel Wilberforce at the British Association meeting in Oxford in 1860, which countinues to draw the attention of academia and the general public. It projected the scientific controversy over Darwinism into appearing to be a conflict between science and theology, instead of essentially within the former, it projected Huxley into the broad public view more quickly than would otherwise have been the case, and it reinforced his recognition of the importance of public speaking. The episode demonstrated that Huxley could not only clearly communicate the findings of science, but could also boldly and effectively defend science from its detractors, including powerful and eloquent leaders within the established church. His assertiveness emboldened younger scientists in their efforts to gain freedom from scientific traditionalism and ecclesiastical dogma. It cemented the closeness of Huxley and Darwin, entrenching the latter's gratefulness, as he expressed it twenty years later shortly before his death in a letter to Huxley: "I well know how great a part you have played in establishing and spreading the belief in the descent-theory, ever since that grand review in the *Times* and the battle royal at Oxford up to the present day."[1]

In the third decade of his active professional life, at the age of fifty-one, his 1876 lecture tour of the United States became another significant rhetorical milestone, as it expanded his influence to the broader world scene. It had a bonding effect between Huxley and scientists, educators, and publishers in the American republic celebrating its centenary. It tied him more firmly to individuals and to their research findings, to the membership of the American Association for the Advancement of Science, and to the birthing of Johns Hopkins University. He inspired scientists and science educators throughout the country, especially those who advocated evolution. The tour entrenched his reputation as one of the foremost English scientific leaders, as a talented lecturer, and as a leader in behalf of freedom from the constraints of academic and ecclesiastical traditionalism. He inspired many nineteenth-and twentieth-century Americans whose lives were embroiled in public controversy.[2] More importantly, perhaps, his rhetorical legacy has persisted by his being cited, up to the present time, in American textbooks in public speaking, persuasion, rhetoric, and communication, and in speech anthologies and college readers. Some of his former students secured key positions in American universities and spread not only his scientific ideas and methodologies, but also his rhetorical emphases. In 1925 a knowledgeable science educator asserted, "I know that more than six hundred students are now profiting annually by this Huxleyan method [extemporaneous lecturing and laboratory experimentation]. . . . in American, Canadian, and British universities."[3]

In the English-speaking world Huxley still serves as an outstanding example of a scientist who is capable of clarifying scientific material to all types of audiences—learned and lay as well as students. He could render complicated subject matter understandable and appealing without sacrificing accuracy and without becoming trivial. An admirer, Moncure Conway, wrote in his autobiography:

> I never missed on of his [Huxley's] lectures, whether at the Hunterian, Royal, or London institutions, or at workingmen's institutes, and at St. George's Hall. . . . Huxley was a perfect lecturer,—as artistic and finished in speaking to workingmen as when addressing a learned audience. Without notes, without a hesitating or a superflous word, simple, lucid, he carried every mind with him.[4]

Just as Huxley spent much of his time translating German and other works into English, so he also fulfilled the rhetorical role of translating complex scientific material into everyday language.

Huxley is equally remembered today as a highly effective advocate, a skilled, intelligent, articulate, and vigorous controversialist. His numerous rhetorical contributions from 1860 until his death in 1895, in lectures before varying audiences, in periodicals such as the *Fortnightly Review* and the *Nineteenth Century*, in books and prefaces to books, and in letters to the *Times*, placed him in the front lines of what he perceived to be a battle with the adherents of orthodox theology in his defense of science in general, and Darwinism in particular. During the decade following his retirement, he remained unusually active rhetorically, as theologically grounded foes stirred his fighting spirit to new heights. He is acknowledged by most, including many of his adversaries, to be a principled advocate fighting honorably for a cause that he believed to be true and good. "To him," an admirer in 1925 rather gushingly reminisced, "a man's principal duty was to hold and defend the truth, and to let nothing in life come between him and it. We had in Huxley a perfect example of zeal in preaching: there never was a more faithful servant of the truth."[5] Huxley carried with him a strong moral fervor, what one has called "the power of wrath,"[6] much akin to the righteous indignation of an Old Testament prophet. Detractors would call the trait excessive combativeness, a chronic pugnacious flailing at foes. Some would say that while "Huxley was capable of shedding light, . . . he took too much pleasure in engendering heat."[7] That he did indeed enjoy it, despite his many denials, seems quite clear.

All would agree that it took much courage for him to speak out as he did. In the first Huxley Memorial Lecture, delivered in 1900, his fellow X Club member, John Lubbock, now Lord Avebury, said, "It required much courage to profess his opinions,. . . . we owe much to him for the inestimable freedom which we now enjoy."[8] In 1925 another person paying tribute to Huxley emphasized, "The great event of Huxley's career was his defence of Darwin, leading on to something much wider and deeper, the defence of freedom for thought."[9] Unquestionably he was a leader, not afraid to be the first to step into the jungle and to remain there slashing away at the brush, clearing a path. In his vigorous life of advocacy, it is important to note that former students committed to orthodox theology have verified that he scrupulously kept his controversial theological views out of the classroom.[10]

His rhetorical stance was one in which a hero figure was fighting the forces of falsehood and superstition. In this simplistic, two-valued mindset, he was engaged in warfare on behalf of science. A respected historian of science recently asserted that "the polematically attractive warfare thesis is historially bankrupt. . . . [for] it assumes the existence of two static entities, 'science' and 'religion', . . . it distorts a complex relationship that rarely, if ever, found scientists and theologians in simple opposition [and]; it celebrates the triumphs of science in whiggish fashion."[11] More specifically, in this confrontation between good and evil, Huxley was adopting a rhetorical stance more similar to theologians than he would probably care to acknowledge. Rhetorically he was a secular theologian. He reflected an attitude of being an inspired messenger, but his "revelations" came not from a God-inspired Scripture, but from what nature had revealed to him and to other scientist through human observation, experimentation, and reason. He harbored a strong sense of having been "called" by nature to do what he was doing. He was "saved" from ignorance, whereas his foes were not. He viewed himself as a roadblock remover, engaged in the task of getting rid of dangerous obstacles standing in the pathway of science and humankind. This central metaphor generated a vivid hero's image, for he thus became a courageous servant of his fellowmen, seeking only to remove an unwanted obstruction. he was a positive, constructive individual engaged not in tearing down something but in creating an opening through which his fellowmen could stream unharrassed into the promised land. He felt assured of final victory, for "Truth" was on his side.

Just as major religions such as Christianity, Judaism, and Islam pride themselves on being mono-theisms, so Huxley was driven by a sense of oneness, of unity, in his outlook and in his resultant rhetoric. His Eastbourne Catholic neighbor, Wilfrid Ward, reminisced, "He [Huxley] said to me once, in 1894, 'Faulty and incorrect as is the Christian definition of Theism, it is nearer the truth than the creed of some agnostics who conceive of no unifying principle in the world'."[12] Darwinism provided for him that unifying principle, a sense of structure to all natural knowledge, an orderliness to life and the universe, which appealed to his mechanical engineer proclivity. Looking back on his life, Huxley wrote, "What I cared for was the architectural and engineering part of the business [natural science], the working out the wonderful unity of plan in the thousands and thousands of diverse living constructions, and the modifications of similar apparatuses to serve diverse ends."[13] A former student of his reminisced that in his classroom lectures "the interest of morphology stood out clearest and central to all"; Huxley had once told him, "'You see, I should have been an engineer!'"[14] Another person looking back on Huxley's life, wrote, "Surveying the whole field of Nature, he [Huxley] sought to formulate a comprehensive schema as the plan of all natural plans. ... His cardinal tenets [were] one order of Nature, one evolutionaray process."[15] Evolution provided a sense of symmetry and completeness, bringing order out of chaos.

Huxley's yearning for oneness worked itself out in many ways. As a biologist he was concerned with bringing together botany and zoology, and his leadership brought together the ethnologists and anthropologists. He sought to integrate the laboratory, museum, classroom, public platform, and printed page into one great learning enterprise. He blended the theoretical and practical, and academia and the larger society, seeking to have scientific advancements work for practical benefits, for the grander enrichment of all humanity. As one contemporary scholar of Huxley has put it, "Always Huxley envisioned science as a great social and intellectual venture, a synthesis of knowledge in an endeavor that had been vital to humanity since the beginning of civilization."[16] A former student summarized it this way: "Breadth and depth, culture from every source, ... faith in the educational value of science without prejudice to the classics, these were the keynotes of Huxley's influence as a teacher and writer.''[17] Huxley viewed science and the humanities as harmonious bedfellows, as long as the latter gave the former his share of the bed. They were two sides of the same coin, complementary not opposites, like the yin and yang of Eastern religions. In fact, he even felt that science and the true religious spirit were one, for it was the dogmatic ecclesiastical spirit, the superstitious frame of mind, buttressed by a powerful clerical hierarchy that he was fighting. Stephen Jay Gould has put it well when he writes that Huxley, "though not anti-religious, was uncompromisingly and pugnaciously anticlerical.''[18]

Comtemporary American and British historians of science have drawn some astute observations regarding the similarity of Huxley's rhetoric to that of theological rhetoric. Frank Turner has asserted that "the dogmatc science" of Huxley and his allies "nurtured a new variety of honest doubter who questioned the all-sufficiency of contemporary scientific concepts, theories, and categories to describe and interpret every facet of life" just as the dogmatic religionists had created honest doubters like Huxley.[19] David Knight has pointed out that "the process whereby men of science began to take upon themselves the role of wise men or prophets, who can advise their contemporaries on all kinds of topics, has continued from the nineteenth century when men like T. H. Huxley took over this role from the clergy.''[20]

He stands as a prime example to would-be rhetoricians, that to be successful in one's advocacy one needs to possess a high ethos, that is, qualities of expertness and trustworthiness, which auditors and readers can perceive and honor. It has been seen that while he was weakening the traditional religious element in Victorian society, he was actually bolstering other important social, political, economic, educational, and moral values, and hence was a highly respected person. Many eulogies emphasize that it was Huxley the person which influenced them, rather than any specific ideas he was advocating. His personal traits of honesty, candor, sensitivity to injustice, sense of duty, and integrity were acknowledged, even by foes.

As a writer and speaker Huxley left a legacy of distinct characteristics. He demonstrated that thoughts and words must mesh, and that style should reflect the authenticity of the uniqueness of the person. He exemplified the importance of thoroughly being in command of one's subject matter, and of engaging in a disciplined and conscientious construction of multi-drafts in the preparation process. His carefully chosen words and phrases and cadence brought clarity and beauty to his expressions, so that, as one former student said, "lectures in zoology became also a lesson in the English language."[21] The editors of the four volumes of his scientific memoirs, Foster and Lankester, in their preface hoped that younger scientists would read them not only for their scientific information, but to "be brought to know models of style, patterns of sincerity and lucidity of exposition, which haply they may set before themselves as standards towards which they may strive."[22] Joined by his wit and bitter tongue, his expressions achieved memorability; as one biographer put it, Huxley "had a gift for the apt and acid phrase which reverberates after weaker words are forgotten."[23] He was one who used concrete illustrations and examples effectively, defined terms and concepts carefully, and organized clearly. He is still cited as a master of the colorful use of anaolgies and metaphors without distortion of content. He integrated science and literature with ease, weaving into his works much insightful and appealing literary references and allusions. Sir Leslie Stephen, with his literary insights, asserted that "Huxley's best essays deserve to be put on a level with the finest examples of Swift" or other great literary figures.[24]

Additional characteristics are part of his legacy as a lecturer in and out of the classroom. He was a skillful practitioner of the extemporaneous mode of delivery, being able to hold the attention of audiences for a long period of time. His punctuality in beginning lectures and his no-nonsense, businesslike progression in a concise and direct manner were trademarks. While testimonies differ as to the amount of humor he employed, there is universal acclaim of his ever-present use, whenever feasible, of visual aids, particularly his skillful colored chalk sketches on blackboards. He serves as an example that a speaker can be effective without having a strong commanding voice, vigorous gestures, or flamboyant manner, and that nervous tension can be controlled through effort and time. Of course, voices of the indifferent our unimpressed seldom appear in selective tributes, but at least one former student helps to give some balance, when he reminisced that Huxley's lectures "were too didactic, the treatment too special and detailed for my taste. . . . [He] had a definite tendency to pontificate. . . . As a lecturer, apart from his fluency, he made no special impression upon me, but his blackboard drawings were fascinating."[25]

To view only the public rhetoric of a person and overlook his private communication networks is to catch only a portion of that person. Just as we have explored the important private interaction with his three confidantes early in life, so we have analyzed the behind-the-scenes X Club network, with which Huxley regularly and frequently interacted for decades. His public rhetorical battles were greatly bolstered by being a part of such a group of close scientific friends, which served as an intimate fraternity and a scientific cuacus, a source of intellectual stimulation, and a significant forum for evaluating each other's work. The club became a source of nominators and supporters helping members gain various preferments. It was instrumental in developing connections with American publishers and scientists. The members of the club successfully marshaled their efforts in the furtherance of their views as against foes within science, religion, education, or politics. The club played a large role in the affairs of the Royal Society, the Royal Institution, the British Association, various learned societies, and science education in general. While difficult to measure exactly the effect of the X Club, it can be said that the Victorian scientific scene and the lives of the club members would have been significantly less rich without the X Club, and it surely was pivotal to the life of Huxley. To understand the dynamics of the X Club is to acknowledge the admonition recently made. "Historians of science are becoming aware that the true value of their contribution to learning lies more and more in recognizing the so-called nonscientific factors that once molded the endeavors of any individual."[26] Scholars of communication likewise are becoming increasingly alert to the importance of private communication networks in organization decision-making and in the personal fortunes of individuals.

The most private interpersonal communication network of all of course, was his family, to whom he was deeply devoted. Nettie outlived him by nineteen years, and late in life she left a brief reminiscence, which reveals some of his characteristics and their life together:

> It was the eternal goodness in him that set our lives upon a plane far higher than that of most people. He was so simply truthful—grand in the performance of duty—unswerving from what he thought to be right. . . . His keen sense of fun, his ready wit & stores of knowledge, & intellect of the highest order, would of themselves have made our joint lives interesting. But it was the rich brightness of his great enfolding love for me, that for our forty years of wedded life knew no shadow of change, save increase of love, that brought about something of the divine light into our house. The eternal goodness in him drew me on unconsciously to better things. . . . There was a strong dualism in his nature. To a hard logical incisive intellect was united the tenderest & most loving of hearts. To the outside lookers on, especially before his whole fine character became known, intellect was all they saw.[27]

His extremely busy life did not leave much time for being with the children, but as one person put it, Huxley "loved to imagine that he was entirely ruled by his family and spoke of himself as chicken-pecked as well as hen-pecked."[28] His biographer-son Leonard has penned some family memories,[29] and such distinguished grandsons as Sir Julian, Aldous, and Sir Andrew have perpetuated the legacy of Thomas Henry.

Tributes to Huxley the man and his rhetorical powers abound. In 1881 C.S. Minot gave a concise précis of Huxley's efforts and their effect up to that point in time:

> The employment of his very rare gifts has exerted a profound influence over the lives and welfare of many Englishmen. He has dealt frankly, ably, and courageously with many burning questions of life and faith. He has scattered broadcast the yeast of new ideas; leavening public opinion with doubt of the traditions of authority and with distrust of the child-like faith our fathers often had.[30]

By the end of his life most critics had greatly mellowed their views toward him, and the public saw him in a considerably more favorable light than they had in earlier decades. As one biographer has summarized it, Huxley was "at first only a brilliant young scientist, then a dangerous infidel, finally a revered oracle."[31] Numerous obituary tributes following his death can be found among the Huxley papers in the Imperial College archives.[32] In 1900 his friend John Lubbock concisely stated, "The truth is that Huxley was one of those all-around men who would have succeeded in almost any walk of life."[33] More recently, the historian J. H. Plumb has written:

> Victorian biology could have had no better publicist than T. H. Huxley. . . . [He was] a rugged spirit, full of courage and compassion. And he was a splendid writer—clear, pungent, convincing—a man who was as true to himself as to his ideas.[34]

A contemporary scholar has appropriately concluded the following about Huxley's rhetorical legacy:

> [Huxley] was not only a determined and forthright speaker in the cause [of science], but a writer so highly regarded that his place in English literature is secure. It was not too difficult to earn the reputation of a controversialist; but very few men can back up the reputation with writings of enduring quality, and fewer yet can say as much of value as Huxley did about so many different subjects.[35]

Numerous tangible reminders of Huxley have come into being: the Huxley Memorial Tablet in Ealing Public Library, old and new Huxley buildings at the Imperial College, a statue in the British Museum (Natural Science), numerous busts and portraits, memorial lectures, and even tiny Huxley Island off the coast of New Guinea. But even more enduring of course is the multi-sided intellectual and rhetorical legacy he has left in his writings and in his speeches. His voluminous works stand for ready reference, and he still is being frequently quoted and cited in the fields of science and rhetoric, as the centenary of his death approaches. Few can claim such longevity. Few there are about whom it can be said, that after the passage of a century they still stand as acknowledged premier communicators for science.

Appendix

Some American textbooks that have perpetuated Huxley's rhetorical legacy include: (1) speech anthologies, (2) general public-speaking textbooks, (3) argumentation and persuasion textbooks, (4) books on interpretive reading and interpersonal communication, (5) textbooks on rhetoric/composition/communication, and (6) general college readers.

(1) David J. Brewer, *The World's Best Orations* (St. Louis, 1901); Houston Peterson, *A Treasury of the World's Great Speeches* (New York, 1954); Carroll C. Arnold, Douglas Ehninger, and John C. Gerber, *The Speaker's Resource Book* (Chicago, 1961); Wil A. Linkugel, R. R. Allen, and R. L. Johannesen, *Contemporary American Speeches: A Sourcebook of speech Forms and Principles* (Belmont, Calif., 1965, 1969); James H. McBath and Walter R. Fisher, *British Public Address, 1828–1960* (Boston, 1971).

(2) J. Berg Esenwein, *How to Attract and Hold an Audience* (New York, 1902); James A. Winans, *Public Speaking: Principles and Practice* (Ithaca, N.Y., 1915); William Doll, *The Art of Public Speaking* (Chicago, 1927); John M. Clapp and Edwin A. Kane, *How to Talk* (New York, 1928); Charles H. Woolbert and A. T. Weaver, *Better Speech*, rev. ed. (New York, 1932); Charles H. Woolbert and Joseph F. Smith, *Fundamentals of Speech: A Textbook of Delivery*, 3rd ed. (New York, 1934); Edith E. Gattis, *Vitalize Your Speech* (Caldwell, Idaho, 1938); John Dolman, Jr., *A Handbook of Public Speaking* (New York, 1944); Lew Sarett and William T. Foster, *Basic Principles of Speech,* rev. ed. (Boston, 1946); John Dixon, *How to Speak* (New York, 1949); Wilbur E. Gilman, Bower Aly, and Loren D. Reid, *The Fundamentals of Speaking*, 3rd ed. (New York, 1960); John F. Wilson and Carroll C. Arnold, *Public Speaking as a Liberal Art* (Boston, 1964, 1968, 1974, 1978, 1983); Kenneth G. Hance, D. C. Ralph, and M. J. Wiksell, *Principles of Speaking* (Belmont, Calif., 1965, 1969); Horace G. Rahskopf, *Basic Speech*

Improvement (New York, 1965); Carl H. Weaver, *Speaking in Public* (New York, 1966); Jane Blankenship, *Public Speaking: A Rhetorical Perspective* (Englewood Cliffs, N.J., 1966).

(3) George P. Baker, *Specimens of Argumentation* (Boston, 1893); George P. Baker, *Principles of Argumentation* (Boston, 1895); William T. Foster, *Argumentation and Debating* (Boston, 1908, 1932); J. H. Gardiner, *The Making of Arguments* (Boston, 1912); Harry F. Covington, *The Fundamentals of Debate* (New York, 1918); Harold F. Graves and Carle B. Spotts, *The Art of Argument* (New York, 1927); George P. Baker and H. B. Huntington, *The Principles of Argumentation*, rev. ed. (Boston, 1925); Wayne C. Minnick, *The Art of Persuasion* (Boston, 1957); W. W. Fearnside and W. B. Holther, *Fallacy: The Counterfeit of Argument* (Englewood Cliffs, N.J., 1959).

(4) Harry B. Gough, L. Rousseau, Mary E. Cramer, and J. W. Reeves, *Effective Speech: A Textbook for Beginning Courses* (New York, 1930); A. T. Weaver, Gladys L. Borchers, and Charles H. Woolbert, *The New Better Speech* (New York, 1938); Donald K. Darnell and Wayne Brockriede, *Persons Communicating* (Englewood Cliffs, N.J., 1976).

(5) Harrison Ross Steeves, *Representative Essays in Modern Thought: A Basis for Composition* (New York, 1913); George Sensabaugh and Virgil K. Shitaker, *Purposeful Press: A Statement of Principles, with Selections* (New York, 1951); Francis Connolly, *A Rhetorical Case Book* (New York, 1959); William E. Buckler and W. C. McAvoy, *American College Handbook of English Fundamentals* (New York, 1960); J. W. Corder and Lyle H. Kendall, Jr., *A College Rhetoric* (New York, 1962); Richard E. Hughes and P. A. Duhamel, *Rhetoric: Principles and Usage* (Englewood Cliffs, N.J., 1962); James L. Sanderson and W. K. Gordon, *Exposition and the English Language* (New York, 1963); Lawrence D. Brennan, *Modern Communication Effectiveness* (Englewood Cliffs, N.J., 1963); John E. Jordan, *Using Rhetoric* (New York, 1965); Jim W. Corder, *Rhetoric: A Text-Reader on Language and Its Uses* (New York, 1965); W. Ross Winterowd, *Rhetoric and Writing* (Boston, 1965); Edward P. J. Corbett, *Classical Rhetoric for the Modern Student* (New York, 1965); Phillips Damon, John Espey, and Frederick Mulhauser, *Language, Rhetoric and Style* (New York, 1966); Newman P. Birk and G. B. Birk, *Understanding and Using English*, 4th ed. (New York, 1967); W. Ross Winterowd, *Rhetoric*:

A Synthesis (New York, 1968); William Pratt, *The College Writer: Essays for Composition* (New York, 1969); Cleanth Brooks and Robert Penn Warren, *Modern Rhetoric*, 3rd ed. (New York, 1970); Eilene R. Rall, Karl E. Snyder, Caroline D. Eckhardt, James F. Holahan, and David Stewart, *The Wiley Reader: Designs for Writing* (New York, 1976).

(6) Harrison Hayford and H. P. Vincent, *Reader and Writer* (Boston, 1954); Harold C. Martin and Richard M. Ohmann, *Inquiry and Expression: A College Reader* (New York, 1958); Lawrence V. Ryan, *A Science Reader* (New York, 1959); N. P. Birk and G. B. Birk, *Ideas and Style* (New York, 1960, 1969); James Kruezer and Lee Cogan, *Studies in Prose Writing* (New York, 1961); Kenneth L. Knickerbocker, *Ideas for Writing* (New York, 1962); George Levine and Owen Thomas, *The Scientist vs. The Humanist* (New York, 1963); Marvin Laser, R. S. Cathcart, and Fred H. Marcus, *Ideas and Issues: Readings for Analysis and Evaluation* (New York, 1963); Michael W. Alssid and William Keeney, *The World of Ideas: Essays for Study* (New York, 1964); Jim W. Corder, *Readings for College Rhetoric* (New York, 1964); Leslie Fiedler and Jacob Vinocur, *The Continuing Debate: Essays on Education for Freshmen* (New York, 1964); John Wasson, *Subject and Structure: An Anthology for Writers*, 2nd ed. (Boston, 1966); William R. Seat, Jr., Paul S. Burtness, and W. U. Ober, *The University Reader* (New York, 1966); Ralph H. Singleton and Stanton Millet, *An Introduction to Literature* (Cleveland, 1966); Paul A. Jorgensen and F. B. Shroyer, *A College Treasury: Prose*, 2nd ed. (New York, 1967); Mark Schorer, Philip Durham, and E. L. Jones, *Harbrace College Reader* (New York, 1968, 1972); K. L. Knickerbocker and H. W. Reninger, *Interpreting Literature*, 4th ed. (New York, 1969); William Pratt, *The College Writer: Essays for Composition* (New York, 1969); Arthur F. Kinney, K. W. Kuiper, and L. Z. Bloom, *Symposium* (Boston, 1969).

Notes

Introduction

1. *The Pall Mall Gazette*, 24 October 1888.
2. Stephen Jay Gould, "Knight Takes Bishop?" *Natural History* (May 1986): 95:33.
3. Huxley is being rather modest here, for despite lack of training, his artistic skill was considerable.
4. T. H. Huxley, *Autobiography*, in *Collected Essays*, 9 vols. (New York: D. Appleton, 1897), 1:3–4 (hereafter cited as *Autobiography*).
5. Leonard Huxley, *Life and Letters of Thomas Henry Huxley*, 2 vols. (New York: D. Appleton, 1916), 1:69 (hereafter cited as *LL*).
6. *Autobiography*, 8.
7. Ibid., 8–9.
8. Ibid., 13–14.
9. Ibid., 6–7.
10. Ibid., 12.
11. Ibid.
12. *LL*, 1:27, 29.
13. Huxley to Henrietta Heathorn, 16 September 1852, Huxley-Heathorn Correspondence, fol. 222, Imperial College (hereafter cited as Huxley-Heathorn Correspondence).

Chapter 1. Early Confidantes

1. David A. Roos, "Neglected Bibliographical Aspects of the Works of Thomas Henry Huxley," *Journal of the Society for the Bibliography of Natural History* 8 (May 1978) :419. See also *LL*, 1:15. As an appendix to his excellent article, Roos has included Huxley's small journal (pp. 413–20). The original is to be found in the Huxley Manuscripts, vol. 23, Imperial College.
2. Roos, "Neglected Bibliographical Aspects," 419; *LL*, 1:15.
3. *LL*, 1:38.
4. Julian Huxley, ed., *T. H. Huxley's Diary of the Voyage of H.M.S. Rattlesnake* (Garden City, N.Y.: Doubleday, Doran & Co., 1936), 72–73 (hereafter cited as *Rattlesnake Diary*).
5. *LL*, 1:29. For additional sources on Huxley's experiences on this scientific expedition, see M. Bassett, *Behind the Picture: H.M.S. Rattlesnake's Australia-New Guinea Cruise* (Melbourne: Oxford University Press, 1966); A. Lubbock, *Owen Stanley R.N. 1811–50: Captain of the Rattlesnake* (Melbourne: William Heinemann, 1968); A. J. Marshall, *Darwin and Huxley in Australia* (Sydney: Hodder & Stoughton, 1970); J. Macgillivray, *Narrative of the Voyage of H.M.S.

Rattlesnake (London: T. & W. Boone, 1852); T. H. Huxley, "Science at Sea," *Westminster Review* 61 (January 1854): 53–63.

6. *LL*, 1:36.

7. *Rattlesnake Diary*, 71.

8. This refers to Miss Henrietta Heathorn, his fiancée.

9. *Rattlesnake Diary*, 71.

10. Ibid., n. 1; Ronald W. Clark, *The Huxleys* (London: Heinemann, 1968), 14–15, 26.

11. *LL*, 1:40.

12. Ibid., 41.

13. Ibid., 47–48.

14. Ibid., 69.

15. Ibid., 66.

16. Ibid., 69.

17. Ibid., 67.

18. Ibid., 103–4.

19. Ibid., 109; Huxley Papers, vol. 31, fol. 20, Imperial College.

20. *LL*, 1:114.

21. Ibid.

22. Ibid.

23. Ibid., 116. For insight into Huxley's rising and falling hopes for the Toronto post, see Huxley-Heathorn Correspondence, fols. 159–61, 168–70, 181, 185; *Rattlesnake Diary*, 285, 287; *LL*, 1:100, 108, 116.

24. *LL*, 1:127 (italics in original).

25. Ibid., 129.

26. Ibid., 127.

27. Ibid., 169; Huxley Papers, vol. 31, fol. 24. The Huxley's second child and first daughter, was named after Jessie, Lizzie's daughter who had died in 1850 (ibid.; *LL*, 1:67).

28. *LL*, 1:498.

29. Henrietta Huxley, "Reminiscences," in Cyril Bibby, ed., *The Essence of T. H. Huxley* (London: Macmillan, 1967), 27.

30. For accounts of their courtship, see ibid., 27–29; *Rattlesnake Diary*, 61–66; Clark, *Huxleys*, 21–23.

31. *Rattlesnake Diary*, 63.

32. Ibid., 64–66.

33. Ibid., 66.

34. Ibid., 63.

35. *LL*, 1:42.

36. Ibid., 67.

37. *Rattlesnake Diary*, 78.

38. Ibid., 99.

39. *LL*, 1:40.

40. Ibid., 48.

41. Ibid., 42.

42. *Rattlesnake Diary*, 135.

43. Ibid., 208.

44. Ibid., 276.

45. Henrietta Heathorn Journal, *Rattlesnake Diary*, 235.

46. 10 August 1849, ibid.

47. Now and throughout their lives, she called him "Hal," not "Tom."

48. 11 April 1850, *Rattlesnake Diary*, 244.
49. Ibid., 228.
50. Ibid., 229–30.
51. *LL*, 1:67.
52. Ibid., 110.
53. Huxley-Heathorn Correspondence, fol. 220.
54. *LL*, 1:109.
55. Ibid., 110.
56. Ibid., 89.
57. Huxley-Heathorn Correspondence, fol. 190.
58. *LL*, 1:109.
59. Huxley-Heathorn Correspondence, fol. 222.
60. *LL*, 1:110–11.
61. Ibid., 91.
62. Huxley-Heathorn Correspondence, fol. 216.
63. *LL*, 1:117. See also Huxley's *Autobiography*, 15.
64. Huxley-Heathorn Correspondence, fol. 280; *LL*, 1:118–19.
65. Huxley-Heathorn Correspondence, fol. 281. For some additional letters that discuss his 1854 successes, see ibid., fols. 260–62, 267, 271, 275, 276; *LL*, 1:127–29; Huxley to Rev. John Barlow, 8 May, 3 July, 1854, T. H. Huxley Letters, Royal Institution, London.
66. *LL*, 1:117, 119, 128.
67. Ibid., 137.
68. Huxley-Heathorn Correspondence, fol. 186.
69. Huxley to Dr. Dyster, 6 May 1855, *LL*, 1:136.
70. 21 November 1850, ibid., 67.
71. 28 December 1852, Huxley-Heathorn Correspondence, fol. 238.
72. 1 February 1852, ibid., fol. 185.
73. Ibid., fols. 185, 266; Huxley Papers, vol. 11, fols, 206–7. In 1855 Busk resigned from active surgical practice and settled in London where he devoted all his time to scientific pursuits.
74. Huxley-Heathorn Correspondence, fol. 238.
75. Ibid., fol. 221; Huxley Papers, vol. 11, fols. 208–9.
76. For references to this translation enterprise, see Huxley Papers, vol. 11, fols. 210–14; vol. 19, fols. 276, 278–79.
77. Ibid., vol. 11, fols. 215–16.
78. Huxley-Heathorn Correspondence, fols. 281, 285, 287; Tyndall Correspondence, vol. 9, fol. 2866, Royal Institution.
79. *LL*, 1:135.
80. Huxley-Heathorn Correspondence, fols. 165, 185.
81. Ibid., fol. 165 (italics in original).
82. Ibid., fol. 185.
83. Ibid., fol. 165.
84. Ibid., fol. 216.
85. Ibid., fol. 238 (italics in original).
86. Ibid., fol. 163.
87. Ibid., fol. 165 (italics in original).
88. Mr. and Mrs. William Fanning lived in London from May 1850 until August 1852, when they started on their return voyage to Sydney (Huxley-Heathorn Correspondence, fols. 130–31, 135, 137, 144–45, 154, 160, 167, 169–70, 176, 182, 192, 214, 216–18; *Rattlesnake Diary*, 280).

89. Huxley-Heathorn Correspondence, fol. 185.
90. Ibid., fol. 216.
91. Ibid., fol. 238.
92. Ibid., fol. 281.
93. Ibid., fols. 165, 185, 216, 223.
94. Ibid., fol. 165.
95. Ibid., fol. 136.
96. He apparently had left London on 9 or 10 August (Ibid., fol. 281).
97. Ibid., fol. 285.
98. Ibid., fol. 287.
99. Tyndall Journals, vol. 3, fol. 744.
100. H. Huxley, "Reminiscences," 29.
101. Huxley Papers, vol. 15, fols. 61, 67.
102. Huxley-Heathorn Correspondence, fol. 375.
103. Ibid., fol. 382.
104. Ibid., fol. 385.
105. Journals of Thomas Archer Hirst, vol. 3, fol. 1517, Royal Institution (hereafter cited as Hirst Journals; italics in original).
106. Ibid., vol. 5, fol. 2728.
107. Huxley Papers, vol. 31, fol. 31.
108. H. Huxley, "Reminiscences," 30.
109. Ibid., 32.

Chapter 2. Maiden Public Address, 1852

1. To trace the role that Forbes played in getting Huxley started on his career, see Huxley-Heathorn Correspondence, fol. 138, 143, 144, 156, 158, 159, 209, 221, 180; *LL*, 1:27, 29 ,30, 42, 46, 64, 65, 68, 71–73, 94, 96, 102–4, 112–13, 116–20, 122–26, 128–29; *Rattlesnake Diary*, 25, 259, 283; *The Athenaeum* (London), 12 July 1851, p. 754; *Report of the Sixteenth Meeting of the British Association for the Advancement of Science* (London: John Murray, 1848), 95.
2. Huxley-Heathorn Correspondence, fol. 189.
3. Huxley Papers, vol. 31, fol. 19; *LL*, 1:108.
4. *Autobiography*, 15.
5. *Rattlesnake Diary*, 44.
6. *Autobiography*, 15.
7. Huxley-Heathorn Correspondence, fol. 156.
8. Huxley to Dr. Thomson, 27 July 1851; *Rattlesnake Diary*, 284.
9. Huxley-Heathorn Correspondence, fol. 156.
10. *LL*, 1:96. See Huxley Papers, vol. 37, fols. 12, 43.
11. Huxley-Heathorn Correspondence, fol. 157.
12. Ibid., fol. 158.
13. Huxley Papers, vol. 12, fol. 67.
14. Ibid., vol. 31, fol. 67.
15. Tyndall Correspondence, vol. 9, fol. 2859 (italics in original). See Geoffrey Parr, ed., *Michael Faraday's Advice to a Lecturer* (London: Royal Institution, 1960), passim.
16. For a description of the homemade towing net used by Huxley and Macgillivray, the naturalist on the *Rattlesnake* expedition, see John Macgillivray,

Narrative of the Voyage of H.M.S. Rattlesnake, 2 vols. (London: T. & W. Boone, 1852), 1:27.

17. *Autobiography*, 13–14.

18. *Rattlesnake Diary*, 78.

19. *LL*, 1:40.

20. Ibid., 49.

21. For a list of his writings, see ibid., 81–82, 99–100. 116; 2:488-89.

22. *Rattlesnake Diary*, 8.

23. *LL*, 1:69.

24. Huxley-Heathorn Correspondence, fols. 189, 192 (italics in original).

25. Ibid., fol. 189.

26. *LL*, 1:64–65, 68–71.

27. Ibid., 64.

28. For these Royal Society successes, see Huxley-Heathorn Correspondence, fols. 138, 142, 144, 152, *Rattlesnake Diary*, 283; *LL*, 1:72–76, 87, 99, 103–5, 109–13.

29. *The Athenaeum*, 12 July 1851, p. 754; *LL*, 1:98.

30. *LL*, 1:98.

31. Ibid., 75, 76, 87.

32. *Rattlesnake Diary*, 56–57.

33. *LL*, 1:99–106, 114.

34. Ibid., 23–24; *Rattlesnake Diary*, 15–17.

35. Huxley-Heathorn Correspondence, fol. 191.

36. Edward Forbes to Royal Society (Committee of Papers), 27 July 1852, Referee's Report 2, item 113. See also item 114, Royal Society of London.

37. Huxley-Heathorn Correspondence, fol. 136.

38. *LL*, 1:69 (italics in original).

39. Ibid., 87.

40. See ibid., 27, 64–65, 68, 74, 102–3; *Rattlesnake Diary*, 280.

41. *LL*, 1:102.

42. Huxley-Heathorn Correspondence, fol. 191 (itlaics in original). In publishing this letter, Leonard Huxley left out Owen's name (*LL*, 1:105).

43. *LL*, 1:67.

44. Huxley to W. Macleay, 9 November 1851, ibid., 100.

45. Huxley Papers, vol. 31, fol. 19; *LL*, 1:108 (italics in original).

46. Huxley-Heathorn Correspondence, fols. 195–96.

47. Huxley Papers, vol. 31, fols. 17–19; *LL*, 1:107.

48. *LL*, 1:4, 104; Huxley-Heathorn Correspondence, fol. 147. For some of his letters to his mother, see *LL*, 1:30, 33–34, 36–38, 41–42, 46–47, 49. In May 1851 Huxley wrote to Lizzie that he was planning to move his lodgings, which would be "close to my mother's, against whose forays I shall have to fortify myself" (*LL*, 1:104).

49. Huxley-Heathorn Correspondence, fol. 200.

50. Thomas Martin, *The Royal Institution* (London: Royal Institution, 1961), 67. Other brief accounts of the life of the Institution are A. D. R. Caroe, *The House of the Royal Institution* (London: Royal Institution, 1963); and K. D. C. Vernon, "The Foundation and Early Years of the Royal Institution," *Proceedings of the Royal Institution* 39 (1963): 364–402 (reprint in pamphlet form).

51. The current system of spreading the twenty lectures over the whole academic year began in 1929, with eight in the fall term, eight in the winter term, and four in the short spring term.

52. Martin, *Royal Institution*, 44.

53. Huxley-Heathorn Correspondence, fol. 189.

54. Ibid., fol. 192.

55. Huxley Papers, vol. 31, fol. 19; *LL*, 1:108.

56. Huxley to John Fiske, HM 13255, Huntington Library, San Marino, Calif. (hereafter cited as H.L.).

57. A. S. Eve and C. H. Creasey, *Life and Work of John Tyndall* (London: Macmillan, 1945), 58.

58. Huxley-Heathorn Correspondence, fol. 189. See also ibid., fol. 200.

59. Faraday, *Advice to a Lecturer*, 3.

60. Huxley to Lizzie, 3 May 1852, Huxley Papers, vol. 31, fol. 19; *LL*, 1:108. See also Huxley to Henrietta, 30 April 1852, Huxley-Heathorn Correspondence, fol. 200.

61. Upon Huxley's return to England in November 1850 and until April 1851 he had stayed with George and his wife (Huxley-Heathorn Correspondence, fols. 129, 139, 162, 167, 176, 221, 267, 279, 287; Huxley to Lizzie, 20 May 1851, *LL*, 1:104) and Huxley had written to George from Sydney (Huxley Papers, vol. 31, fols. 47, 50, 52). See also *LL*, 1:92, 268, for Huxley's amicable relationship with George and Polly.

62. John Barlow to Huxley, 24 April 1852, Huxley Papers, vol. 10, fol. 229.

63. Huxley-Heathorn Correspondence, fol. 189.

64. File 108 (*Index for Friday Evening Meetings*, 1842–65), 52, Royal Institution Archives. The index lists the date, lecturer, subject, and total attendance for each meeting, and occasionally the name of the person in the chair.

65. John Barlow to Huxley, 24 April 1852, Huxley Papers, vol. 10, fol. 229.

66. Huxley Papers, vol. 38, fols. 1–52.

67. Vol. 1 (1851–54): 184–89. Reprinted in *The Scientific memoirs of Thomas Henry Huxely*, ed. Michael Foster and E. Ray Lankester, vol. 1:146–151.

68. The phrase, "hot and copper sky," is used in Coleridge's poem.

69. Huxley Papers, vol. 38, fol. 10.

70. Ibid., fols. 11–12.

71. *Proceedings of the Royal Institution*, vol. 1 (1851–54): 185–88 (italics in original).

72. *Rattlesnake Diary*, 52.

73. Huxley Papers, vol. 37, fol. 42.

74. Ibid., fol. 43.

75. *Rattlesnake Diary*, 52.

76. *LL*, 1:100.

77. Huxley-Heathorn Correspondence, fol. 189.

78. Ibid.

79. Ibid., fol. 192.

80. Huxley Papers, vol. 31, fol. 19; *LL*, 1:108.

81. Huxley-Heathorn Correspondence, fol. 200.

82. The lectures began promptly at 9:00 P.M., and stopped promptly at 10:00 P.M. No introduction was given; the speaker simply walked into the theater to the lecture table and began. Attending Friday evening discourses in recent years I have noticed with much interest that these procedures still exist. A buzzer indicates when the hour is up, and the lecturer stops if he has not already finished. Faraday felt that in order not to tire the audience, lectures should not exceed one hour (*Advice to a Lecturer*, 5).

83. Huxley-Heathorn Correspondence, fol. 200. For an extensive and very interesting account by Huxley's friend, John Tyndall, when the latter, a year later

gave his first Friday evening lecture at the Royal Insitution (Huxley was in the audience), see 9, 10, 11 February 1853, Tyndall Journals, vol. 2, fols. 599–600.

84. Huxley-Heathorn Correspondence, fol. 200. He continued: "There will be one day in my life like it—the day when we meet again—When I shall ask Nettie do you love me? And you shall once again put your arms lovingly around me and say 'yes indeed I do love you'—And that day Menen shall last all the rest of our lives." See also *Rattlesnake Diary*, 64–65.

85. This rapid heart reference was not merely a trite figure of speech familiarly claimed by most public speakers facing a tense situation, for Huxley suffered from occasional attacks of rapid palpitation of the heart. For instance, when he was in the Azores in October 1850 on the way back to England, he joined a group that ascended the eight thousand-foot peak on the island of Pico, but he had to remain behind just a short distance from the summit due to a sudden attack of heart palpitation (*Rattlesnake Diary*, 273–75).

86. Huxley Papers, vol. 31, fol. 19; *LL*, 1:108.

87. The Lecture Theatre at the Royal Institution has always been noted for its excellent acoustics.

88. *LL*, 1:94.

89. *Autobiography*, 12.

90. *LL*, 1:94.

91. Huxley-Heathorn Correspondence, fol. 200 (italics in original).

92. Huxley Papers, vol. 31, fol. 19; *LL*, 1:108. Clark (*Huxleys*, 43) is somewhat off the mark when he says that this lecture "had not repeated the success of his impromptu speeches at Ipswich."

93. Huxley-Heathorn Correspondence, fol. 200.

94. Huxley, Papers, vol. 31, fol. 19; *LL*, 1:108.

95. Huxley-Heathorn Correspondence, fol. 200.

96. Ibid., fol. 209.

97. 25 February 1853, *LL*, 1:124.

98. File 113 (*Index for Friday Evening Meetings, 1866–1939*), 66, 74, Royal Institution. It is interesting to note that Huxley's record attendance on 2 March 1877 was achieved after he had arranged to postpone his scheduled January appearance due to ill health. On 9 January 1877 he wrote to his friend John Lubbock:

> to ask if you would mind changing days with me at the Royal Institution. I am down for the 26th of this month & you for the 2nd March. I have been rather shaky lately & although much better again I should be very glad, if I could, to postpone my Friday Evening. Tyndall told me last night he thought you might not be disinclined to change; but pray do not think of inconveniencing yourself as I can give the lecture if I *must* (Avebury Papers, 49642, fol. 116b, British Library; italics in original).

See also Add Mss 49644, fol. 167, B.L. Fortunately for Huxley, Lubbock agreed to the exchange of dates.

99. Huxley-Heathorn Correspondence, fol. 200.

100. Huxley Papers, vol. 31, fol. 19; *LL*, 1:108.

101. It was a paper on the structure of the Ascidians, and related to his work at the British Museum.

102. 16 September 1852, Huxley-Heathorn Correspondence, fol. 222 (italics mine).

103. *LL*, 1:111.

104. Ibid., 112. For a draft of his speech, see Huxley Papers, vol. 31, fols. 139–40.

105. 6 February 1853, *LL*, 1:114. It is interesting that Huxley repeated this dove and ark allusion thirty-six years later in his *Autobiography*.

106. Ibid., 116.

Chapter 3. "Debate" with Bishop Wilberforce, 1860

1. See, for instance, the work of Gould, "Knight Takes Bishop?" 18–33; A. MacC. Armstrong, "Samuel Wilberforce v. T. H. Huxley: A Retrospect," *The Quarterly Review* 296 (October 1958): 426–37; J. R. Lucas, "Wilberforce and Huxley: A Legendary Encounter," *The Historical Journal* 22 (1979): 313–30; Sheridan Gilley and Ann Loades, "Thomas Henry Huxley: The War Between Science and Religion," *The Journal of Religion* 61 (July 1981): 285–308; Sheridan Gilley, "The Huxley-Wilberforce Debate: A Reconsideration," in *Religion and Humanism*: Papers read at the Eighteenth Summer Meeting and the Nineteenth Winter Meeting of the Ecclesiastical History Society, Keith Robbins, ed. (Oxford: Basil Blackwell, 1981), 325–40. Approximately the first 40% of the last two sources are identical, except for very minor differences.

2. Charles S. Blinderman, "The Great Bone Case," *Perspectives in Biology and Medicine* 14 (Spring 1971): 377.

3. James R. Moore, *The Post-Darwinian Controversies: A Study of the Protestant Struggle to Come to Terms with Darwin in Great Britain and America, 1870–1900* (Cambridge: Cambridge University Press, 1979), 60.

4. Josef L. Altholz, "The Huxley-Wilberforce Debate Revisited," *Journal of the History of Medicine and Allied Sciences* 35 (July 1980):314.

5. Nora Barlow, ed., *The Autobiography of Charles Darwin* (London: Collins, 1958), 121–22.

6. Ibid., 124. His nonchalance on accreditation is of course open to question. His friends certainly wanted him to publish and get the credit.

7. Charles Darwin, *The Origin of Species* (New York: New American Library, 1958), 17–25. At the end of the nineteenth century Edward Clodd wrote an interesting historical survey of the contributions to the idea of evolution prior to Darwin in *Pioneers of Evolution from Thales to Huxley* (London: G. Richards, 1897). For some readers on early ideas on evolution, see Robert Ames and Philip Siegelman, eds., *The Idea of Evolution: Readings in Evolutionary Theory and Its Influence* (Minneapolis: Meyers, 1957); Harold Y. Vanderpool, ed., *Darwin and Darwinism* (Lexington, Mass.: Heath, 1973); Bentley Glass, Owsei Temkin and William J. Straus, Jr., eds., *Forerunners of Darwin, 1745–1859*, rev. ed. (Baltimore: Johns Hopkins University Press, 1968). Gertrude Himmelfarb (*Darwin and the Darwinian Revolution* [New York: Doubleday, 1959]) fully developed the point that Darwin culminated rather than initiated the theory of evolution, and Dov Ospovat carefully analyzed the two decades prior to 1859 (*The Development of Darwin's Theory: Natural History, Natural Theology, and Natural Selection, 1838–1859* [New York: Cambridge University Press, 1981]).

8. C. Darwin, *Origin*, 30.

9. Ibid. See the provocative article by Robert M. Young, "Darwin's Metaphor: Does Nature Select?" *The Monist* 55 (July 1971): 442–503.

10. C. Darwin, *Origin*, 450.

11. Ibid., 443.

12. Ibid., 450.

13. Francis Darwin, *The Life and Letters of Charles Darwin*, 2 vols. (New York: D. Appleton, 1897), 1:550–52 (hereafter cited as *Darwin*). See also *LL*, 1:182–83.

14. *LL*, 1:171. In the conclusion of his *Origin* Darwin used similar phrasing. "We can dimly foresee that there will be a considerable revolution in natural history" (447).

15. Barlow, *Autobiography of Darwin*, 122; Sir Gavin de Beer, *Charles Darwin: Evolution by Natural Selection* (London: Thomas Nelson & Sons, 1963), 2:1, 149; Alvar Ellegard, "Public Opinion and the Press: Reactions to Darwinism," *Journal of the History of Ideas* 19 (1958) :383.

16. Barlow, *Autobiography of Darwin*, 122.

17. George Levine, "Darwin and the Evolution of Fiction," *New York Times Book Review*, 5 October 1986, p. 1.

18. George Rolleston to John Lubbock, 1 December 1859, Lubbock Letters, Add. MSS 49638, fol. 175, British Library.

19. Darwin Papers, vol. 98, fols. 11–13, Cambridge University Library; *LL*, 1:188–89.

20. *Macmillan's Magazine*, December 1859, p. 146.

21. *Darwin*, 2:34. See also Hirst Journals, vol. 3, fol. 1517.

22. For Huxley's account of how he was given the opportunity to write the review, and how hastily he wrote it, see *LL*, 1:189–90; *Darwin*, 2:49–50; Huxley to Hooker, 31 December 1859, Huxley Papers, vol. 2, fols. 57–58.

23. *Darwin*, 2:47–48.

24. Ibid., 144 (italics in original).

25. Ibid., 49.

26. Lyell to George Ticknor, 9 January 1860, in Mrs. Charles Lyell, ed., *Life, Letters and Journals of Sir Charles Lyell*, 2 vols. (London: Murray, 1881), 1:329 (hereafter cited as *Lyell*).

27. *Darwin*, 2:76. See also Hirst Journals, vol. 3, fol. 152.

28. *Darwin*, 2:79.

29. Vol. 225 (1860): 251–75.

30. Vol. 73 (1860): 295–310.

31. *Darwin*, 2:94 (italics in original).

32. Ibid., 101. Darwin's former Cambridge mentor, the highly respected botanist, Rev. J. S. Henslow, wrote to Darwin, "I don't think it is at all becoming in one Naturalist to be better against another any more than for one sect to burn the members of another" (5 May 1860, in Nora Barlow, ed., *Darwin and Henslow—The Growth of an Idea—Letters 1831–1860* [Berkeley: University of California Press, 1967], 203).

33. See, for example, *Darwin*, 2:15, 17, 28, 31, 35, 47, 58, 61–62, 84, 93, 96, 100–2, 109–10; Francis Darwin and A. C. Seward, eds., *More Letters of Charles Darwin*, 2 vols. (New York: D. Appleton, 1903), 1:156–57, 161 (hereafter cited as *More Letters*).

34. *Jackson's Oxford Journal*, 7 July 1860, p. 4; Roy MacLeod and Peter Collins, eds., *The Parliament of Science: The British Association for the Advancement of Science, 1831–1981* (Northwood, Middlesex: Science Reviews, 1981), 280. The British Association had met in Oxford on two previous occasions, 1832 and 1847.

35. 7 July 1860, p. 656. See also *The Athenaeum*, 7 July, p. 19.

36. *The Athenaeum*, 30 June, p. 886. See also *Jackson's Oxford Journal*, 30 June, p. 4; *The Times*, 28 June, p. 12.

37. *LL*, 1:29.

38. Huxley-Heathorn Correspondence, fol. 191. Owen's name is omitted in the excerpt included in *LL*, 1:106.

39. Clark, *Huxleys*, 45; *LL*, 1:153.

40. *LL*, 1:169.

41. Ibid., 1:172.

42. Ibid., 168.

43. Huxley-Mrs. Huxley Correspondence, fol. 448; *LL*, 1:166.

44. For some insight into Huxley's decade of tension with Owen, see Tyndall Journals, vol. 3, fol. 744; Huxley-Heathorn Correspondence, fol. 191; Huxley Papers, vol. 31, fol. 25; *LL*, 1:102, 169; Stephen Jay Gould, "The *Archaeopteryx* flap," *Natural History* 95 (September 1986): 16–25; Blinderman, "The Great Bone Case," 370–93; Evelleen Richards, "A Question of Property Rights: Richard Owen's Evolutionism Reassessed," *British Journal for the History of Science* 20 (1987): 129–71; David Knight, *The Age of Science: The Scientific World-View in the Nineteenth Century* (Oxford: Oxford University Press, 1986), 100–2, 115; Mario A. de Gregorio, *T. H. Huxley's Place in Natural Science* (New Haven: Yale University Press, 1984), 35–44; Moore, *Post-Darwinian Controversies*, 87–88.

45. Barlow, *Autobiography of Darwin*, 104–5.

46. *The Athenaeum*, 7 July, p. 26. See also *LL*, 1:193–94.

47. *The Press*, 7 July, p. 656.

48. Jack Morrell and Arnold Thackray, *Gentleman of Science: Early Years of the British Association for the Advancement of Science* (Oxford: Clarendon Press, 1981), 395. For an 1860 engraving of the new museum, see ibid., plate 25.

49. Ibid., 394.

50. Rev. W.Tuckwell, *Reminiscences of Oxford*, 2d ed. (London: Smith, Elder and Co., 1970), 51.

51. Morrell and Thackray, *Gentleman of Science*, 395.

52. *Jackson's Oxford Journal*, 7 July, p. 4.

53. (Mrs. Isabel Sidgwick), "A Grandmother's Tales," *Macmillan's Magazine* 78 (May-October 1898): 433. For attribution of authorship, see Walter E. Houghton, ed., *The Wellesley Index of Victorian Peridoicals, 1824–1900*, 3 vols. (Toronto: University of Toronto Press, 1966), 1:656. See also Tuckwell, *Reminiscences*, 53.

54. 14 July, p. 65.

55. *The Evening Star*, 2 July, p. 3; *Darwin*, 2:114; *LL*, 1:195; Benjamin Peirce's Journal of a European Trip, 30 June 1860, in Nathan Reingold, ed., *Science in Nineteenth-Century America* (New York: Hill and Wang, 1964), 197. For bringing this last source to my attention, I wish to thank Nathan Reingold, senior historian, Department of the History of Science and Technology, National Museum of American History, Smithsonian Institution, Washington, D.C.

56. *LL*, 1:195.

57. *The Athenaeum*, 7 July, p. 19; Lucas, "Wilberforce and Huxley," 319, 323.

58. Lucas, "Wilberforce and Huxley," 330; Gilley, "Huxley-Wilberforce Debate," 333.

59. *Darwin*, 2:114.

60. Rev. A. S. Farrar to Leonard Huxley, 12 July 1899, Huxley Papers, vol. 16, fol. 13.

61. Tuckwell, *Reminiscences*, 55. See also *Jackson's Oxford Journal*, 7 July, p. 2; *Letters of John Richard Green*, Lesile Stephen, ed. (London: Macmillan, 1901), 44 (hereafter cited as *Green*).

62. Altholz, "Huxley-Wilberforce Debate," 316.

63. *The Evening Star*, 2 July, p. 3.

64. *British Association Report*, 115–16; *The Athenaeum*, 14 July, pp. 64–65; *Green*, 44; Huxley Papers, vol. 16, fol. 13. The title of Draper's paper was, "On the Intellectual Development of Europe, Considered with Reference to the Views of Mr. Darwin and Others that the Progression of Organisms Is Determined by Law." Draper's paper appeared in a book in 1863, entitled, *A History of the Intellectual Development of Europe*.

65. *The Evening Star*, 2 July, p. 3.

66. Tuckwell, *Reminiscences*, 53.

67. When journalists mentioned dignitaries at the conference, Bishop Wilberforce was one of them, so he was a central figure throughout (e.g., *The Times*, 28 June, p. 12; *Jackson's Oxford Journal*, 30 June, p. 4). J. S. Henslow, the presiding officer, in the center; to his right was Wilberforce, then Dr. Draper. To Henslow's left was Huxley, Sir Benjamin Brodie, Professor Beale, John Lubbock, Joseph Hooker, and Mr. Dingle (*LL*, 1:195, 202).

68. Wilberforce played a central role in the discussion following a report from David Livingstone in Africa (*Jackson's Oxford Journal*, 14 July, p. 2).

69. *LL*, 1:197.

70. *The Evening Star*, 2 July, p. 3.

71. 7 July, p. 19. See also *The Press*, 7 July, p. 656; *The Evening Star*, 2 July, p. 3; and *Jackson's Oxford Journal*, 7 July, p. 2. Some supporters of Darwin, such as Lyell (*Lyell*, 2:333) and J. S. Henslow (*Macmillan's Magazine*, 3 [February 1861]:336) carefully insisted on referring to Darwin's hypothesis, not his theory.

72. (A. R. Ashwell) and Reginald G. Wilberforce, *Life of the Right Reverend Samuel Wilberforce, D.D.*, 3 vols. (London: Murray, 1881), 2:449 (hereafter cited as *Wilberforce*). The bishop was not as ill-informed as the Darwin camp contended, and their suspicion that Owen had coached Wilberforce was perhaps exaggerated. However, in 1887 Huxley finally felt that proof now did exist for the claim that Owen had indeed primed the bishop at Oxford (Huxley Papers, vol. 41, fols. 133–34).

73. Lynn A. Phelps and Edwin Cohen, "The Wilberforce-Huxley Debate," *Western Speech* 37 (Winter 1973): 57–60.

74. Lucas, "Wilberforce and Huxley," 317–22.

75. 7 July, p. 656.

76. Ibid.; *Green*, 44.

77. *Lyell*, 2:335. Lucas, in his effort to rehabilitate Wilberforce, insists that "it cannot have been what was actually said" ("Wilberforce and Huxley," 324), and is, for instance, too quick to denigrate Lyell's account merely because it was second hand and because Lyell had heard different versions. Actually, multiple versions, presumably trustworthy ones (even though likely pro-Darwin), reported to Lyell so soon after the event, and he, a highly trustworthy (though pro-Darwin) individual, reporting so soon to his correspondent, could, on the contrary, add up to Lyell's version having a high probability of accuracy. Six months after Oxford, a writer in *Macmillan's Magazine* lamented that opponents of Darwinism would stoop "to ask a professor if he should object to discover that he had been developed out of an ape" (Henry Fawcett, "A Popular Exposition of Mr. Darwin on the Origin of Species," *Macmillan's Magazine* 3 [December 1860]:88).

78. Rev. W. H. Feemantle's account: "I should like to ask Professor Huxley . . . as to his belief in being descended from an ape. Is it on his grandfather's or his grandmother's side that the ape ancestry comes in?" (*LL*, 1:200). Rev. A. S. Farrar's account: "If any one were to be willing to trace his descent similarly on the

side of his *grandmother*?'' (italics in original) (Huxley Papers, vol. 16, fol. 14). Farrar felt that Wilberforce's words "did not appear vulgar, nor insolent, nor personal, but flippant" (ibid., fol. 13).

79. "Was it through his grandfather or his grandmother that he claimed his descent from a monkey?" (*Macmillan's Magazine* 78 [October 1898]: 433).

80. "Then the Bishop spoke the speech that you know, and the question about his [Huxley's] mother being an ape, or his grandmother" (*LL*, 1:196).

81. A. G. Vernon-Harcourt's account: "The Bishop had rallied your father as to the descent from a monkey, asking ... how recent this had been, whether it was his grandfather or further back" (ibid, 199).

82. *Wilberforce*, 2:451. See also Tuckwell, *Reminiscences*, 53.

83. O. J. R. Horwarth, *The British Association for the Advancement of Science: A Retrospect*, 2d ed. (London: B.A.A.S., 1931), 63.

84. *LL*, 1:202.

85. Tuckwell, *Reminiscences*, 54–55.

86. *Green*, 44.

87. 7 July, p. 19. See also *The Evening Star*, 2 July, p. 3.

88. Tuckwell, *Reminiscences*, 55.

89. 7 July, p. 656.

90. *Green*, 45 (italics in original). Both Huxley and Farrar claimed that the term *equivocal* had not been used (*LL*, 1:199, n.; Huxley Papers, vol. 16, fol. 14). Green's account is included in *Bartlett's Familiar Quotations*, 15th ed. (Boston: Little, Brown, 1980), 596.

91. *Lyell*, 2:335.

92. See Darwin to Huxley, 5 July 1860, Huxley Papers, vol. 5, f. 123. Francis Darwin, working on his father's biography in 1886, wrote to Huxley: "I wish I had some account of the celebrated Oxford meeting. It is a thousand pities that my father destroyed his letters. There seems to have been one from you. . . . " (Huxley Papers, vol. 13, fols. 44–45).

93. Huxley to Dr. F. D. Dyster, 9 September 1860, Huxley papers, vol. 15, fols. 117–19. Until a portion of this letter was first brought to public view by D. J. Foskett in 1953 in *Nature*, 172:920, it was assumed that Huxley had left no account of his retort. Portions of the letter can be found in *Scientific American* 190 (1954): 52; *The Scientific Monthly* 84 (1957): 171–72; de Beer, *Charles Darwin*, 166–67; Garrett Hardin, ed., *Population, Evolution, and Birth Control: A Collage of Controversial Readings* (San Francisco: Freeman, 1964), 154–55; Cyril Bibby, *The Essence of T. H. Huxley* (London: Macmillan, 1967), 12–13; Clark, *Huxleys*, 59–60; Bibby, *Scientist Extraordinary: The Life and Scientific Work of Thomas Henry Huxley* (Oxford: Pergamon Press, 1972), 41. The phrasing mentioned by Huxley at the end of his letter to Dyster refused to die, and when Reginald Wilberforce included it in volume two (p. 451) of his biography of his father, Huxley insisted that the author correct it, which was done with the following errata placed at the beginning of volume three (1882): " 'I would rather be descended from an ape than a bishop' ought to be 'If I had to choose between being descended from an ape or from a man who would use his great powers of rhetoric to crush an argument, I should prefer the former'."

94. *Macmillan's Magazine*, 3:88.

95. *LL*, 1:197–202; *Darwin*, 2:114–16. At the end of the century, Sidgwick reminisced that Huxley had said, "He was not ashamed to have a monkey for his ancestor; but he would be ashamed to be connected with a man who used great gifts to obscure the truth" ("A Grandmother's Tales," 434).

96. See Janet Browne, "The Charles Darwin-Joseph Hooker Correspondence: An Analysis of Manuscript Resources and Their Use in Biography," *Journal of the Society for the Bibliography of Natural History* 8 (May 1978): 360–63. See also Roos, "Neglected Bibliographial Aspects," 403–10.

97. Lucas, "Wilberforce and Huxley," 323.

98. *The Athenaeum*, 7 July, p. 19; *The Evening Star*, 2 July, p. 3; *Jackson's Oxford Journal*, 7 July, p. 2; *John Bull*, 7 July, p. 422.

99. 14 July, p. 65.

100. Hooker to Darwin, 2 July 1860, in Leonard Huxley, *Life and Letters of Sir Joseph Dalton Hooker*, 2 vols. (London: Murray, 1918), 1:526 (hereafter cited as *Hooker*). Later in his autobiography Darwin characterized Hooker as "very impulsive and somewhat peppery in temper" (Barlow, *Darwin's Autobiography*, 105), and a mid twentieth-century biographer described Hooker as "nervous and highly strung and . . . sometimes hasty" (William Bertram Turrill, *J. D. Hooker, Botanist, Explorer, and Administrator* [London: T. Nelson, 1963], 201).

101. *LL*, 1:200.

102. *The Athenaeum*, 14 July, p. 65.

103. *Hooker*, 1:526; Darwin to Huxley, 3 July, Huxley Papers, vol. 5, fol. 121. Lyell's 4 July letter to Bunbury also stresses Hooker's effectiveness (*Lyell*, 2:335).

104. Farrar to Leonard Huxley, 7 July 1899, Huxley Papers, vol. 16, fol. 16 (italics in original). See also ibid., fol. 19. A late twentieth-century church historian has perhaps stated it too strongly when he writes, "It is clear that the speech of J. D. Hooker, and not the speech of Huxley, made the big impression on the audience in countering the bishop's arguments . . . [Huxley] attacked rather the tone and rhetoric than the argument, and contemporaries were agreed that the man who answered the arguments was Hooker" (Owen Chadwick, *The Victorian Church*, 2 vols. [London: Adam & Charles Black, 1966], 2:10–11). One eyewitness later wrote that "Hooker led the devotees" (Tuckwell, *Reminiscences*, 56) of Darwin, but that means *after* Huxley had spoken.

105. Huxley Papers, vol. 16, fol. 19. See also fol. 15.

106. *The Evening Star*, 2 July, p. 3; *Jackson's Oxford Journal*, 7 July, p. 2; *John Bull*, 7 July, p. 422.

107. See the accounts, for example, by Green, Sidgwick, and Vernon-Harcourt.

108. Huxley Papers, vol. 15, fol. 117 (italics mine).

109. Samuel Wilberforce Diary, Dept. e. 327, Bodleian Library, Oxford. I am indebted to Mary Clapinson, keeper of western manuscripts, Bodleian Library, for her assistance in securing a photocopy of a portion of the Wilberforce Diary and for securing permission for me to use it.

110. Peirce's Journal, in Reingold, ed., *Science in Nineteenth-Century America*, 197.

111. Sir Mountstuart E. Grant Duff, *Notes from a Diary, 1851–1872*, 2 vols. (London: Murray, 1897), 1:139.

112. Tuckwell, *Reminiscences*, 56.

113. Ibid. See also *Hooker*, 1:527.

114. 14 July, pp. 65, 68.

115. 30 June, p. 5.

116. See Alvar Ellegard, *Darwin and the General Reader: The Reception of Darwin's Theory of Evolution in the British Periodical Press, 1859–1872* (Goteborg: Goteborgs Universitets Arsskrift, 1958), 64–65.

117. 2 July, p. 3.

118. *Green*, 44.

119. *Lyell*, 2:335.

120. Huxley Papers, vol. 15, fol. 118.

121. Since the tightly packed room "was crowded to suffocation long before the protagonists appeared" (*LL*, 1:195), the "debate" perhaps should not be given full credit for the effect!

122. Sidgwick, "A Grandmother's Tales," 425, 434. She was about twenty-five years old at the time.

123. Huxley Papers, vol. 16, fol. 15. Somehow, published versions of this portion of Farrar's letter have inaccurately inserted the adjective "perfect" before "gentlemen."

124. *LL*, 1:203–4. It seems that Lucas ("Wilberforce and Huxley," 323) is straining considerably when he cites Foster's account as a piece of evidence for the claim that at the end of the debate the majority were with Wilberforce.

125. *LL*, 1:201.

126. As quoted in Browne, "Darwin-Hooker Correspondence," 361, and Gould, "Knight Takes Bishop?", 21. It is surprising that Gould makes so much of the fact that here was actually a scientist who gave that judgment, for as has been noted, many scientists were not in Darwin's corner, and a major point in Gould's article is that in science, as well as in organized religion, there are differing views. For a fine discussion of Gould's exciting but controversial contributions to contemporary science, see John Lyne and Henry F. Howe, "'Punctuated Equilibriua': Rhetorical Dynamics of a Scientific Controversy," *Quarterly Journal of Speech* 72 (May 1986): 132–47.

127. Peirce's Journal, in Reingold, ed., *Science in Nineteenth Century America*, 197–98. Of course, critics of Wilberforce used the slippery soap metaphor in the negative sense!

128. As quoted in Altholz, "Huxley-Wilberforce Debate," 315.

129. *LL*, 1:202.

130. *Wilberforce*, 2:450–51.

131. *LL*, 1:203.

132. 7 July, p. 422. The italics are mine, to call attention to the similarity in wording to the Freemantle account cited above, but from the opposite point of view.

133. 7 July, p. 19.

134. *Darwin*, 2:101, 112, 117; Huxley Papers, vol. 5, fol. 122.

135. *Darwin*, 2:116–17.

136. Ibid., 117; Huxley Papers, vol. 5, fols. 121, 123.

137. Barlow, *Autobiography of Darwin*, 106.

138. John Angus Campbell, "The Invisible Rhetorician: Charles Darwin's 'Third Party' Strategy," *Rhetorica* 7 (Winter 1989): 55–85. For additional excellent rhetorical analyses of Darwin's works by Professor Campbell, see "Darwin and *The Origin of Species*: The Rhetorical Ancestry of an Idea," *Speech Monographs* 37 (March 1970): 1–14; Charles Darwin and the Crisis of Ecology: A Rhetorical Perspective, *Quarterly Journal of Speech* 60 (December 1974): 442–49; "The Polemical Mr. Darwin," *Quarterly Journal of Speech* 61 (December 1975): 375–90; "Scientific Revolution and the Grammar of Culture: The Case of Darwin's *Origin*," *Quarterly Journal of Speech* 72 (November 1986): 351–76. See also Barbara Warnick, "A Rhetorical Analysis of Episteme Shift: Darwin's *Origin of the* [sic] *Species*," *Southern Speech Communication Journal* 49 (Fall 1983): 26–42.

139. Huxley to Mivart, 12 November 1885, *LL*, 2:121.

140. For a recent thorough analysis of these debates, see David Zarefsky, "The Lincoln-Douglas Debate Revisited: The Evolution of Public Argument," *Quarterly Journal of Speech* 72 (May 1986): 162–84.

141. de Beer, *Charles Darwin*, 166.

142. Tuckwell, *Reminiscences*, 63.

143. *The Times*, 29 November 1887; Huxley Papers, vol. 41, fol. 133.

144. Wilberforce Diary, Dep. 3. 327, Bodleian.

145. As quoted in Altholz, "Huxley-Wilberforce Debate," 315. See also *LL*, 1:196; Tuckwell, *Reminiscences*, 53.

146. Huxley Papers, vol. 16, fol. 13.

147. *British Association Report*, 136; *The Athenaeum*, 7 July, p. 28.

148. An early evolutionist, Chambers had published anonymously in 1844 a highly controversial and not so highly respected treatise on evolution, *Vestiges of the Natural History of Creation*.

149. Indeed, in his diary for Saturday, 30 June, Huxley recorded departure times for the train to Reading (Huxley Papers, vol. 70, fol. 3). Mrs. Huxley's sister and her family (the Fannings) had returned to England from Australia eighteen months earlier (ibid., vol. 31, fol. 31).

150. *LL*, 1:202.

151. *Darwin*, 2:101.

152. Darwin, to Huxley, 3 July 1860, Huxley Papers, vol. 5, fol. 121. See also fol. 122.

153. *Darwin*, 2:101.

154. Darwin to Huxley, 5, 20, July 1860, Huxley Papers, vol. 5, fols. 124, 126.

155. *Darwin*, 2:109, 120, 124.

156. As quoted in Altholz, "Huxley-Wilberforce Debate," 315.

157. *Green,* 44.

158. *LL*, 1:203.

159. Huxley Papers, vol. 15, fols. 117–18.

160. Huxley to Hooker, 6 August 1860, Huxley Papers, vol. 2, fol. 73.

161. 7 July 1860, p. 656.

162. Tuckwell, *Reminiscences*, 56.

163. *Darwin*, 2:147.

164. "A Popular Exposition of Mr. Darwin," 81.

165. As quoted in Howarth, *British Association*, 41–42.

166. To cite two examples, Huxley was not selected in 1853 for a position at King's College, London (J. W. C. Law to Huxley, 13 May 1853, Huxley Papers, vol. 21, fol. 175); and his religious views were a negative factor in applying for a chair at Oxford in 1856 (Huxley to [Frederick James] Furnival, 24 November 1856, Huntington MSS: FU 429, H.L.).

167. Lucas notes that "the Darwinians, who were a small minority in 1860, became the dominant majority over the next twenty years, but never lost the sense of being persecuted" ("Wilberforce and Huxley," 329).

168. *Darwin*, 2:113–14.

169. *LL*, 1:196–204.

170. See, for example, Edward Clodd, *Thomas Henry Huxley* (New York: Dodd, Mead, 1902), 20–23; J. R. Ainsworth Davis, *Thomas H. Huxley* (London: J. M. Dent, 1907), 52–54; Clarence Ayres, *Huxley* (New York: Norton, 1932), 50–52; William Irvine, *Apes, Angels, and Victorians: Darwin, Huxley, and Evolution* (Cleveland: World Publishing Co., 1955), 3–8; Bibby, *Essence of Huxley* 157; Clark, *Huxleys*, 54–62; Bibby, *Scientist Extraordinary*, 40–41; de Beer, *Darwin and Huxley: Autobiographies*, xiii.

171. Barlow, *Darwin and Henslow*, 209, n. 1.

172. Phelps and Cohen, "Wilberforce-Huxley Debate," 60. The authors also show their pro-Huxley bias in the way in which they refer to the sons who wrote

their father's biographies: Reginald Wilberforce is "the reverend's son and therefore not an altogether objective source," (ibid.) but Leonard Huxley is simply "Huxley's son and biographer" (61).

173. Howarth, *British Association*, 65.

174. David L. Edwards, *Leaders of the Church of England, 1828–1944* (London: Oxford University Press, 1971), 103.

175. Gilley and Loades, "War Between Science and Religion," 289.

176. Moore, *Post-Darwinian Controversies*, passim.

177. *Oxford University Museum*, p. 1.

178. This impression of mine when I viewed the program is similar to that expressed by Lucas, "Wilberforce and Huxley," 313, Gilley, "Huxley-Wilberforce Debate," 325, and Gilley and Loades, "War Between Science and Religion," 285.

179. *Green*, 44; Donald Fleming, "John William Draper," in *Dictionary of Scientific Biography*, Charles Coulston Gillispie, ed., 16 vols. (New York: Scribner, 1971), 4:181–83.

180. *LL*, 1:200.

181. Ibid., 199.

182. 7 July, p. 18.

183. MacLeod, in *The Parliament of Science*, 22.

184. However, Huxley in his April 1860 *Westminster Review* article had defended Darwin against being called an ape, so Huxley no doubt took this Oxford episode as a repeated taunt and hence no longer funny.

185. Huxley to Dyster, 9 September 1860, Huxley Papers, vol. 15, fol. 117.

186. Ibid., fol. 116.

187. It could have been a father-son relationship not only in age but even in looks, and indeed, a stranger that week had thought Huxley was the bishop's son (*LL*, 1:198, n.). For photos of Huxley in 1857 and of Wilberforce, see de Beer, *Darwin, Huxley, Autobiographies*, 86, 102. For a photograph of Huxley taken at the British Association meeting in 1860, see Tuckwell, *Reminiscences*, 55.

188. George J. Allman to Huxley, 9 July 1860, Huxley Papers, vol. 10, fol. 79.

189. *LL*, 2:377–78, 381.

190. Ibid., 1:202.

191. Ibid., 193.

192. Altholz, "Huxley-Wilberforce Debate," 313.

193. Gilley and Loades, "War between Science and Religion," 294.

194. Wilberforce Diary, Dep. e. 327, Bodleian.

195. Ibid.; *John Bull*, 7 July 1860, p. 422.

196. *John Bull*, 7 July, p. 432; *Jackson's Oxford Journal*, 14 July, p. 3; Great Britain, *Hansard's Parliamentary Debates*, 3d ser., vol. 159 (1860): cols. 1513–15.

197. *Wilberforce*, 2:450–51.

198. Standish Meacham, *Lord Bishop: The Life of Samuel Wilberforce*, 1805–1873 (Cambridge: Harvard University Press, 1970), 215–17.

199. This was the first issue of a publication that Huxley helped to found.

200. 3 January 1861, MS Wilberforce, C13, fols. 1–2, Bodleian. This also has been published in Clark, *Huxleys*, 61–62 (but misdated as June), and in Bibby, *Scientist Extraordinary*, 46.

201. George Macaulay Trevelyan, *The Life of John Bright* (Boston: Houghton, 1913), 38.

202. Wilberforce to Huxley, 30 January 1871, Huxley Papers, vol. 29, fol. 25.

203. 29 November and 1 December 1887, Huxley Papers, vol. 41, fols. 133–34. See Hirst Journals, vol. 5, fol. 2473.

204. 2 July, p. 3.

205. Tuckwell, *Reminiscences*, 57.

206. Morrell and Thackray, *Gentlemen of Science*, 395.

207. Lucas, "Wilberforce and Huxley," 330.

208. Morrell and Thackray, *Gentleman of Science*, 395.

209. Ibid.

210. A. Hunter Dupree, *Asa Gray* (Cambridge: Harvard University Press, 1959), 294.

211. Gilley and Loades, "War between Science and Religion," 289.

212. *British Association Report*, lxxv. See also *The Athenaeum*, 30 June, p. 891.

213. Ellegard, *Darwin and the General Reader*, 63–64.

214. *More Letters*, 1:156–57.

215. *LL*, 1:204. See also Howarth, *British Association*, 65.

Chapter 4. Lecture Tour of the United States, 1876

1. For a list of honorary degrees and memberships in academic societies, see *LL*, 2:499–502. Huxley's letter to M. C. Vesseloffsky, 2 July 1865, accepting the nomination to be a Corresponding Member in the Section of Biology in the Imperial Academy of Sciences of St. Petersburg, is in the American Philosophical Society Library in Philadelphia (*Letters of Scientists*, 509 L56. m.).

2. Victor Purcell, *The Boxer Uprising* (Cambridge: Cambridge University Press, 1963), 103, 109, 113; W. Scott Morton, *China: Its History and Culture* (New York: McGraw-Hill, 1980), 178; James Reeve Pusey, *China and Charles Darwin* (Cambridge: Harvard University Press, 1983), 83, 155–57.

3. See Huxley Papers, vol. 82, fol. 16.

4. Youmans to Huxley, 9 April 1864, ibid., vol. 29, fol. 256.

5. Youmans to Spencer, 20 March 1866, ibid., fol. 257.

6. Huxley to Joseph N. Lockyer, 21 November 1868, ibid., vol. 21, fol. 248.

7. Huxley to Lockyer, 9 July 1869, ibid., fol. 249.

8. John Fiske, "Reminiscences of Huxley," *Smithsonian Institution Annual Report, 1900*, 713.

9. James Tyson to Huxley, 24 October 1869, Huxley Papers, vol. 28, fol. 63.

10. "Professor Huxley," *Nation* 11 (1870): 407. See also E. L. Youmans, "Prof. Huxley," *Popular Science Monthly*, 9 (1876): 621–22.

11. Georg Weitbrecht to Huxley, 12 February 1871, Huxley Papers, vol. 28, fol. 226.

12. 30 December 1873, ibid., fol. 187.

13. William Peirce Randel, "Huxley in America," *Proceedings of the American Philosophical Society* 114 (April 1970): 74–75.

14. Huxley Papers, vol. 16, fols. 80–85.

15. J. B. S. Pearce to Huxley, 29 June 1875, ibid., vol. 24, fol. 88.

16. *LL*, 2:500–1; Warren R. Dawson, *The Huxley Papers: A Descriptive Catalogue of the Correspondence, Manuscripts, and Miscellaneous Papers of the Rt. Hon. Thomas Henry Huxley, Preserved in the Imperial College of Science and*

Technology, London (London: Macmillan, 1946), 180–81.

17. Barlow, *Autobiography of Darwin*, 106–7.

18. P. Chalmers Mitchell erroneously spoke of Huxley's "several trips to America" (*Thomas Henry Huxley: A Sketch of His Life and Work* [New York: Putnam, 1901], 276).

19. Wayne C. Minnick, "British Speakers in America, 1866–1900," Ph.D. diss., Northwestern University, 1949, passim.

20. New York *Tribune*, 18 December 1869, p. 6.

21. *The American Commonwealth*, 2 vols. (New York: Macmillan, 1919), 2:867.

22. Huxley to Michael Foster, Huxley Papers, vol. 4, fol. 114.

23. Ibid., vol. 31, fols. 44–47.

24. *LL*, 1:115.

25. Ibid., 450–51 (italics in original).

26. See Katherine Russell Sopka, "John Tyndall: International Populariser of Science," *John Tyndall: Essays on a Natural Philosopher*, W. H. Brock, N. D. McMillan, and R. C. Mollan, eds. (Dublin: Royal Dublin Society, 1981), 193–203. Being a bachelor at that time without Huxley's family expenses, Tyndall graciously turned his profits into a fund for American students in physics. After 1876 Americans sometimes got Tyndall and Huxley mixed up.

27. Huxley Papers, vol. 16, fols. 86–91. Researchers will forever thank Fiske for his beautiful legible handwriting! Huxley is another matter!

28. *LL*, 1:451.

29. New York *World*, 6 August 1876, p. 5; 8 August 1876, p. 5.

30. *LL*, 1:493.

31. 9 August 1876, as quoted in Randel, "Huxley in America," 77.

32. Ibid., 75.

33. *LL*, 1:492–93.

34. Ibid., 493.

35. "Prof. Tyndall," *Nineteenth Century* 35 (January 1894): 6.

36. George M. Smalley, "Mr. Huxley," *Scribner's Magazine* 18 (July-December 1895): 421–22. A similar account is in the New York *World*, 8 August 1876, p. 5.

37. Randel, "Huxley in America," 78; New York *World* 6 August, p. 5.

38. P. Thomas Carroll, "American Science Transformed," *American Scientist* 74 (September-October 1986): 474.

39. As quoted in Randel, "Huxley in America," 79.

40. 12 January 1877, Spencer papers, Athenaeum Collection, MS 791, item 116ii, U.L.C.

41. As quoted in Randel, "Huxley in America," 82.

42. Ibid., 83.

43. 14 September 1876, p. 7.

44. As quoted in Randel, "Huxley in America," 83.

45. Ibid., n. 36.

46. Ibid., 85.

47. Alexander Winchell, a science professor at Vanderbilt, a kindred spirit in tune with Huxley, was unfortunately out of town. Three years later he would be fired for his writings on evolution (Kenneth L. Jones, "Thomas H. Huxley's One Visit to the United States," *Michigan Academician* 17 [Spring 1985]: 351).

48. As quoted in Randel, "Huxley in America," 86. For other surveys of Huxley's Nashville visit, see James N. Smith, "Thomas Henry Huxley in Nashville," *Tennessee Historical Quarterly* 33 (Summer 1974): 191–203, 33 (Fall

1974): 332–41; William J. Baker, "Thomas Huxley in Tennessee," *The South Atlantic Quarterly* 73 (Autumn 1974): 475–86.

49. Smith, "Huxley in Nashville," 335.

50. Ibid., 336.

51. Ibid., 340.

52. Daniel Coit Gilman, *The Launching of a University* (New York: Dodd, Mead, 1906), 19–20.

53. Randel, "Huxley in America," 88.

54. Gilman, *Launching of a University*, 21–22.

55. *The Pall Mall Gazette*, 24 October 1888.

56. *Collected Essays* 3:254–55.

57. Ibid., 260–61.

58. Ibid., 261. Entrance exams began the next day and classes commenced on 3 October.

59. Ibid.

60. *LL*, 1:501.

61. Less than two moths later, 4 November, Sir Andrew also gave the address at the official opening of the new Huxley Building at the Imperial College of Science and Technology in London. Sir Andrew, a Nobel Prize winner in Medicine in 1963, became president of the Royal Society in 1983—one hundred years after his grandfather had been president—and currently is master of Trinity College, Cambridge. See his interesting paper, "Grandfather and Grandson," *Notes and Records of the Royal Society of London* 38 (March 1984): 147–51.

62. Gilman, *Launching of a University*, 22.

63. Huxley Papers, vol. 17, fol. 54. The cataloger of the Huxley Papers, Warren Dawson, misled by Folwell's handwriting, ascribed the letter to "Wm. W. Forbes."

64. Ibid., fol. 56.

65. Ibid., fol. 57.

66. For some details on various elements surrounding the lectures, see Randel, "Huxley in America," 91–97; and Wayne C. Minnick, "Thomas Huxley's American Lectures on Evolution," *The Southern Speech Journal* 17 (May 1952): 225–33. Manuscripts of Lectures 1 and 2 are in Huxley Manuscripts, vol. 82, fols. 38–59. The first is more full, the second becomes sketchy and more in outline form.

67. 19, 21, 23 September, pp. 5, 4, 4.

68. 19, 21, 23 September, pp. 4, 8, 10, 1.

69. 19, 21, 23 September, pp. 5, 4, 4.

70. 8 August, p. 5.

71. 19, 21 September, pp. 4, 8, 10.

72. *American Addresses* (New York: D. Appleton, 1877), 14, 17. Italics are mine here and in subsequent quotations. Future page citations are in the body in parentheses.

73. 19 September, p. 8.

74. Ibid., p. 4.

75. Ibid., p. 8.

76. Ibid.

77. Examples of negative reactions are "Three Lectures on Evolution," *The Catholic World* 24 (1876–77): 616–32; A. M. Kirsch, "Professor Huxley on Evolution," *The American Catholic Quarterly Review* 2 (1877): 644–64; New York *World*, 20, 24 September 1876, pp. 5, 4; New York *Times*, 24 September 1876, p. 6. One that is fairly neutral is E. L. Godkin, "Professor Huxley's Lectures," *The Nation* 33 (1876): 192–93. Positive reactions are in the New York *Tribune*, 25

September 1876, pp. 3–4; E. L. Youmans, "Professor Huxley's Lectures," *Popular Science Monthly*, 10 (1876): 103–4; E. Ray Lankester, "Huxley's American Lectures," ibid., 11 (1877): 709–13. For a general discussion of reactions see Minnick, "Huxley's American Lectures," 228–31, and Randel, "Huxley in America," 97.

78. 24 September, p. 4.

79. "Professor Huxley in New York," *International Review* 4 (January 1877): 50, 34.

80. 108 (October 1877): 257–58.

81. Dee Brown, *The Year of the Century: 1876* (New York: Scribner, 1966), 293.

82. *LL*, 1:496; Huxley Papers, vol. 13, fol. 135; vol. 15, fol. 224; vol. 29, fol. 100.

83. Randel, "Huxley in America," 83, n. 36; Huxley Papers, vol. 11, fols. 106–7; vol. 15, fol. 223; vol. 24, fol. 198.

84. Pilkington Jackson to Huxley, 22 September 1876, Huxley Papers, vol. 19, fol. 11.

85. *LL*, 1:493.

86. Minnick, "Huxley's American Lectures," 225.

87. Randel, "Huxley in America," 99.

88. New York *World*, 24 September, p. 4.

89. 6 October, p. 4.

90. Huxley Papers, vol. 4, fols. 133–34; vol. 31, fols. 105–8; *LL*, 1:502–4.

91. Huxley to Lockyer, 12 October 1876, Huxley Papers, vol. 21, fol. 273. It was published in the issue of 19 October 1876, pp. 546–50.

92. *LL*, 1:305.

93. Ibid., 2:500–1; Dawson, *Huxley Papers*, 180–81; Huxley Papers, vol. 32.

94. Huxley stipulated that he would accept membership only "as long as I am not understood to be committed to any particular method or procedure—such as the legal enforcement of abstinence. . . ." (Huxley Papers, vol. 23, fols. 238–39).

95. Donnelly to Huxley, 18 February 1882, ibid., vol. 13, fol. 306.

96. Mrs. Mary H. Phelps to Mrs. Huxley, 11 January 1889. ibid., vol. 24, fol. 115. The ambassador's wife received the photographs (14 January 1889, ibid., fol. 116).

97. John Calhoun Stallcup to Huxley, 14 May 1890, ibid., vol. 26, fol. 210.

98. Wallace Wood to Huxley, 4 March 1892, ibid., vol. 29, fol. 90.

99. Franklin W. Hooper to Huxley, 3 May 1894, ibid., vol. 30, fol. 197.

100. Some typical tributes were T. N. Gill, "Huxley and His Work," *Smithsonian Annual Report, 1895*, 759–79; W. H. Flower, "Reminiscences of Professor Huxley," *North American Review* 161 (1895): 279–86; "Huxley's Greatest Service," *Nation* 61 (1895): 5–6; O. C. Marsh, "Thomas Henry Huxley," *American Journal of Science* 50 (1895): 177–83.

Chapter 5. Rhetorical Combatant, 1860–1895

1. Thomas Henry Huxley, *On a Piece of Chalk*, Loren Eiseley, ed. (New York: Scribner, 1967), 13.

2. *LL*, 1:247.

3. This annual series of lectures began in 1855 (Huxley-Heathorn Correspondence, fol. 278).

4. *LL*, 1:209.

5. Ibid., 211.

6. Ibid., 210–12, 214.

7. Ibid., 218–19.

8. Ibid., 217.

9. *Lyell*, 2:363; Huxley, *Collected Essays* (hereafter cited as *CE*), 7:viii.

10. *LL*, 1:211, 216, 220–22, 245, 273, 275–76, 289, 298, 319, 323, 335–36, 386, 391–92, 442, 514.

11. Ibid., 222–23; *CE*, 2:vi–vii. Reprinted in ibid., 303–475. The person Huxley permitted to take shorthand notes and publish them, apparently made much money, so Huxley later regretted not publishing them himself (*LL*, 1:223).

12. 18 December 1862, ibid.

13. 2 July 1863, ibid., 266.

14. Ibid.

15. Ibid., 271.

16. Huxley to Dyster, 26 January 1865, Huxley Papers, vol. 15, fol. 130. Huxley, Darwin, and some of their friends helped launch *The Reader* in January 1863, but it lasted only three years. See Huxley Papers, vol. 5, fols. 223–24; vol. 7, fols. 118–19; vol. 15, fol. 130; vol. 22, fol. 194.

17. Reprinted in T. H. Huxley, *Lay Sermons, Addresses, and Reviews*, introduction by Oliver Lodge (New York: Appleton, 1910), 1–19; *CE*, 1:18–41. *The Fortnightly Review* had been founded in 1865. John Morley was its distinguished editor from 1867 until 1882.

18. *LL*, 1:325.

19. Huxley to Haeckel, 21 January 1868, ibid.

20. John Morley, *Recollections*, 2 vols. (London: Macmillan, 1917), 1:90.

21. 12 September, *LL*, 1:319.

22. Ibid., 229, 319.

23. Ibid., 322–23.

24. Ibid., 336.

25. *CE*, 5:239.

26. Huxley to Charles Albert Watts, 10 September 1883, Huxley Papers, vol. 28, fol. 196.

27. Ibid., fol. 197. See also Hirst Journals, vol. 5, fol. 2578.

28. Huxley to [unknown], 28 November 1883, Letters to T. H. Huxley, Wellcome Institute for the History of Medicine Library, London (hereafter cited as W.L.). These seventy-five overlooked Huxley letters, uncataloged and unarranged in a file folder, are a valuable resource.

29. R. H. Hutton, "Pope Huxley," *Spectator* 43:135–36. The term was again publicized in the 1 October 1870 *Spectator* (43:1170–71). It came to be applied to Herbert Spencer's famous doctrine of the Unknowable and he readily accepted it. In June 1876 Lesile Stephen gave the term a dramatic and literary flavor when, at the death of his wife, he wrote "An Agnostic's Apology" in the *Fortnightly Review*. See also George W. Hallam, "Source of the Word 'Agnostic'," *Modern Language Notes* 70 (1955): 265–69; Priscilla Metcalf, *James Knowles: Victorian Editor and Architect* (Oxford: Clarendon Press, 1980), 214; Bernard Lightman, *The Origins of Agnosticism: Victorian Unbelief and the Limits of Knowledge* (Baltimore: Johns Hopkins University Press, 1987), passim.

30. Reprinted in *CE*, 1:166–98.

31. A summary of this address appears in ibid., 6:192–211.

32. *LL*, 1:361.

33. Reprinted in *CE*, 2:120–86.

34. In the July 1871 issue of the *Quarterly Review*, a review hostile to Darwin's work was published anonymously, but Huxley correctly suspected that Mivart was the author (*CE*, 2:122). See also *Hooker* 2:128.

35. Mivart, "Some Reminiscences of T. H. Huxley," *Nineteenth Century* 42 (1897): 985–98. See also Huxley to Knowles, 24 June 1876, Letters of Huxley, W.L.

36. Huxley to Tyndall, 1 January 1873, *LL*, 1:419–20.

37. 1 and 2 March 1874, ibid., 439.

38. Reprinted in *Macmillan's Magazine* and in *CE*, 3:1–27.

39. *LL*, 1:442.

40. Reprinted in *Science and Culture*, 206–52 and in *CE*, 1:199–250.

41. *LL*, 1:476–79.

42. Ibid., 491.

43. Reprinted in *Science and Culture*, 281–316; and in *CE*, 2:187–226.

44. Reprinted in *CE*, 6:3–240.

45. Reprinted in ibid., 2:227–43.

46. Reprinted in the *Nineteenth Century*, in *Science and Culture*, 135–55, and in *CE*, 4:1–23.

47. Reprinted in *Science and Culture*, 7–30; and in *CE*, 3:134–59.

48. Reprinted in *CE*, 2:244–47. A longer obituary for the Royal Society was finally completed in 1888. It is reprinted in ibid., 253–302. In February 1888 he wrote to a friend: "I have been reading the *Origin* slowly again for the *n*th time, with the view of picking out the essentials of the argument, for the obituary notice. Nothing entertains me more than to hear people call it easy reading" (*LL*, 2:202–3). See also ibid., 204–5.

49. Darwin Papers, vol. 106/7, sec. 5, fols. 204–5, C. U. L.

50. See Cyril Bibby, "Huxley: Prince of Controversialists," *Twentieth Century* 161 (March 1957): 268–76.

51. This article appeared in America in the *Popular Science Monthly* in February 1886. It was reprinted in *Controverted Questions*, 56–73; and in *CE*, 4:139–63.

52. Reprinted in the *Popular Science Monthly*, April 1886; *Controverted Questions*, 74–100; *CE*, 4:164–200. See Huxley to Knowles, 15 and 20 January 1886, Letters of Huxley, W.L., and *LL*, 2:125.

53. Reprinted in *Controverted Questions*, 101–62, and *CE*, 4:287–372.

54. *LL*, 2:154. See aslo ibid., 149.

55. Ibid., 154.

56. Ibid., 155.

57. The article was reprinted in the *Popular Science Monthly*, February 1887; and in *Controverted Questions*, 163–83.

58. *LL*, 2:156.

59. Ibid.

60. 13 December 1886, ibid.

61. Ibid., 167–68. The article, "Scientific and Pseudo-Scientific Realsim," was reprinted in the *Popular Science Monthly* for April, *Controverted Questions*, 184–205; and *CE*, 5:59–89.

62. *LL*, 2:168; Huxley to Knowles, 9 March 1887, Letters of Huxley, W.L. The article, "Science and Pseudo-Science," was reprinted in the June issue of the *Popular Science Monthly*, *Controverted Questions*, 206–31; and *CE*, 5:90–125.

63. George Jacob Holyoake to Huxley, 20 April 1887, Huxley Papers, vol. 18, fol. 216.

64. *LL*, 2:169. The article, "An Episcopal Triology," was reprinted in *Controverted Questions*, 232–5; and *CE*, 5:126–69. Huxley's friend Hirst wrote in his journal for 16 October 1887: "Huxley paid me a visit. . . . He was in good form, and very cheery. He is writing in the 19th Century against the Duke of Argyle" (vol. 5, fol. 2461).

65. *LL*, 2:171.

66. Letters of Huxley, W.L. See also *LL*, 2:235.

67. Huxley to Knowles, 3 June 1888, Letters of Huxley, W.L.; *LL*, 2:212–13.

68. *LL*, 2:235.

69. The article was reprinted in *Controverted Questions*, 256–93; and in *CE*, 5:209–62.

70. 5 February 1889, vol. 5, fol. 2578. See also fol. 2585.

71. Reprinted in the September issue of the *Popular Science Monthly*, *Controverted Questions*, 294–316; and *CE*, 5:160–91.

72. 1 March 1889, vol. 5, fol. 2583.

73. Huxley to Knowles, 28 February 1889, Letters of Huxley, W.L.; *LL*, 2:237.

74. *LL*, 2:237.

75. Ibid., 238.

76. Huxley to Knowles, 15 March, Letters of Huxley, W.L.; *LL*, 2:239. The article, "Agnosticism, a Rejoinder," was reprinted in *Controverted Questions*, 317–65; and *CE*, 5:263–308.

77. 13 April 1889, vol. 5, fol. 2592.

78. 30 April 1889, vol. 5, fol. 2598.

79. Huxley to Edward Clodd, 15 April 1889, *LL*, 2:245.

80. Reprinted in *Controverted Questions*, 350–90; and *CE*, 5:309–65.

81. *LL*, 2:240.

82. Hirst Journals, 12 June 1889, vol. 5, fol. 2607.

83. Huxley to Knowles, 6 May, Letters of Huxley, W.L.; *LL*, 2:241 (italics in original). See also Huxley to Knowles, 14 May 1889, Letters of Huxley, W.L.

84. Huxley to Knowles, 4 May 1889, *LL*, 2:241.

85. 22 May 1889, Letters of Huxley, W.L.; *LL*, 2:242.

86. 30 May 1889, *LL*, 2:240.

87. Huxley to Knowles, 14 April 1889, Letters of Huxley, W.L.; *LL*, 2:239.

88. 22 May 1889, *LL*, 2:249.

89. For example, see the following articles in the *North American Review*: Robert Ingersoll, "Professor Huxley," 149 (1888): 157–63; John Burroughs, "The Corroboration of Professor Huxley," ibid., 560–68.

90. See William George (Lord) Armstrong to Huxley, 8 January 1891, Huxley Papers, vol. 10, fol. 138.

91. Hooker to Tyndall, 11 December 1889, Huxley Papers, vol. 8, fol. 421.

92. Reprinted in *Controverted Questions*, 391–417; and *CE* 4:201–38.

93. Houston Peterson, *Huxley, Prophet of Science* (London: Longmans Green, 1932), 261.

94. *CE*, 4:207.

95. Reprinted in *Controverted Questions*, 418–37; and *CE*, 5:366–92.

96. Reprinted in the *Popular Science Monthly* in August 1891.

97. Reprinted in the August *Popular Science Monthly*, *Controverted Questions*, 437–55; and *CE*, 5:393–419.

98. Hirst Journals, vol. 5, fol. 2759.

99. Sir Mountstuart Grant-Duff to Leonard Huxley, 4 November 1898, *LL*, 1:381.

100. *LL*, 2:289.

101. Ibid., 291. The battle with the Salvation Army is brought together in *CE*, 9:188–334.

102. Reprinted in *Controverted Questions*, 456–89; and *CE*, 4:239–86.

103. Reprinted in *CE*, 5:192–208.

104. Reprinted in ibid., 1–59.

105. See *LL*, 2:370–81. Published in *CE*, 9:46–86. It was also published in America in the November and December 1893 issues of the *Popular Science Monthly*.

106. Huxley Papers, vol. 8, fol. 281; *LL*, 2:377–78. See also ibid., 381.

107. Huxley's use of the extended analogy of the gardener throughout this address stems from the fact that he was spending much of his time happily tending his garden in retirement at Eastbourne.

108. Tyndall to Spencer, 25 November 1893, Spencer Papers, Athenaeum Collection, MS. 791, item 224, U.L.C.

109. Papers of Huxley, W.L.

110. *LL*, 1:162. See also ibid., 69, 510.

111. *CE*, 1:16–17.

112. "Prof. Tyndall," *Nineteenth Century*, 1.

113. C.K. Thomas, "The Rhetoric of Thomas Henry Huxley," Ph.D. diss., Cornell University, 1930, p. 303.

Chapter 6. Rhetorical Stance: Secular Theologian

1. Gould, "Knight Takes Bishop?", 33.

2. *CE*, 5:313. Throughout this chapter citations are from this nine-volume collection, unless otherwise noted, and will be cited in the body in parentheses. They are of course only a few representative items used to illustrate the points being made.

3. David Knight, *The Age of Science: The Scientific World-view in the Nineteenth Century* (Oxford: Basil Blackwell, 1986), 4.

4. 1 October 1880, *CE*, 3:150. This address is also available in an anthology of *British Public Addresses, 1828–1960*, ed. James McBath and Walter Fisher (Boston: Houghton, 1971), 376–87.

5. Huxley to Kingsley, 30 April 1863, *LL*, 1:258.

6. Ibid.

7. 19 November 1876, ibid., 505.

8. Ibid., 235.

9. Ibid., 75, 91.

10. *CE*, 3:239 (italics mine).

11. *LL*, 2:120.

12. Ibid., 172.

13. Huxley to Dohrn, 7 July 1871, ibid., 1:389.

14. As quoted by E. B. Poulton, "Thomas Henry Huxley," *Nature* 115 (9 May 1925): 708.

15. Huxley to Kingsley, 23 September 1860, *LL*, 1:238.

16. Huxley to M. Henri Gadeau de Kerville, February 1887, *LL*, 2:172.

17. See also Huxley to C. A. Watts, 10 September 1883, Huxley Papers, vol. 28, fol. 196.

18. Moore, *Post-Darwinian Controversies*, 99.

19. "Knight Takes Bishop?" 33 (italics in original).

Chapter 7. Communicating with Close Friends: The X Club

1. Vol. 4, fol. 1702. See also Hirst's minutes of the meeting in X Club Notebooks, Royal Institution, vol. 1, p. 1: Tyndall Journals, vol. 3, fol. 1260; Herbert Spencer, *An Autobiography*, 2 vols. (New York: D. Appleton, 1904), 2:133; Sir Edward Frankland, *Sketches from the Life of Edward Frankland* (London: Spottiswoode & Co., 1902), 150.
2. Huxley Papers, vol. 70, item 7.
3. "Tyndall," 10.
4. Spencer, *Autobiography*, 2:134. See X Club Notebooks, 5 January 1865, 2 February 1865, 1 March 1988.
5. "Tyndall," 10.
6. Spencer, *Autobiography*, 2:134. See also ibid., 132; Hirst Journals, vol. 4, fols. 1702, 1735; Huxley, "Tyndall," 10.
7. For additional details of the X Club and further documentation, interested readers may wish to consult Roy M. MacLeod, "The X-Club: A Social Network of Science in Late-Victorian England," *Notes and Records of the Royal Society of London* 24 (1970): 305–22; J. Vernon Jensen, "The X Club: Fraternity of Victorian Scientists," *The British Journal for the History of Science* 3 (1970): 63–72; J. Vernon Jensen, "Interrelationships Within the Victorian 'X-Club'," *The Dalhousie Review* 51 (1971–72): 539–52; J. Vernon Jensen, "Tyndall's Role in the 'X-Club'," *John Tyndall: Essays on a Natural Philosopher*, chap. 12, eds., W. H. Brock, N. D. McMillan, and R. C. Mollan (Dublin: Royal Dublin Society, 1981); Ruth Barton, "The X Club: Science, Religion, and Social Change in Victorian England," Ph.D. diss., University of Pennsylvania, 1976; Ruth Barton, " 'An Influential set of Chaps': The X Club and Royal Society Politics 1864–85," *British Journal for the History of Science* 23 (March 1990): 53–81.
8. Prof. Roy MacLeod discovered the notebooks among the Hirst and Tyndall papers in the Royal Institution. I had the notebooks microfilmed in 1970; a copy is in my possession and the negative remains in the Royal Institution.
9. See Frankland, *Sketches*, 150–61; *Hooker*, 1:541–44.
10. "Reminiscences" in Bibby, *Essence of Huxley*, 30. See also Tyndall Correspondence, vol. 9, fols. 2918, 2944, 2945, 2950, 2951, 2973, 3024, 3026, 3027; Huxley Papers, vol. 9, fol. 2983A.
11. *LL*, 1:168.
12. Tyndall Correspondence, vol. 12, fol. 3975. See also, Huxley Papers, vol. 16, fol. 248.
13. Hirst Journals, vol. 2, fols. 1290, 1302. See also, ibid., vol. 3, fol. 1514.
14. Ibid., vol. 3, fols. 1494, 1510, 1511, 1514.
15. "Reminiscences," in Bibby, *Essence of Huxley*, 30.
16. Spencer, *Autobiography*, 1:485; Tyndall's Journals, vol. 3, fol. 730; *Fortnightly Review*, 55 (February 1894): 141–48.
17. Lubbock Letters, 1862–64, Add. MSS 49639, fols. 47, 64, 89, B. L.
18. In 1886 Hirst wrote in his journal, "I may truly say that of all the Institutions of which I am or have been a member none has contributed so much as the Athenaeum Club to my convenience and well being" (vol. 5, fol. 2299).
19. "Tyndall," 10. See also Spencer, *Autobiography*, 2:135.

20. *Autobiography*, 2:134. Also unintelligible to researchers would be such expressions as in the following letter from Tyndall to Huxley: "On reaching this place [his home, Hind Head] last night through the snow I found your algebraic equation. What am I to do? I cannot go; to stay I am ashamed" (6 January 1886, Huxley Papers, vol. 1, fol. 179).

21. Spencer to Mrs. Lecky, 28 October 1876, Mrs. C. E. Lecky Correspondence MS 1931.20, Trinity College, Dublin. See also same to same, 24 May 1875, ibid., 1931.11; Huxley to (William) Carruthers, 16 March 1887, H 981.30, A.P.S. Library, Philadelphia.

22. X Club Notebooks, vol. 1, p. 1; Frankland, *Sketches*, 162.

23. For some interesting discussions of these XX excursions, see Hirst Journals, vol. 4, fols. 1735, 1786, 2000; X Club Notebooks, vol. 1, p. 8 et passim; Huxley Papers, vol. 8, fol. 168; vol. 70, item 16; Spencer, *Autobiography*, 2:136; Frankland, *Sketches*, 150.

24. Spencer Papers, Athenaeum Collection, MS 791, item 109i, U. L. C.

25. Frankland, *Sketches*, 161.

26. "Tyndall," 10–11.

27. Spencer, *Autobiography*, 2:135 (italics in original).

28. 4 December 1885, David Duncan, *Life and Letters of Herbert Spencer*, 2 vols. (New York: Appleton, 1908), 1:333.

29. Hirst Journals, vol. 4, fol. 1842.

30. Spencer, *Autobiography*, 2:132.

31. 16 February 1870, vol. 5, fol. 1859. See also ibid., fols. 2198, 2200, 2202.

32. For Tyndall's deep appreciation for the wedding gift given by his X Club friends, see Huxley Papers, vol. 8, fol. 367. See also ibid., fols. 365–66; Spencer Papers, Athenaeum Collection, MS 791, items 18, 113, U. L. C.

33. "Tyndall," 7.

34. Mivart, "Reminiscences of Thomas Henry Huxley," 985.

35. X Club Notebooks, 2 November 1865.

36 Hirst Journals, vol. 4, fols. 1712, 1713, 1734. See also ibid., vol. 3, fols. 1540, 1542; Tyndall Journals, vol. 3, fol. 163.

37. X Club Notebooks, 29 June 1867 (italics in original). See also ibid., 1 October 1868; Lubbock Letters, Add Mss, 49460, fol. 10, B. L.

38. For example, see Huxley Papers, vol. 8, fol. 388; Royal Society MS 7.323; Metcalf, *James Knowles*, 214.

39. For example, see R. S. Referee Reports, 3.183; 4.154, 157, 252; 5.119, 124; 7.496.

40. Hirst Journals, vol. 4, fol. 2092.

41. *LL*, 1:419.

42. Hirst Journals, vol. 5, fol. 1859.

43. Horatio Gordon Hutchinson, *Life of Sir John Lubbock, Lord Avebury*, 2 vols. (London: Macmillan, 1914), 1:117–18.

44. Ibid., 325; Huxley Papers, vol. 8, fol. 388.

45. Spencer Papers, Athenaeum Collection, MS 791, items 250, 264.

46. Hutchinson, *Lubbock*, 2:164–66; Duncan, *Spencer*, 2:200.

47. Hirst Journals, vol. 4, fol. 2130; Huxley Papers, vol. 11, fol. 61, vol. 26, fol. 209, vol. 27, fol. 95; Hutchinson, *Lubbock*, 1:197.

48. Huxley Papers, vol. 8, fols. 359–62, 365, 369.

49. Hirst Journals, vol. 5, fol. 2744. See also ibid., fols. 2293, 2302, 2306, 2676–77, 2680, 2682–83, 2686–87, 2747. When summing up his views on various individuals for his autobiography in 1876, the kindly Darwin wrote: "Herbert

Spencer's conversation seemed to me very interesting, but I did not like him particularly, and did not feel that I could easily have become intimate with him. I think that he was extremely egotistical. ... His deductive manner of treating every subject is wholly opposed to my frame of mind. His conclusions never convince me" (Barlow, *Autobiography*, 108–9).

50. Huxley Papers, vol. 7, fol. 243.

51. Ibid.

52. Ibid., vol. 8, fol. 420. See also Hooker's lengthy letter to Huxley on the same day, ibid., vol. 3, fols. 352–53.

53. Ibid., vol. 8, fol. 421.

54. Duncan, *Spencer*, 2:37.

55. Ibid.

56. For those interested in delving into the details of the Huxley-Spencer rift, see Huxley Papers, vol. 3, fol. 360, vol. 7, fols. 242, 244, vol. 8, fols. 411–13, 421–22, vol. 12, fols. 285–87, vol. 18, fol. 123; Spencer Papers, Athenaeum Collection, MS 781, item 224, U. L.C.; Huxley to Knowles, 21 November 1889, Huxley Letters, W.L.; *LL*, 2:258–59, 264; Duncan, *Spencer*, 1:197–98, 359–61, 369–71, 2:26–27. For tensions between Spencer and other X Club members, see Huxley Papers, vol. 3, fols. 353, 360, vol. 8, fol. 413; Duncan, *Spencer*, 1:220; Hirst Journals, vol. 5, fol. 1891.

57. Mrs. Huxley to J. W. Troughton, Spencer Papers, Athenaeum Collection, MS 791, item 350, U. L. C.

58. Commenting on how Spencer depended on X Club and other conversations for securing information, Irvine (*Apes, Angles, and Victorians*, 236) asserted in Churchillian fashion, "No modern thinker has read so little in order to write so much." In his old age, Spencer found it very exhausting and difficult to converse even with close friends.

59. The eight were elected Fellows in the following years: Hooker (1847), Busk (1850), Huxley (1851), Tyndall (1852), Frankland (1853), Spottiswoode (1853), Lubbock (1857), and Hirst (1861).

60. Spencer to Hooker, 28 March 1874, Duncan, *Spencer*, 1:223. Spencer declined invitations to membership in the American Philosophical Society and in other foreign academies (Spencer to the American Philosophical Society, 22 April 1885, A.P.S.).

61. *Hooker*, 1:543; X Club Notebooks, 6 January 1870.

62. Frankland, *Sketches*, 160; X Club Notebooks, 2 March 1871.

63. Hirst Journals, vol. 4, fol. 1963. See also Hooker to Spottiswoode, 26 February 1873, MC9.502, R.S.

64. Tyndall Journals, vol. 3, fol. 1260.

65. Lubbock Letters, 1868–70, Add Mss, 49641, fol. 59, B.L.

66. Hirst Journals, vol. 4, fol. 914. See also Busk to Tyndall, 19 April 1871, 21 April 1880, Tyndall Correspondence, vol. 1, fols. 180, 181.

67. Hirst Journals, vol. 4, fol. 2130. See also *Proceedings of the Royal Society of London*, 36:74; Huxley to Tyndall, 9 November 1883, *LL*, 2:66.

68. Tyndall Correspondence, vol. 9, fol. 3112.

69. Hirst Journals, vol. 5, fol. 2555.

70. Ibid., fol. 2685.

71. Hooker was one of the original forty-seven members; Busk, Huxley and Tyndall were elected in 1855, Frankland in 1859, Lubbock in 1860, Spottiswoode in 1861, and Hirst in 1865.

72. For instance, see Tyndall to Hooker, undated 1868, Huxley Papers, vol. 8,

fol. 344; *LL*, 1:432; *Hooker*, 1:542, 2:108; Frankland, *Sketches*, 155: X Club Notebooks, 7 February 1867.

73. Frankland, *Sketches*, 157. See also X Club Notebooks, 7 March 1867, 7 November 1867, 9 January 1868, 6 February 1868, 4 March 1869.

74. Lubbock to Dr. Sharpey, 28 September 1870, MC9.123, R.S.

75. Spencer, *Autobiography*, 2:256.

76. Ibid., 331–32.

77. Huxley Papers, vol. 8, fols. 356, 357.

78. Hirst Journals, vol. 4, fol. 2116.

79. For example, see Lubbock Letters, 1865–67, Add Mss, 49640, fols. 24, 25, 133, B.L.; Tyndall Correspondence, vol. 12, fols. 3964, 3971. Huxley notified the club that he had accepted the presidency of the Ethnological Society (X Club Notebooks, 5 June 1868).

80. "Tyndall," 5.

81. Hirst Journals, vol. 5, fol. 2416. See also X Club Notebooks, 5 October 1865, 5 December 1867.

82. *Hooker*, 1:541. See also Spencer, *Autobiography*, 2:139; X Club Notebooks, 3 November 1864.

83. Vol. 4 fol. 1702. See also Frankland, *Sketches*, 150.

84. Spencer, *Autobiography*, 2:137. See also Spencer to Huxley, 25 December 1864, Huxley Papers, vol. 7, fols. 118, 119.

85. Huxley Papers, vol. 15, fol. 130.

86. Duncan, *Spencer*, 1:153. At the same time Spencer also requested the aid of Sir John F. W. Herschell, MS 16.495, 496, R.S.

87. Huxley Papers, vol. 5, fols. 223, 224.

88. Spencer, *Autobiography*, 2:140.

89. Ibid.

90. Ibid., 138.

91. Ibid., 14, 268–69; John Fiske, "Edward L. Youmans," in *A Century of Science and Other Essays* (Boston: Houghton Mifflin, 1899), 89–97; Youmans to Huxley, 28 April 1871, Huxley Papers, vol. 29, fol. 259.

92. *Hooker*, 1:543.

93. Add Mss 49644, fol. 11, B.L.

94. Rhees MSS: RH 3963–3971, 3973–3980, H. L. The Huntington Library possesses twenty-six Tyndall letters. John F. Frazer Papers, F865.h, A. P. S.; Sir John Lubbock Papers, B:L961, A. P. S.; Hirst Journals, vol. 5, fol. 2200.

95. Huntington MSS: HM 13718–24, 13727, 13729–31, 13749, H. L.; Fiske MSS: FK 1141, 1146, H. L.; Fiske, *Essays, Historical and Literary*, 2 vols. (New York: Macmillan, 1902), 2: 204, 247–48. Fiske was a guest at an X Club meeting on 4 December 1873 (X Club Notebooks).

96. Huntington MSS: HM 13245, 13253, 13254, H. L.; T. H. Huxley Papers, B:H981.21, A. P. S.

97. Huntington MSS: HM 13426, 13255, H. L.; Fiske, *American Political Ideas Viewed from the Standpoint of Universal History* (New York: Harper & Bros., 1885), preface; John Spencer Clark, *The Life and Letters of John Fiske*, 2 vols. (Boston: Houghton, 1917), 2:126–28, 131, 139–41, 143, 145, 149–53.

98. Huntington MSS: HM 13739, 13741, 13759, H. L.; Edward L. Youmans, *Herbert Spencer on the Americans and the Americans on Herbert Spencer* (New York: D. Appleton, 1883).

99. Fiske to Spencer, 23 April 1882, Spencer Papers, Athenaeum Collection, MS 791, item 162i, U. L. C.

100. Huntington MSS: HM 13743, H. L.; Fiske, *Essays*, 2:248; Clark, *Fiske*, 2:269–91.

101. Huntington MSS: HM 13754, 13755, 13243, 13256, 13757, H. L.

102. *Hooker*, 1:542; X Club Notebooks, 4 January 1866.

103. Ibid., 4 February 1869.

104. Ibid., 3 December, 1868.

105. Hirst Journals, vol. 4, fol. 1840.

106. Ibid., vol. 6, fol. 2585.

107. Huxley Papers, vol. 8, fol. 176.

108. For example, see ibid., fols. 374, 375, 376, 386.

109. Spencer Papers, Athenaeum Collection, MS 791, item 60, 61, 77, 94, U. L. C. At Spencer's death, Mrs. Huxley wrote that she was looking forward to reading his autobiography, many pages of which "were years and years ago submitted to my husband for criticism. To prevent any publication of it without his [Spencer's] consent, he would have, say pages 1 & 13–40 printed by one printer, 18–30 & 60 by another," etc. (Mrs. Huxley to J. W. Troughton, 16 February 1904, ibid., item 350).

110. Huxley Papers, vol. 8, fol. 902. Darwin was present as a guest at an X Club meeting at least once (X Club Notebooks, 5 March 1868).

111. Vol. 4, fol. 1702.

112. Frankland, *Sketches*, 51.

113. *Hooker*, 1:542; X Club Notebooks, 4 January 1866, 5 December 1867.

114. *Hooker*, 1:542; X Club Notebooks, 1 February 1866.

115. *Hooker*, 1:543; X Club Notebooks, 7 January 1869.

116. For a discussion of this "Ayrton Affair," see *Hooker*, 2:159–77; Turrill, *Hooker*, 123–25; Eve and Creasey, *Tyndall*, 160–66; George Bentham to William Spottiswoode, 16 July 1872, Huxley Papers, vol. 10, fols. 303–05.

117. Some of Tyndall's vigorous writings on the subject were published in 1887 by William Blackwood and Sons in a one-penny pamphlet entitled, "Mr. Gladstone and Home Rule." See Tyndall to Lord Wolmer [sic—should be Woolner], 2, 4 December 1888, MS Selbourne 13.37, 38, Western MSS, Bodleian Library.

118. Huxley Papers, vol. 16, fol. 273. For Huxley's opposition to Home Rule see *LL*, 2:132–34, 144–45, 179, 187–88. For a discussion of the Unionist views of men of science in general, see J. L. Hammond, *Gladstone and the Irish Nation* (London: Longmans, Green, 1938), 540–53.

119. 1 January 1888, Huxley Papers, vol. 8, fol. 262. See also Hooker to Tyndall, 29 December 1887, ibid., fol. 410.

120. 4 January 1888, ibid., fol. 263.

121. 9 November 1866, ibid., fol. 322.

122. X Club Notebooks, 7 December 1865.

123. Ibid., 3 January 1867.

124. Ibid., 9 January 1868.

125. Ibid., 4 March 1869.

126. Ibid., 6 October 1870.

127. Ibid., 3 November 1870.

128. Hirst had attended the December 1891 and January 1892 X Club meetings (Hirst Journals, vol. 6, fols. 2833–34, 2848), so he literally was active in the club until his death.

129. Huxley Papers, vol. 8, fol. 441.

130. Spencer Papers, Athenaeum Collection, MS 791, item 226, U. L. C.

131. Hooker to Mrs. Huxley, 24 October 1897, Huxley Papers, vol. 3, fol. 431.

132. For information on the declining years of the X Club, see: *LL*, 2:128, 209, 353; *Hooker*, 2:350, 358; Huxley Papers, vol. 2, fol. 409, vol. 3, fols. 283, 320, 325, 379, 384, 389, 391, 394, 400, vol. 8, fols. 275, 413, 416, 437, 438, 439, 442, 443, 445, vol. 9, fols, 229, 231, 236; Hutchinson, *Lubbock*, 1:258–59, 325, 2:269; Duncan, *Spencer*, 2:23; Frankland, *Sketches*, 161–62.

133. Spencer Papers, Athenaeum Collection, MS 791, item 289, U. L. C.

134. Ibid., item 313. See also Duncan, *Spencer*, 2:219.

135. Hutchinson, *Lubbock*, 2:204, 215, 284.

136. As quoted in ibid., 298.

137. Ibid., 303.

138. *Autobiography*, 2:134.

139. *LL*, 2:120.

140. Ibid., 1:281.

141. Ibid., 282.

142. "Tyndall," 11.

143. Ibid.

144. *Autobiography*, 2:135.

145. Ibid.

146. As quoted in MacLeod, "X-Club," 305.

147. Ibid., 318–19.

148. James R. Moore. Review of *The Origins of Agnosticism: Victorian Unbelief and the Limits of Knowledge*, by Bernard Ligthman. *Isis*, 79 (September 1988): 511.

149. Huxley to Hooker, 22 March 1889, *LL*, 2:246.

Chapter 8. Rhetorical Legacy

1. Huxley Papers, vol. 49, fol. 59.

2. *Autobiography*, 9.

3. *LL*, 1:128.

4. "Tyndall," 5.

5. *Pall Mall Gazette*, 24 October 1988.

6. *LL*, 2:65.

7. Huxley Papers, vol. 49, fol. 59.

8. *LL*, 2:42.

9. Ibid., 173.

10. 14 May 1889, Letters of Huxley, W.L.

11. *Huxley Papers*, p. v.

12. C. S. Minot, "Huxley's Writings," *International Review* 11 (1881): 536.

13. *Darwin*, 2:34.

14. Barlow, *Darwin's Autobiography,*106.

15. Huxley Papers, vol. 31, fol. 71.

16. Spencer, *Autobiography*, 1:467.

17. Huxley to G. S., 9 November 1893, *LL*, 2:387.

18. Huxley Papers, vol. 49, fol. 57.

19. Ibid., fol. 58.

20. *LL*, 1:344.

21. *Hooker*, 2:337.

22. *Public Speaking and Debate*, 9th ed. (London: T. F. Unwin, n.d.), 226.

23. Huxley Papers, vol. 27, fol. 238.

24. William Irvine, *Thomas Henry Huxley* (London: Longmans, Green, 1960), 37.

25. Huxley Papers, vol. 49, fols. 57–58.

26. Ibid., vol. 31, fol. 71.

27. Barlow, *Darwin's Autobiography*, 106.

28. *LL*, 1:519, n.

29. Holyoake, *Public Speaking*, 226.

30. An unidentified, undated symposium, Huxley Papers, vol. 49, fol. 58.

31. *Autobiography*, 9. See also Roos, "Neglected Bibliographical Aspects," 405.

32. "Tyndall," 5.

33. *Problems and Persons* (London: Longmans, Green, 1903), 249. See also *Pall Mall Gazette*, 24 October 1888.

34. *CE*, 6:vi.

35. "Tyndall," 3. See also Roos, "Neglected Bibliographical Aspects," 406.

36. Cyril Bibby, "The Huxley-Wilberforce Debate: A Postcript," *Nature* 176 (20 August 1955): 363; Charles S. Blinderman, "Semantic Aspects of T. H. Huxley's Literary Style," *Journal of Communication* 12 (September 1962): 175.

37. *Towards the Mountain: An Autobiography* (New York: Scribner, 1980), 70.

38. *LL*, 1:255.

39. L. Robert Stevens, "Darwin's Humane Reading: The Anaesthetic Man Reconsidered," *Victorian Studies*, 26 (Autumn 1982): 51–63.

40. "Reminiscences of Huxley," in *Essays Historical and Literary*, 2:205–7.

41. "Semantic Aspects," 177.

42. 8 May 1876, *LL*, 1:491.

43. E. A. Parkyn, "Oratory," *Westminster Review* 156 (November 1901): 559.

44. "Huxley's Collected Essays," *Nature* 49 (1 February 1894): 310.

45. *Pall Mall Gazette*, 24 October 1888.

46. Ibid.

47. Huxley Papers., vol. 25, fol. 254; *LL*, 2:372–75, 378.

48. *Pall Mall Gazette*, 24 October 1888. See also *LL*, 1:444–46; E. Ray Lankester, "Huxley's Collected Essays," *Nature* 49 (1 February 1894): 310–11.

49. *Autobiography*, 3.

50. Ibid., 15.

51. *Pall Mall Gazette*, 24 October 1888.

52. Ibid.

53. "Tyndall," 5.

54. *Autobiography*, 13.

55. *LL*, 1:107–8, 154; *CE*, 1:15.

56. *Pall Mall Gazette*, 24 October 1888.

57. *LL*, 1:438.

58. Ibid., 499. See also Baker, "Huxley in Tennessee," 428.

59. Randel, "Huxley in America," 88–89 ,93.

60. *New York Times*, 19 September 1876, p. 8.

61. *LL*, 2:377.

62. Huxley Papers, vol. 25, fol. 255.

63. MS Engl. misc. d. 177, fol. 465, Bodleian.

64. Huxley Papers, vol. 8, fol. 281; *LL*, 2:377.

65. Wilfrid Ward, *Problems and Persons*, 244.

66. *LL*, 2:376–78.

67. Blinderman, "Semantic Aspects," 171.

68. Alistair Cooke, *The Patient Has the Floor* (New York: Knopf, 1986), 13.
69. Huxley Papers, vol. 15, fol. 55 (italics in original). See also 6 May 1855, ibid., fol. 65.
70. Mivart, "Reminiscences of Huxley," 996.
71. T. H. Huxley, *On the Origin of Species: or the Causes of the Phenomena of Organic Nature. A Course of Six Lectures to Working Men* (New York: D. Appleton, 1863), 4.
72. Blinderman, "Semantic Aspects," 171.
73. *CE*, 8:viii.
74. 4 December 1859, Hirst Journals, vol. 3, fol. 1517.
75. *CE*, 8:v-vii.
76. *LL*, 1:124, 2:380;*CE*, 9:vii.
77. Huxley Papers, vol. 49, fols. 56–57.
78. Minot, "Huxley's Writings," 530.
79. R. M'Cheyne Edgar, "The Logic of Evolution," *The British and Foreign Evangelical Review* 145 (July 1888): 447.
80. 2 July 1895, Huxley Papers, vol. 82, fol. 16.
81. Jean Pradal, *The Literature of Science Popularisation: A Study of the Present Situation in Member States of the Council for Cultural Co-operation* (Strasbourg: Council of Europe, n.d., c. 1970), 22–23.
82. Gray to Charles L. Brace, (?) 1861, *Letters of Asa Gray*, ed. Jane Loring Gray, 2 vols. (London: Macmillan, 1893), 2:458.
83. "T. H. Huxley," *The Scientific Monthly* 84 (April 1957): 175.
84. For examples, see *LL*, 1:476; *New York Times*, 21 September 1876, p. 10.
85. Ward, *Problems and Persons*, 231.
86. Huxley Papers, vol. 49, fol. 59.
87. *LL*, 1:345.
88. See, for example, Thomas M. Sawyer, "Rhetoric in an Age of Science and Technology," *College Composition and Communication* 23 (1972): 390–98.
89. See, for instance, Greg Myers, "Nineteenth-Century Popularizations to Thermodynamics and the Rhetoric of Social Prophecy," *Victorian Studies* 29 (Autumn 1985): 60–65; Joseph H. Gardner, "Huxley Essay as "Poem'," *Victorian Studies* 14 (December 1970): 177–91; Oma Stanley, "T. H. Huxley's Treatment of Nature," *Journal of the History of Ideas* 18 (1957): 120–27; Thomas, "Rhetoric of Huxley," 159–65, 207–10, 228–30; D. J. Foskett, "T. H. Huxley and His Presentation of Scientific Material," M. A. thesis, Birkbeck College, University of London, 1955, passim; Donald Watt, "Soul-Facts: Humour and Figure in T. H. Huxley," *Prose Studies, 1800–1900* 1 (1978): 30–40.
90. Darwin Papers, vol. 98, fol. 13, C. U.; *LL*, 1:189.
91. Huxley to Sir J. Donnelly, 10 October 1890, *LL*, 1:171.
92. Spencer to Leonard Huxley, 6 November 1900, Huxley Papers, vol. 7, fol. 253.
93. See, for example, Jo Manton, *Elizabeth Garrett Anderson* (London: Meuthen, 1965), 120.
94. Huxley Papers, vol. 49, fol. 58.
95. *Autobiography*, 16–17.
96. Himmelfarb, *Darwinian Revolution*, 219.
97. Minot, "Huxley's Writings," 536.
98. Smalley, "Mr. Huxley," 514.
99. 5 December 1893, Letters of Huxley, W. L.
100. 30 June 1883, Huxley Papers, vol. 2, fol. 250.

101. David C. Somervell, *English Thought in the Nineteenth Century* (London: Methuen, 1929), 116.

102. "Huxley," 905.

103. Horace Traubel, *With Walt Whitman in Camden*, 4 vols. (New York and Philadelphia: M. Kennerley, 1914–53), 1:262.

104. Huxley Papers, vol. 49, fol. 37.

105. *LL*, 1:345.

106. 23 February 1899, Huxley Papers, vol. 20, fol. 200.

107. 4 May 1889, *LL*, 2:241.

108. Spencer to Huxley, 7 December 1885, Huxley Papers, vol. 7, fol. 169.

109. Barlow, *Darwin's Autobiography*, 106.

110. *Problems and Persons*, 233.

111. *LL*, 1:364.

112. Mivart, "Reminiscences of Huxley," 995.

113. Peterson, *Prophet of Science*, 16.

114. Huxley to Donnelly, 14 September 1886, *LL*, 2:148.

115. Edward B. Poulton, *Charles Darwin and the Origin of Species* (New York: Longmans, Green, 1909), 25–26.

116. *The Nation* 61 (1985): 5.

117. "Thomas Henry Huxley," *American Journal of Science*, 50 (1895): 183.

118. Hooker to W. H. Harvey, 3 February 1858, *Hooker*, 1:401.

119. 16 July 1967, *LL*, 1:311.

120. *LL*, 1:233.

121. *Problems and Persons*, 243.

122. Huxley to Knowles, 14 April 1889, Letters of Huxley, W. L.; *LL*, 2:239.

123. Minot, "Huxley's Writings," 527.

124. Eva Ingersoll Wakefield, ed., *The Letters of Robert G. Ingersoll* (New York: Philosophical Library, 1951), 310.

125. *The Works of Robert G. Ingersoll*, 12 vols. (New York: Dresden, 1912), 4:53.

126. E. J. Bunker to Huxley, 13 June 1889, Huxley Papers, vol. 11, fol. 188.

127. Charles Fluhrer to Huxley, 2 June 1892, ibid., vol. 16, fol. 140.

128. Traubel, *With Whitman*, 1:126, 137, 262.

129. For a list of some of these textbooks, see the Appendix.

130. Gilman, *Launching a University*, 51–52.

131. *Nature*, 115 (1925): 726. For a summary of Huxley's influence in placing specific young scientists in key positions in Britain and throughout the world, see Bibby, *Scientist Extraordinary*, 3.

132. Emily Morison Beck, et al., eds., *Bartlett's Familiar Quotations*, 15th ed. (Boston: Little, Brown, 1980).

133. George Seldes, compiler, *The Great Thoughts* (New York: Ballantine Books, 1985).

134. William L. Rivers and Cleve Mathews, *Ethics for the Media* (Englewood Cliffs, N.J.: Prentice-Hall, 1988), 11.

Conclusion

1. 11 April 1880, *Darwin*, 2:416–17.

2. For example, see his influence on the journalist, H. L. Mencken (Douglas C.

Stenerson, *H. L. Mencken: Iconoclast from Baltimore* (Chicago: University of Chicago Press, 1971), 102, 141, 157, 167, 229.

3. Henry Fairfield Osborn, "Enduring Recollections," *Nature* 115 (May 1925): 726.

4. *Autobiography, Memories and Experiences*, 2 vols. (Boston: Houghton Mifflin, 1904), 2:192.

5. Stephen Paget, "Truth and Righteousness," *Nature* 115 (May 1925): 749.

6. T. D. A. Cockerell, "Huxley's Message to Modern World," ibid., 750.

7. Bibby, "The Prince of Controversialists," 272.

8. "Huxley's Life and Work," *Nature* 63 (November 1900): 118.

9. E. B. Poulton, "Thomas Henry Huxley," ibid., 115 (May 1925): 709.

10. Rev. E. G. Russell, "A Student's Reminiscences," ibid., 752; Mivart, "Reminiscences of Huxley," 991.

11. Ronald Numbers, "Science and Religion," *Osiris*, 2d series, 1 (1985): 80.

12. *Problems and Persons*, 241.

13. *Autobiography*, 7.

14. Patrick Geddes, "Huxley as Teacher," *Nature* 115 (May 1925): 742.

15. C. Lloyd Morgan, "Processes of Life and Mind," ibid., 740.

16. James G. Paradis, *T. H. Huxley: Man's Place in Nature* (Lincoln: University of Nebraska Press, 1978), 9.

17. Osborn, "Enduring Recollections," 726.

18. "Knight Takes Bishop?" 31.

19. *Between Science and Religion: The Reaction to Scientific Naturalism in Late Victorian England* (New Haven: Yale University Press, 1974), 3.

20. *The Nature of Science: The History of Science in Western Culture Since 1600* (London: Andre Deutsch, 1976), 195.

21. W. J. Sollas, "The Master," *Nature* 115 (May 1925): 747.

22. Michael Foster and E. Ray Lankester, eds., *The Scientific Memoirs of Thomas Henry Huxley*, 4 vols. (London: Macmillan, 1898), preface.

23. Peterson, *Huxley*, vii.

24. "Thomas Henry Huxley," *Nineteenth Century* 46 (December 1900): 908.

25. H. E. Armstrong, "Huxley's Message in Education," *Nature*, 115 (May 1925): 743.

26. Paul J. McCartney, review of *Richard Griffith, 1784–1878: Papers Presented at the Centenary Symposium Organised by the Royal Dublin Society, 21 and 22 September 1978, Isis* 72 (December 1981): 687.

27. "Reminiscences," Bibby, *Essence of Huxley*, 31–32; Huxley Papers, vol. 62, fol. 1.

28. Osborn, "Enduring Recollections," 728.

29. "Home Memories," ibid., 698–702; *Thomas Henry Huxley: A Character Sketch* (Freeport, N.Y.: Books for Libraries Press, 1920, reprinted 1969).

30. "Huxley's Writings," 537.

31. Peterson, *Huxley*, 80. See also *LL*, 1:346. For Huxley's comments on this shift in public opinion, see *CE*, 7: x–xi.

32. See vol. 82.

33. "Huxley's Life and Work," 93.

34. *New York Times Book Review*, 30 June 1968, p. 1.

35. Randel, "Huxley in America," 98.

Select Bibliography

Primary Sources

MANUSCRIPT SOURCES

American Philosphical Society Library, Philadelphia
  T. H. Huxley Papers, Sir John Lubbock Papers, John Fries Frazer Papers
Bodleian Library, Oxford
  Selbourne MSS, Wilberforce MSS
British Library, London
  Additional MSS, Sir John Lubbock Letters, Tyndall Papers
University Library, Cambridge
  Darwin Papers
Henry E. Huntington Library, San Marino, Calif.
  Huntington MSS, Fiske MSS, Furnival MSS. Rhees MSS, Huxley Letters,
  Tyndall Letters
Imperial College of Science, Technology, and Medicine, London
  Huxley Papers and Huxley Manuscripts
University of London Library Collection
  Herbert Spencer Papers, Athenaeum Collection, Overstone Papers
Royal Institution, London
  John Tyndall Correspondence and Journals, Journals of T. A. Hirst, T. H.
  Huxley Letters, Faraday MSS
Royal Society, London
  Herschel Papers, Lubbock Letters, Sabine MSS, Referee Reports
Trinity College, Dublin
  Mrs. C. E. Lecky Correspondence
The Wellcome Institute for the History of Medicine Library, London
  Letters of T. H. Huxley

PUBLISHED WORKS OF HUXLEY

"Science at Sea." *Westminster Review* 61 (January 1854): 53–63.
Lay Sermons, Addresses, and Reviews. London: Macmillan, 1870.
Critiques and Addresses. London: Macmillan, 1873.
American Addresses. New York: D. Appleton, 1877.
*Science and Culture and Other Essays.*London: Macmillan, 1881.
Essays on Some Controverted Questions. London: Macmillan, 1892.

"Professor Tyndall." *Nineteenth Century* 203 (January 1894): 1–11.

Collected Essays. 9 vols. London: Macmillan, 1893–94. Reprint 1968.
   1. *Methods and Results*; 2. *Darwiniana*; 3. *Science and Education*; 4. *Science and Hebrew Tradition* ; 5. *Science and Christian Tradition*; 6. *Hume, With Helps to the Study of Berkeley;* 7. *Man's Place in Nature, and Other Anthropological Essays*; 8. *Discourses, Biological and Geological*; 9. *Evolution and Ethics, and Other Essays.*

The Scientific Memoirs of Thomas Henry Huxley. Edited by Michael Foster and E. Ray Lankester. 5 vols. London: Macmillan, 1898–1903.

Aphorisms and Reflections from the Works of T. H. Huxley. Selected by Henrietta A. Huxley. London: Macmillan, 1907.

Autobiography and Selected Essays by Thomas Henry Huxley. Edited by Ada L. F. Snell. Boston: Houghton Mifflin, 1909.

Lectures and Lay Sermons by Thomas Huxley. Edited by Oliver Lodge. London: J. M. Dent, 1910.

Huxley, Leonard. *Life and Letters of Thomas Henry Huxley.* 2 vols. New York: D. Appleton, 1916. Reprint 1968.

Copy of galley proof of unpublished part of "Mr. Balfour's Attack on Agnosticism." In *Huxley: Prophet of Science* by Houston Peterson, 315–27. New York: Longmans, Green, 1932.

T. H. Huxley's Diary of the Voyage of H.M.S. Rattlesnake. Edited by Julian Huxley. Garden City, N.Y.: Doubleday, Doran, 1936.

Selections from the Essays of T. H. Huxley. Edited by Alburey Castell. New York: Appleton-Century-Crofts, 1948.

On a Piece of Chalk. Edited by Loren Eiseley. New York: Charles Scribner's Sons, 1967.

The Essence of T. H. Huxley: Selections from His Writings. Edited by Cyril Bibby. London: Macmillan, 1967.

MAJOR RHETORICAL WORKS OF HUXLEY RELATIVE TO THE CONFLICT
BETWEEN SCIENCE AND THEOLOGY

Sources are cited for those works that appeared first as written discourse; all other works first appeared as oral discourse.

1859—"The Darwinian Hypothesis" (London *Times*)

1860—"The Origin of Species" (*Westminster Review*)

1863—"Six Lectures to Working Men on Our Knowledge of the Causes of the Phenomena of Organic Nature"

1863—*Evidence as to Man's Place in Nature*

1864—"Criticism on 'The Origin of species' " (*Natural History Review*)

1866—"On the Advisableness of Improving Natural Knowledge"

1868—"On the Physical Basis of Life"

1869—"Scientific Education: Notes of an After-Dinner Speech"

1870—"On Descrates' 'Discourse Touching the Method of Using One's Reason Rightly, and the Seeking Scientific Truth' "

1871—"Mr. Darwin's Critics" (*Contemporary Review*)

1874—"Joseph Priestley"

1874—"On the Hypothesis that Animals Are Automata, and Its History"

1876—"Three Lectures on Evolution"

1878—*Hume* (in the English Men of Letters series)

1880—"The Coming of Age of 'The Origin of Species' "

1880—"On the Method of Zadig"

1880—"Science and Culture"

1882—"Charles Darwin" (*Nature*)

1885—"The Interpreters of Genesis and the Interpreters of Nature" (*Nineteenth Century*)

1886—"Mr. Gladstone and Genesis" (*Nineteenth Century*)

1886—"The Evolution of Theology: An Anthropological Study" (*Nineteenth Century*)

1886—"Science and Morals" (*Fortnightly Review*)

1887—"Scientific and Pseudo-Scientific Realism" (*Nineteenth Century*)

1887—"Science and Pseudo-Science" (*Nineteenth Century*)

1887—"An Episcopal Trilogy" (*Nineteenth Century*)

1888—"Darwin Obituary" (*Proceedings of the Royal Society*)

1889—"Agnosticism" (*Nineteenth Century*)

1889—"The Value of Witness to the Miraculous" (*Nineteenth Century*)

1889—"Agnosticism: A Rejoinder" (*Nineteenth Century*)

1889—"Agnosticism and Christianity" (*Nineteenth Century*)

1890—"The Lights of the Church and the Light of Science" (*Nineteenth Century*)

1890—"The Keepers of the Herd of Swine" (*Nineteenth Century*)

1890–91—"Social Diseases and Worse Remedies" (letters to the London *Times*)

1891—"Illustrations of Mr. Gladstone's Controversial Methods" (*Nineteenth Century*)

1891—"Hasisadra's Adventure" (*Nineteenth Century*)

1892—"Possibilities and Impossibilities" (*Agnostic Annual*)

1892—"An Apologetic Irenicon" (*Fortnightly Review*)

1892—"Prologue" (*Controverted Questions*)

1893—"Evolution and Ethics"

1894—"Prolegomena" (*Collected Essays*, vol. 9)

1895—"Mr. Balfour's Attack on Agnosticism" (*Nineteenth Century*)

AUTOBIOGRAPHIES, COMMENTARIES, LETTERS, MEMOIRS, AND WORKS BY SOME OF HUXLEY'S CONTEMPORARIES

Brooks, William K. "The Lesson of the Life of Huxley." *Smithsonian Institution Annual Report, 1900*, 801–11.

Burroughs, John. "The Corroboration of Professor Huxley." *North American Review* 149 (1889): 560–68.

Clodd, Edward. *Memories*. 3d ed. London: Chapman and Hall, 1916.

Conway, Moncure Daniel. *Autobiography: Memories and Experiences*. 2 vols. Boston: Houghton, Mifflin, 1904.

Darwin, Charles. *The Origin of Species*. London: John Murray, 1859. Reprint. New York: Mentor Books, 1958.

_____. *The Autobiography of Charles Darwin*. Edited by Nora Barlow. London: Collins, 1958.

_____. *The Life and Letters of Charles Darwin*. Edited by Francis Darwin. 2 vols. New York: D. Appleton, 1897–99.

_____. *More Letters of Charles Darwin*. Edited by Francis Darwin and A. C. Seward. 2 vols. New York: D. Appleton, 1903.

_____ and J. S. Henslow. *Darwin and Henslow: The Growth of an Idea—Letters, 1831–1860*. Edited by Nora Barlow. Berkeley: University of California Press, 1967.

_____ and T. H. Huxley. *Charles Darwin and Thomas Henry Huxley: Autobiographies*. Edited by Gavin DeBeer. London: Oxford University Press, 1974.

Dawson, J. W. "Professor Huxley in New York." *International Review* 4 (January 1877): 34–50.

Faraday, Michael. *Michael Faraday's Advice to a Lecturer*. Edited by Geoffrey Parr. London: Royal Institution, 1960.

Fawcett, Henry. "A Popular Exposition of Mr. Darwin on the Origin of Species." *Macmillan's Magazine* 3 (December 1860): 81–92.

Fiske, John. "Reminiscences of Huxley." *Essays Historical and Literary* 2:199–226. 2 vols. New York: Macmillan, 1902.

_____. *Edward Livingston Youmans: A Sketch of His Life, with Selections from His Published Writings and Extracts from His Correspondence with Spencer, Huxley, Tyndall and Others*. Freeport, N.Y.: Books for Libraries Press, 1894. Reprint 1972.

_____. *The Life and Letters of John Fiske*. Edited by John Spencer Clark. 2 vols. Boston: Houghton Mifflin, 1917.

Flower, W. H. "Reminiscences of Professor Huxley." *North American Review* 161 (1895): 279–86.

Foster, Michael. "A Few More Words on Thomas Henry Huxley." *Nature* 52 (1895): 318–20.

_____. "Thomas Henry Huxley." *Proceedings of the Royal Society of London* 49 (1896): xlvi–lxvi.

Frankland, Edward. *Sketches from the Life of Edward Frankland*. London: Spottiswoode, 1902.

Gill, T. N. "Huxley and His Work." *Smithsonian Annual Report, 1895*, 759–79.

Gilman, Daniel Coit. *The Launching of a University, and Other Papers: A Sheaf of Remembrances*. New York: Dodd, Mead, 1906.

Godkin, E. L. "Professor Huxley's Lectures." *The Nation* 33 (1876): 192–93.

Grant Duff, Mountstuart E. *Notes from a Diary, 1851–1872*. 2 vols. London: John Murray, 1897.

Gray, Asa. *Letters of Asa Gray*. Edited by Jane Loring Gray. 2 vols. Boston: Houghton Mifflin, 1894.

Green, J. R. *Letters of John Richard Green*. Edited by Leslie Stephen. London: Macmillan, 1901.

Hooker, Joseph Dalton. *Life and Letters of Sir Joseph Dalton Hooker*. Edited by Leonard Huxley. 2 vols. London: John Murray, 1918.

Huxley, Leonard. *Thomas Henry Huxley: A Character Sketch.* Freeport, N.Y.: Books for Libraries Press, 1920. Reprint 1969.

_____. "Huxley and Agassiz: Some Unpublished Letters." *Cornhill Magazine* 55, n.s., (1923): 366–82.

_____. "Home Memories." *Nature* 115 (May 1925): 698–702.

Ingersoll, Robert G. *The Works of Robert G. Ingersoll.* 12 vols. New York: Dresden, 1912.

_____. *The Letters of Robert G. Ingersoll.* Edited by Eva Ingersoll Wakefield. New York: Philosophical Library, 1951.

Kirsch, A. M. "Professor Huxley on Evolution." *The American Catholic Quarterly Review* 2 (1877): 644–64.

Lankester, E. Ray. "Huxley's American Lectures." *Popular Science Monthly* 11 (1877): 709–13.

_____. "Huxley's Collected Essays." *Nature* 49 (February 1894): 310–11.

Lubbock, John (Lord Avebury). "Huxley's Life and Work." *Nature* 63 (November 1900): 92–96, 116–19.

Lyell, Charles. *Life, Letters and Journals of Sir Charles Lyell.* Edited by Mrs. Lyell, 2 vols. London: John Murray, 1881.

Macgillivray, John. *Narrative of the Voyage of H.M.S. Rattlesnake.* London: T. & W. Boone, 1852. Reproduced, Adelaide: Libraries Board of South Australia, 1967.

Marsh, Othniel C. "Thomas Henry Huxley." *American Journal of Science* 50 (1895): 177–83.

Minot, Charles S. "Huxley's Writings." *International Review* 11 (1881): 527–37.

Mivart, St. George. "Some Reminiscences of Thomas Henry Huxley." *Nineteenth Century* 42 (December 1897): 985–98.

Morley, John. *Recollections.* 2 vols. London: Macmillan, 1917.

Nature 115 (May 1925): 697–752. Special Supplement of twenty-three brief tributes by former students and others who had first-hand knowledge of Huxley, in commemoration of his centenary.

Osborn, Henry Fairfield. *Huxley and Education.* New York: Charles Scribner's Sons, 1910.

Poulton, Edward B. *Charles Darwin and the Origin of Species.* London: Longmans, Green, 1909.

Romanes, George John. *The Life and Letters of George John Romanes.* Edited by his wife, E. R. 2d ed. London: Longmans, Green, 1896.

[Sidgwick, Isabel]. "A Grandmother's Tales." *Macmillan's Magazine* 78 (October 1898): 425–35.

Simpson, Jane A. H. "Thomas Henry Huxley in His Relation to Science, Education, and Sunday Observance." *Westminster Review* 144 (1895): 266–72.

Smalley, George W. "Mr. Huxley." *Scribner's Magazine* 18 (July-December 1895): 514–24.

Spencer, Herbert. *An Autobiography.* 2 vols. New York: D. Appleton, 1904. Reproduced, London: Watts & Co., 1926.

_____. *Life and Letters of Herbert Spencer.* Edited by David Duncan. 2 vols. New York: D. Appleton, 1908.

Traubel, Horace. *With Walt Whitman in Camden.* 4 vols. New York: M. Kennerley, 1914–53.

Tuckwell, W. *Reminiscences of Oxford.* 2d ed. London: Smith, Elder, 1907.

Wallace, Alfred Russel. *My Life: A Record of Events and Opinions.* 2 vols. New York: Dodd, Mead, 1906.

Ward, Wilfrid. *Problems and Persons.* London: Longmans, Green, 1903.

Webb, Beatrice. *My Apprenticeships.* London: Longmans, Green, 1926.

Wilson, David. "Huxley and Wilberforce at Oxford and Elsewhere." *Westminster Review* 167 (1907): 311–16.

Youmans, Edward L. "Professor Huxley's Lectures." *Popular Science Monthly* 10 (1876): 102–4.

_____. *Herbert Spencer on the Americans and the Americans on Herbert Spencer.* New York: D. Appleton, 1883.

Secondary Sources

BOOKS

Ainsworth Davis, J. R. *Thomas H. Huxley.* London: J. M. Dent, 1907. Reprint 1970.

Ames, Robert and Philip Siegelman, eds. *The Idea of Evolution: Readings in Evolutionary Theory and Its Influence.* Minneapolis: Meyers, 1957.

Ashforth, Albert. *Thomas Henry Huxley.* New York: Twayne, 1969.

[Ashwell, A. R.] and Reginald G. Wilberforce. *Life of the Right Reverend Samuel Wilberforce, D. D.* 3 vols. London: John Murray, 1881.

Ayres, Clarence. *Huxley.* New York: W. W. Norton, 1932.

Bassett, Marnie. *Behind the Picture: H.M.S. Rattlesnake's Australia-New Guinea Cruise.* Melbourne: Oxford University Press, 1966.

Berman, Milton. *John Fiske: The Evolution of a Popularizer.* Cambridge: Harvard University Press, 1961.

Bevington, Merle Mowbray. *The Saturday Review, 1855–1868: Representative Educated Opinion in Victorian England.* New York: Columbia University Press, 1941.

Bibby, Cyril. *T. H. Huxley, Scientist, Humanist and Educator.* New York: Horizon Press, 1959.

_____. *Scientist Extraordinary: The Life and Scientific Work of Thomas Henry Huxley.* Oxford: Pergamon Press, 1972.

Blau, Eve. *Ruskinian Gothic: The Architecture of Deane and Woodword 1845–1861.* Princeton: Princeton University Press, 1982.

Bonney, Thomas George. *Annals of the Philosophical Club of the Royal Society, Written from Its Minute Books.* London: Macmillan, 1919.

Brantlinger, Patrick, ed. *Energy & Entropy: Science and Culture in Victorian Britain.* Bloomington: Indiana University Press, 1989.

Brock, William H. and Roy M. MacLeod. *Natural Knowledge in Social Context: The Journals of Thomas Archer Hirst, FRS.* London: Mansell, 1980.

Brown, Alan Willard. *The Metaphysical Society: Victorian Minds in Crisis, 1869–1880.* New York: Columbia University Press, 1947.

Caroe, A. D. R. *The House of the Royal Institution.* London: Royal Institution, 1963.

Caudill, Edward, ed. *Darwinism in the Press: The Evolution of an Idea.* Hillsdale, N.J.: Lawrence Erlbaum, 1989.

Chadwick, Owen. *The Victorian Church.* 2 vols. London: Adam & Charles Black, 1966.

Clark, Ronald W. *The Huxleys.* London: Heinemann, 1968.

Clodd, Edward. *Pioneers of Evolution from Thales to Huxley.* London: G. Richards, 1897.

_____. *Thomas Henry Huxley.* New York: Dodd, Mead, 1902.

Cockshut, A. O. J. *The Unbelievers: English Agnostic Thought, 1840–1890.* London: Collins, 1964.

Corsi, Pietro. *Science and Religion: Baden Powell and the Anglican Debate, 1800–1860.* Cambridge: Cambridge University Press, 1988.

Dawson, Warren R. *The Huxley Papers: A Descriptive Catalogue of the Correspondence, Manuscripts and Miscellaneous Papers of the Rt. Hon. Thomas Henry Huxley, Preserved in the Imperial College of Science and Technology, London.* London: Macmillan, 1946.

DeBeer, Gavin. *Charles Darwin: Evolution by Natural Selection.* London: T. Nelson & Sons, 1963.

Desmond, Adrian. *Archtypes and Ancestors: Palaeontology in Victorian London, 1850–1875.* Chicago: University of Chicago Press, 1984.

DiGregoriö, Mario A. *T. H. Huxley's Place in Natural Science.* New Haven: Yale University Press, 1984.

Dupree, A. Hunter. *Asa Gray.* Cambridge: Harvard University Press, 1959.

Edwards, David L. *Leaders of the Church of England, 1828–1944.* London: Oxford University Press, 1971.

Ellegard, Alvar. *Darwin and the General Reader: The Reception of Darwin's Theory of Evolution in the British Periodical Press, 1859–1872.* Göteborg: Göteborgs Universitets Arsskrift, 1958.

Eve, A. S. and C. H. Creasey. *Life and Work of John Tyndall.* London: Macmillan, 1945.

Fiske, John. *A Century of Science and other Essays.* Boston: Houghton Mifflin, 1899.

Glass, Bentley, Owsei Temkin, and William J. Straus, Jr., eds. *Forerunners of Darwin, 1745–1859.* rev. ed. Baltimore: Johns Hopkins Univeristy Press, 1968.

Glick, Thomas F., eds. *The Comparative Reception of Darwinism.* Austin: University of Texas Press, 1974.

Hall, Marie Boas. *All Scientists Now: The Royal Society in the Nineteenth Century.* Cambridge: Cambridge University Press, 1984.

Himmelfarb, Gertrude. *Darwin and the Darwinian Revolution.* New York: Doubleday, 1959. Reprint. Gloucester, Mass.: Peter Smith, 1967.

Houghton, Walter, E., ed. *The Wellesley Index of Victorian Periodicals, 1824–1900.* 3 vols. Toronto: University of Toronto Press, 1966.

Howarth, O. J. R. *The British Association for the Advancement of Science: A Retrospect.* 2d ed. London: B.A.A.S., 1931.

Hutchinson, Horatio Gordon. *Life of Sir John Lubbock, Lord Avebury.* 2 vols. London: Macmillan, 1914.

Huxley, Julian. "Thomas Henry Huxley and Religion." In *Essays in Popular Science*, 137–62. London: Chatto & Windus, 1926.

_____. *Memories*. London: George Allen and Unwin, 1970.

Huxley, Julian and H. B. D. Kettlewell. *Charles Darwin and His World*. New York: The Viking Press, 1965.

Irvine, William. *Apes, Angels, and Victorians: The Story of Darwin, Huxley and Evolution*. New York: McGraw-Hill, 1955. Reprint 1959.

_____. *Thomas Henry Huxley*. London: Longmans, Green, 1960.

Kennedy, James G. *Herbert Spencer*. Boston: Twayne, 1978.

Knight, David M. *Natural Science Books in Englsih, 1600–1900*. London: B. T. Batsford, 1972.

_____. *The Nature of Science: The History of Science in Western Culture since 1600*. London: Andre Deutsch, 1976.

_____. *The Age of Science: The Scientific World-View in the Nineteenth Century*. Oxford. Oxford University Press, 1986.

Leighton, Gerald. *Huxley, His Life and Work*. London: T.C. and E.C. Jack, 1912.

Lightman, Bernard. *The Origins of Agnosticism: Victorian Unbelief and the Limits of Knowledge*. Baltimore: Johns Hopkins University Press, 1987.

Livingstone, David N. *Darwin's Forgotten Defenders: The Encounter between Evangelical Theology and Evolutionary Thought*. Grand Rapids, Mich.: William B. Eerdmans, 1987.

Loewenberg, Bert James. *Darwin, Wallace, and the Theory of Natural Selection, Including the Linnean Society Papers*. New Haven: Yale University Press, 1957.

Lubbock, Adelaide. *Owen Stanley R. N. 1811–50: Captain of the Rattlesnake*. Melbourne: Heinemann, 1968.

Lurie, Edward. *Louis Agassiz: A Life in Science*. Chicago: University of Chicago Press, 1960.

MacBride, Ernest William. *Huxley*. London: Duckworth, 1934.

MacLeod, Roy and Peter Collins, eds. *The Parliament of Science: The British Association for the Advancement of Science, 1831–1981*. Northwood, Middlesex: Science Reviews, 1981.

_____ and Philip F. Rehbock, eds. *Nature in Its Greatest Extent: Western Science in the Pacific*. Honolulu: University of Hawaii Press, 1988.

Marshall, A. J. *Darwin and Huxley in Australia*. Sydney: Hodder & Stoughton, 1970.

Martin, Thomas. *The Royal Institution*. London: Royal Institution, 1961.

Metcalf, Priscilla. *James Knowles: Victorian Editor and Architect*. Cambridge: Harvard University Press, 1970.

Millhauser, Milton. *Just Before Darwin: Robert Chambers and Vestiges*. Middletown, Conn.: Wesleyan University Press, 1959.

Mitchell, P. Chalmers. *Thomas Henry Huxley: A Sketch of His Life and Work*. New York: G. P. Putnam's Sons, 1901

Moore, James R. *The Post-Darwinian Controversies: A Study of the Protestant Struggle to Come to Terms with Darwin in Great Britain and America 1870–1900*. Cambridge: Cambridge University Press, 1979.

Morrell, Jack and Arnold Thackray. *Gentlement of Science: Early Years of the British Association for the Advancement of Science*. Oxford: Clarendon Press, 1981.

Ospovat, Dov. *The Development of Darwin's Theory: Natural History, Natural Theology, and Natural Selection, 1838–1859*. Cambridge: Cambridge University Press, 1981.

Paradis, James G. *T. H. Huxley: Man's Place in Nature*. Lincoln: University of Nebraska Press, 1978.

_____ and Thomas Postlewait, eds. *Victorian Science and Victorian Values: Literary Perspectives*. New York: The New York Academy of Sciences, 1981.

_____ and George C. Williams. *T. H. Huxley's 'Evolution and Ethics' with New Essays on Its Victorian and Sociobiological Context*. Lawrenceville, N.J.: Princeton University Press, 1989.

Peterson, Houston. *Huxley: Prophet of Science*. London: Longmans, Green, 1932.

Pingree, Jeanne. *T. H. Huxley: A List of His Scientific Papers*. London: Imperial College of Science and Technology, 1968.

_____. *Thomas Henry Huxley: List of His Correspondence with Miss Henrietta Heathorn, 1847–1854*. London: Imperial College of Science and Technology, 1969.

Pusey, James R. *China and Charles Darwin*. Cambridge: Harvard University Press, 1983.

Reingold, Nathan, ed. *Science in Nineteenth-Century America*. New York: Hill & Wang, 1964.

_____. *Science in America since 1820*. New York: Science History Publications, 1976.

Richards, Robert J. *Darwin and the Emergence of Evolutionary Theories of Mind and Behavior*. Chicago: University of Chicago Press, 1987.

Roberts, Jon H. *Darwinism and the Divine in America: Protestant Intellectuals and Organic Evolution, 1859–1900*. Madison: University of Wisconsin Press, 1988.

Russett, Cynthia Eagle. *Darwin in America: The Intellectual Response, 1865–1912*. San Francisco: W. H. Freeman, 1976.

Stenerson, Douglas C. *H. L. Mencken: Iconoclast from Baltimore*. Chicago: University of Chicago Press, 1971.

Turner, Frank M. *Between Science and Religion: The Reaction of Scientific Naturalism in Late Victorian England*. New Haven: Yale University Press, 1974.

Turrill, William Bertram. *J. D. Hooker, Botanist, Explorer, and Administrator*. London: T. Nelson, 1963.

Vanderpool, Harold Y., ed. *Darwin and Darwinism*. Lexington, Mass.: D. C. Heath, 1973.

Winston, George. P. *John Fiske*. New York: Twayne, 1972.

ARTICLES

Adams, James Eli. "Woman Red in Tooth and Claw: Nature and the Feminine in Tennyson and Darwin." *Victorian Studies* 33 (1989): 7–27.

Altholz, Josef L. "The Huxley-Wilberforce Debate Revisited." *Journal of the History of Medicine and Allied Sciences* 35 (July 1980): 313–16.

Armstrong, A. MacC. "Samuel Wilberforce v. T. H. Huxley: A Retrospect." *The Quarterly Review* 296 (October 1958): 426–37.

Baker, William J. "Thomas Huxley in Tennessee." *The South Atlantic Quarterly* 73 (Autumn 1974): 475–86.

Bartholomew, Michael. "Huxley's Defence of Darwin." *Annals of Science* 32 (November 1975): 525–35.

Barton, Ruth. "John Tyndall, Pantheist: A Rereading of the Belfast Address." *Osiris*, 2d series, 3 (1987): 111–34.

———. " 'An Influential Set of Chaps': The X Club and Royal Society Politics 1964–85." *British Journal for the History of Science* 23 (March 1990): 53–81.

Bayliss, Robert A. "A Note on T. H. Huxley and the Society of Arts." *Journal of Consumer Studies and Home Economics* 1 (1977): 21–25.

Bibby, Cyril. "The Huxley-Wilberforce Debate: A Postscript." *Nature* 176 (20 August 1955): 363.

———. "Huxley: Prince of Controversialists." *Twentieth Century* 161 (March 1957): 268–76.

———. "Huxley and University Development." *Victorian Studies* 2 (1958): 97–116.

———. "Huxley and the Reception of the 'Origin'." *Victorian Studies* 3 (1959): 76–86.

Bicknell, John W. "Thomas Henry Huxley." In *Victorian Prose: A Guide to Research*, edited by David J. DeLaura, 495–506. New York: Modern Language Association, 1973.

Blinderman, Charles S. "The Oxford Debate and After." *Notes and Queries* 202 (March 1957): 126–28.

———. "Semantic Aspects of T. H. Huxley's Literary Style." *Journal of Communication* 12 (September 1962): 171–78.

———. "T. H. Huxley's Theory of Aesthetics: Unity in Diversity." *Journal of Aesthetics and Art Criticism* 21 (Fall 1962): 49–55.

———. "T. H. Huxley: A Re-evauation of His Philosophy." *Rationalist Annual* 40 (1966): 50–62.

———. "The Great Bone Case." *Perspectives in Biology and Medicine* 14 (Spring 1971): 370–93.

Block, Ed., Jr. "T. H. Huxley's Rhetoric and the Mind-Matter Debate, 1868–1874." *Prose Studies, 1800–1900* 8 (1985): 21–39.

———. "T. H. Huxley's Rhetoric and the Popularization of Victorian Scientific Ideas, 1854–1874." *Victorian Studies* 29 (Spring 1986): 363–86.

Brown, Richard Harvey. "Rhetoric and Science of History: The Debate Between Evolutionism and Empiricism as a Conflict of Metaphors." *Quarterly Journal of Speech* 72 (May 1986): 148–61.

Browne, Janet. "The Charles Darwin-Joseph Hooker Correspondence: An Analysis of Manuscript Resources and Their Use in Biography." *Journal of the Society for the Bibliography of Natural History* 8 (May 1978): 351–66.

Campbell, John Angus. "Darwin and the Origin of Species: The Rhetorical Ancestory of an Idea." *Speech Monographs* 37 (March 1970): 1–14.

———. "Charles Darwin and the Crisis of Ecology: A Rhetorical Perspective." *Quarterly Journal of Speech* 60 (December 1974): 442–49.

_____. "The Polemical Mr. Darwin." *Quarterly Journal of Speech* 61 (December 1975): 375–90.

_____. "Scientific Revolution and the Grammar of Culture: The Case of Darwin's *Origin*." *Quarterly Journal of Speech* 72 (November 1986): 351–76.

_____. "The Invisible Rhetorician: Charles Darwin's 'Third Party' Strategy." *Rhetorica* 7 (Winter 1989): 55–85.

Carroll, P. Thomas. "American Science Transformed." *American Scientist* 74 (September-October 1986): 466–85.

Carter, Neal E. "The Political Side of Science: Communication between Scientists and the Public." *Vital Speeches of the Day* 52 (1 July 1986): 558–61.

Coulson, C. A. "Science and Religion." *Proceedings of the Royal Institution of Great Britain* 41 (1966–67): 480–92.

Eisen, Sydney. "Huxley and the Positivists." *Victorian Studies* 7 (June 1964): 337–58.

Ellegard, Alvar. "Public Opinion and the Press: Reaction to Darwinism." *Journal of the History of Ideas* 19 (1958): 379–87.

Eng, Erling. "Thomas Henry Huxley's Understanding of 'Evolution'." *History of Science* 16 (December 1978): 291–303.

Foskett, D. J. "Wilberforce and Huxley on Evolution." *Nature* 172 (14 November 1953): 920.

Friday, James. "A Microscopic Incident in a Monumental Struggle: Huxley and Antibiosis in 1875." *British Journal for the History of Science* 7 (1974): 61–71.

Gardner, Joseph H. "A Huxley Essay as 'Poem'." *Victorian Studies* 14 (December 1970): 177–91.

Gilbert, Scott F. "Altruism and other Unnatural Acts: T. H. Huxley on Nature, Man, and Society." *Perspectives in Biology and Medicine* 22 (1979): 346–58.

Gilley, Sheridan. "The Huxley-Wilberforce Debate: A Reconsideration." In *Religion and Humanism*, edited by Keith Robbins, 325–40. Oxford: Blackwell, 1981.

_____ and Ann Loades. "Thomas Henry Huxley: The War between Science and Religion." *The Journal of Religion* 61 (July 1981): 285–308.

Gould, Stephen Jay. "Soapy Sam's Logic." *Natural History* 95 (May 1986).

_____. "Knight Takes Bishop? *Natural History* 95 (May 1986)

_____. "The *Archaeopteryx* Flap." *Natural History* 95 (September 1986).

Hall, Marie Boas. "The Royal Society in Thomas Henry Huxley's Time." *Notes and Records of the Royal Society of London* 38 (March 1984): 153–58.

Helfand, Michael S. "T. H. Huxley's 'Evolution and Ethics' " The Politics of Evolution and the Evolution of Politics." *Victorian Studies* 20 (Winter 1977): 159–77.

Heyck, T. W. "From Men of Letters to Intellectuals: The Transformation of Intellectual Life in Nineteenth-Century England." *Journal of British Studies* 20 (Fall 1980): 153–83.

Houghton, Walter E. "The Rhetoric of T. H. Huxley." *University of Toronto Quarterly* 18 (1948–49): 159–75.

Huxley, Aldous. "Thomas Huxley as a Literary Man." In *The Olive Tree, and Other Essays.* London: Chatto & Windus, 1936.

Huxley, Andrew. "Grandfather and Grandson." *Notes and Records of the Royal Society of London* 38 (March 1984): 147–51.

Huxley, Leonard. "Huxley and Agassiz: Some Unpublished Letters." *Cornhill Magazine* 55, n.s., (1923): 266–82.

_____. "Carlyle and Huxley, Early Influences." *Cornhill Magazine* 72, n.s. (1932): 290–302.

Jones, Kenneth L. "Thomas H. Huxley's One Visit to the United States." *Michigan Academician* 17 (Spring 1985): 349–53.

Kohn, David. "Darwin's Ambiguity: The Secularization of Biological Meaning." *British Journal for the History of Science* 22 (July 1989): 215–39.

Levine, George. "Darwin and the Evolution of Fiction." *New York Times Book Review*, 5 October 1986.

Lucas, J. R. "Wilberforce and Huxley: A Legendary Encounter." *Historical Journal* 22 (1979): 313–30.

Lyne, John and Henry F. Howe. "'Punctuated Equilibria': Rhetorical Dynamics of a Scientific Controversy." *Quarterly Journal of Speech* 72 (May 1986): 132–47.

MacLeod, Roy M. "Government and Resource Conservation: The Salmon Acts Administration, 1860–1886." *Journal of British Studies* 7 (May 1968): 114–50.

_____. "The X-Club: A Social Network of Science in Late-Victorian England." *Notes and Records of the Royal Society of London* 24 (June 1970): 305–22.

_____. "Of Medals and Men: A Reward System in Victorian Science." *Notes and Records of the Royal Society of London* 25 (June 1971): 81–105.

McCartney, Jesse F. "The Pedagogical Style of T. H. Huxley in 'On the Physiological Basis of Life'." *Southern Quarterly* 14 (January 1976): 97–107.

Minnick, Wayne C. "Thomas Huxley's American Lectures on Evolution." *Southern Speech Journal* 17 (May 1952): 225–33.

Myers, Greg. "Nineteenth-Century Popularizations of Thermodynamics and the Rhetoric of Social Prophecy." *Victorian Studies* 29 (Autumn 1985): 35–66.

Noland, Richard W. "T. H. Huxley on Culture." *Personalist* 45 (Winter 1964): 94–111.

Numbers, Ronald L. "Science and Religion." *Osiris*, 2d series, 1 (1985): 59–80.

Park, Katharine, Lorraine J. Daston, and Peter L. Galison. "Bacon, Galileo, and Descartes on Imagination and Analogy." *Isis* 75 (June 1984): 287–326.

Phelps, Lynn A. and Edwin Cohen. "The Wilberforce-Huxley Debate." *Western Speech* 37 (Winter 1973): 56–64.

Pingree, Jeanne. "The Huxley Building." *University of London Bulletin* 36 (November 1976): 6–7.

Porter, Roy. "The Descent of Genius: Charles Darwin's Brilliant Career." *History Today* 32 (July 1982): 16–22.

Randel, William Peirce. "Huxley in America." *Proceedings of the American Philosophical Society* 114 (April 1970): 73–99.

Richards, Evelleen. "A Question of Property Rights: Richard Owen's Evolutionism Reassessed." *British Journal for the History of Science* 20 (1987): 129–71.

Roos, David A. "Matthew Arnold and Thomas Huxley: Two Speeches at the Royal Academy of Arts, 1881 and 1883." *Modern Philology* 75 (February 1977): 316–24.

_____. "Neglected Bibliographical Aspects of the Works of Thomas Henry Huxley." *Journal of the Society for the Bibliography of Natural History* 8 (May 1978): 401–20.

Savory, Jerold J. "T. H. Huxley." In *Dictionary of Literary Biography: Victorian Prose Writers After 1867*, edited by William B. Thesing. Detroit: Gale Research Co., 1987. 57:145–57.

Sawyer, Thomas M. "Rhetoric in an Age of Science and Technology." *College Composition and Communication* 23 (1972): 390–98.

Smith, James M. "Thomas Henry Huxley in Nashville." *Tennessee Historical Quarterly* 33 (Summer, Fall 1974): 191–203, 322–41.

Sopka, Katherine Russell. "John Tyndall: International Populariser of Science." In *John Tyndall: Essays on a Natural Philosopher*, edited by W. H. Brock, N. D. McMillan, and R. C. Mollan. Dublin: Royal Dublin Society, 1981.

Stanley, Oma. "T. H. Huxley's Treatment of Nature." *Journal of the History of Ideas* 18 (1957): 120–27.

Stevens, L. Robert. "Darwin's Humane Reading: The Anaesthetic Man Reconsidered." *Victorian Studies* 26 (Autumn 1982): 51–63.

Turner, Frank M. "Rainfall, Plagues, and the Prince of Wales: A Chapter in the Conflict of Religion and Science." *Journal of British Studies* 13 (May 1974): 46–65.

_____. "The Victorian Conflict between Science and Religion: A Professional Dimension." *Isis* 69 (September 1978): 356–76.

_____. "Public Science in Britain, 1880–1919." *Isis* 71 (December 1980): 589–608.

Vernon, K. D. C. "The Foundation and Early Years of the Royal Institution." *Proceedings of the Royal Institution* 39 (1963): 364–402.

Warnick, Barbara. "A Rhetorical Analysis of Episteme Shift: Darwin's *Origin of the* (sic) *Species*." *Southern Speech Communication Journal* 49 (Fall 1983): 26–42.

Watt, Donald. "Soul-Facts: Humour and Figure in T. H. Huxley." *Prose Studies, 1800–1900* 1 (1978): 30–40.

Wickens, G. Glen. "The Two Sides of Early Victorian Science and the Unity of 'The Princess'." *Victorian Studies* 23 (Spring 1980): 369–88.

Young, Robert M. "Darwin's Metaphor: Does Nature Select?" *The Monist* 55 (July 1971): 442–503.

DISSERTATIONS AND THESES

Barton, Ruth. "The X Club: Science, Religion, and Social Change in Victorian England." Ph.D. diss., University of Pennsylvania, 1976.

Boyer, James A. "Thomas Henry Huxley and His Relation to the Recognition of Science in English Education." Ph.D. diss., University of Michigan, 1949.

Foskett, D. J. "T. H. Huxley and His Presentaton of Scientific Material." Master's thesis, Birkbeck College, University of London, 1955.

Kim, Stephen Shin. "Fragments of Faith: John Tyndall's Transcendental Materialism and the Victorian Conflict Between Religion and Science." Ph.D. diss., Drew Univeristy, 1988.

Minnick, Wayne C. "British Speakers in America, 1866–1900." Ph.D. diss., Northwestern University, 1949.

Morrison, John Lee. "A History of American Catholic Opinion on the Theory of Evolution, 1859–1950." Ph.D. diss., University of Missouri, 1951.

Pfeifer, Edward Justin. "The Reception of Darwinism in the United States, 1859–1880." Ph.D. diss., Brown University, 1957.

Roberts, Windsor Hall. "The Reaction of the American Protestant Churches to the Darwinian Philosophy, 1860–1900." Ph.D. diss., University of Chicago, 1936.

Subbiah, Mahalingam. "Popularizing Science: Thomas Henry Huxley's Style." Ph.D. diss., Oklahoma state University, 1987.

Thomas, Charles K. "The Rhetoric of Thomas Henry Huxley." Ph.D. diss., Cornell University, 1930.

Index